ABOUT THE AUTHORS

Laurence Alison began his career in psychology with the Rachel Nickell murder case. As an undergraduate he produced critical analyses of the investigative methods on behalf of early suspect Colin Stagg's defence counsel, and the case formed the basis of his PhD. Professor Alison is now the co-director of the Centre for Critical and Major Incident Research (CAMI) at the University of Liverpool's School of Psychology, where he also holds the chair in forensic psychology. He conducts research on investigative decision-making and leadership, contributes to national police training programmes and publishes on the subject of policing and investigation in internationally recognised journals. He has edited or co-authored a number of books, including *The Forensic Psychologist's Casebook*, and is also an approved behavioural advisor for the National Crime and Operations Facility. Laurence Alison has contributed to a number of major police enquiries, including several particularly complex and controversial investigations. He has also been the key psychological advisor in several major debriefs, including the 2005 London bombings.

Marie Eyre is a research associate working with Professor Alison in the Centre for Critical and Major Incident Research. She is currently involved in projects examining leadership and decision-making in critical incidents and analysing police debriefs of major incidents – ranging from the London bombings to the 'Suffolk Strangler' murders. Marie is specifically interested in the relationships between broad cultural or organisational contexts and the ways in which they influence the cognitive processes of individuals during critical incidents. With a professional background in teaching and a commitment to research with applied value, she supports Laurence Alison's work in advising the police service and helps to deliver training to practitioners in the field.

KILLER
IN THE
SHADOWS

THE MONSTROUS CRIMES
OF ROBERT NAPPER

LAURENCE ALISON
AND MARIE EYRE

First published in paperback 2009
by Pennant Books.

This second edition published December 2009.

Text copyright © 2009 by Laurence Alison and Marie Eyre.

The moral right of the authors has been asserted.

All rights reserved. No part of this publication may be reproduced, stored in a retrieval system, or transmitted, in any form or by any means, electronic, mechanical, photocopying, recording or otherwise, without the prior permission in writing of the publisher, except by a reviewer who wishes to quote brief passages in connection with a review written for insertion in a newspaper, magazine or broadcast.

British Library Cataloguing-in-Publication Data:
A catalogue record for this book is available on request from
The British Library

ISBN 978-1-906015-49-7

Pennant Books' True Crime series is edited by Paul Woods

Design & typeset by Envy Design Ltd

Printed and bound in Turkey by Mega Printing.

Pictures reproduced with kind permission of Mirrorpix,
National Pictures and PA Photos.

Every reasonable effort has been made to acknowledge the ownership of copyright material included in this book. Any errors that have inadvertently occurred will be corrected in subsequent editions provided notification is sent to the publisher.

Pennant Books
PO Box 5675
London W1A 3FB

www.pennantbooks.com

CONTENTS

Acknowledgements		vii
Preface		ix
Chapter 1	Photographs and Fingerprints	1
Chapter 2	Mothers, Murders and the Green Chain Rapes	21
Chapter 3	Fearful Symmetry	47
Chapter 4	Desolated Hearts	71
Chapter 5	Trace, Implicate, Eliminate	99
Chapter 6	Innocent until Profiled Guilty	119
Chapter 7	Stagg Hunting	147
Chapter 8	Sex Murderers	177
Chapter 9	Brought to the Light	211
Chapter 10	Autopsies	231
Chapter 11	Pips in the Heart	257
Further Reading		285

ACKNOWLEDGEMENTS

In producing this book, a number of folk have helped us along the way. We'd like to thank Sean Cunningham and Matt Long for their comments on early drafts, and for picking us up on some police procedural details; Tony Beech, Al Goodwill, Vince Egan and Adrian West for their expertise in relation to the psychology of sex offending and specific comments on chapters relating directly to Napper's crimes; Sheila Owens – Marie's far more technologically competent sister – for her invaluable IT proficiency with maps; and Sean Gregory and John Short – neither of whom are psychologists or police officers, but who, in Sean's case, provided us with the title 'Innocent until Profiled Guilty', and in John's case helped steer us onto a path that the non-expert reader can follow.

At the University of Liverpool Kate Sparks and Kevan Ryan lent us their personal support, but Louise Almond deserves special thanks for always listening patiently to far more detail than was necessary. We must also acknowledge David Canter, who introduced Laurence to this fascinating and tragic subject via his close involvement in the case. We should also like to thank Lucy Roe and Pippa Gregory at the SCAS, both of whom made doubly sure that our numbers and percentages stood up against the SCAS database.

Jonathan Crego provided much needed clarity and has proved himself over and over again to be an oracle of wisdom, as well as a very warm friend.

But most of all, our thanks go to Steve Eyre and Emily Alison, whose contributions did not end at reading our book. Emily spent many hours discussing ideas with Laurence; having worked with countless violent men in a therapeutic environment, she provided a unique insight into Napper and his crimes. With more than thirty years spent working in criminal justice and child protection, Steve's ideas and suggestions were as solidly dependable as the man himself.

Far more challenging to both spouses was the task of showing unstinting support and tolerance while we worked on the book over many months, from first spark to final draft. They accomplished it admirably. This is, of course, the least of the reasons why we admire them so. We thank them also for their love.

Laurence would like to thank Marie: She is affectionately referred to as 'Mum' at the Centre for Critical and Major Incident Psychology because she is the 'go to' person at the time of many a student (or occasionally a staff) crisis. I can't imagine a better mum to have as an emotional core.

Marie's thanks also go to Laurence: For the invitation to co-author a book on a case which constituted a formative part of his professional career. The gesture typifies his generous spirit and complete lack of self-importance, ego or preciousness, despite the important contributions he makes via his work.

PREFACE

"The weight of this sad time we must obey:
Speak what we feel, not what we ought to say."
William Shakespeare, *King Lear*

This is a book about stories. It is not an academic work, though academic themes are drawn upon. Nor is it supposed to serve as an instruction manual for crime investigators. (There are precious few tips for the aspiring detective, though for complete novitiates there may be one or two.) Nor is it a text for students learning about forensic psychology or criminal profiling, though we do refer to both disciplines. It is, rather, a book of stories about peoples' lives, wherein the personal narratives of many individuals collide in profoundly appalling ways.

Many of the stories are bleak, violent, or indeed utterly tragic. For some of the police officers involved in the case it meant broken careers or early retirement through stress. It brought disrepute on the original enquiry team and left a legacy of distrust between the professions of police work and forensic psychology.

There is also sadness in the story of Colin Stagg, then a thirty-year-old virgin who thought he had fallen in love while he was being manipulated by an undercover officer. The consequences of this bogus relationship led him to endure fifteen years of suspicion and outright accusations that he had murdered Rachell Nickell. He was shouted at, attacked and spat at in the street. Even when it was finally clear that there was no case against him, the *Daily Mail* persisted with their campaign of excoriation, unevenly comparing his compensation award by the Home Office with the amounts paid to soldiers injured in Iraq and Afghanistan. Only time will tell whether Robert Napper's conviction will finally release Stagg from both the media's and the general public's suspicion.

Then there is a whole series of tragically interwoven narratives. Robert Napper was the author of all of these, ruining lives and creating secondary victims out of parents, partners and children, several of the latter witnessing the rape or killing of their mother. And all the while, Napper kept the story of his 1992 attack on Rachel as part of his own silent narrative, thereby prolonging the agony for all.

Perhaps the most tragic and certainly the most neglected story as far as the media are concerned relates to Napper's last victims – Samantha Bisset, murdered and mutilated in her own home in an act of almost inconceivable violence, and four-year-old Jazmine, sexually assaulted and suffocated in

PREFACE

her bed. Those of us old enough to remember will recall Rachel's photograph in the media; we struggle hard to recall Jazmine's and Samantha's faces in comparison, but the sole photo used in the press shows a pretty, smiling, tawny-haired hippy, holding her daughter and turning towards the camera, smiling contentedly.

Jazmine would have been twenty years old this year.

Although we purposely chose not to tell the story in the first person, this is also a deeply and unashamedly personal book. In working on Stagg's defence and writing a large chunk of my PhD thesis on the undercover operation, for fifteen years after the offence I was preoccupied with the elusive Napper, a man I didn't know. I would regularly sniff out any morsel that might indicate a breakthrough which would validate my view that Colin Stagg had not committed this crime. And, of course, I speculated as to what sort of man would commit such acts.

For many different reasons, I felt torn about writing this book. I considered the implications of academics writing about crime without the explicit objective of providing scientific insight. I worried about sounding too critical of the police and offender profilers (now called behavioural investigative advisors) – two groups upon which I rely heavily, many of whom are close personal friends. I felt the tensions of the enduring media interest in this case, and how I would have to somehow engage with it – not something I was at all comfortable with.

However, the stories are now sixteen years old and have followed me throughout my career, informing the way I think about crime, criminals, victims, the police and their decision-making processes, profilers, students of crime and witnesses. These are all deeply woven into my professional life, and the killing of Rachel Nickell influenced the pathways that I chose. So a central objective was to give my personal view of the case.

I think that there are important subjective stories to share, and I hope they will inform students and the general public that policing is not just about investigation, or that forensic profiling is just about giving an opinion. I hope they will convey the emotional consequences of crime and demonstrate the far-reaching effects beyond the immediate victims. I also hope they will show how much further ahead policing, profiling and forensic science have moved since the death of Rachel.

The reader will be dragged through some dark areas and witness gross acts of violence. I see no way around being explicit about the level of brutality when we are considering a man able to rape and kill both women and children. However, it was important to Marie and I that we portrayed the horror of it, rather than merely giving a salacious account. I have been utterly appalled by some presentations I've seen at academic conferences or related business forums, where both audience and presenter have revelled in the awfulness of crime-scene details. So we felt it was as important to concentrate on the victims as on Napper, and not to diminish them by failing to describe their lives (as is so often the way in other true crime books).

Despite the awfulness of the crimes and the impact that Napper has had on so many people, my hope is that we end on a note of optimism. The police service has changed

PREFACE

dramatically since the Nickell murder enquiry. There have also been significant developments in the psychology of witness and suspect interviewing, decision making, leadership and motivation, managing stress and, of course, the methodology of psychologists assisting the police via psychological and geographic profiling. They all help to protect other families from the experiences endured by some of Napper's secondary victims.

And all the time forensic science has marched on. Ultimately, its cumulative knowledge and slow but incremental progress would catch up with Robert Napper and force him out of the shadows.

It is strange to consider that the Stephen Lawrence murder enquiry, which happened after Rachel's death, and the recommendations in the subsequent Macpherson Report have moved policing on to an almost unrecognisable place. Profiling has changed profoundly since then, with greater regulation, professionalism and integrity, and far less personality-based media attention. These changes have been almost exclusively positive, so it is my hope that the reader will come to understand that what was then is not now. This case should not be used to cast blame on our contemporary police service or behavioural profilers.

At the same time, the investigation into the Nickell murder is a useful reference point for what can go wrong. As such, it should not be forgotten. We have to recognise the bleak environment and outcome of that initial investigation. We have a responsibility to recognise such errors when we see them.

Laurence Alison, November 2008

DEDICATIONS

For Mum
(Dad, the *next* one's for you)
Laurence

For my men: Steve, Phil, Pete
I love you all.
Marie

CHAPTER ONE
PHOTOGRAPHS AND FINGERPRINTS

"How does this diabolical monster succeed in his infernal work time after time, in the midst of teeming millions of individuals, every one of whom would be only too glad to discover him, and to be the means of bringing him to justice? But no one out of all these multitudes, so far as they are aware, ever get a glimpse of him."

'The Demon of Whitechapel', published in
The Astrologer, volume two, number six, 1888

The words above were penned about Jack the Ripper, the infamous killer who spread raw fear across London's East End like a miasma as he mutilated its most vulnerable female inhabitants. One hundred years later, south London faced a similar problem. There was a man out there, "in the midst of teeming millions of individuals", attacking, mutilating and murdering women, yet nobody seemed able to get a glimpse of him.

Just like his Victorian counterpart, nobody knew the name of this modern-day Ripper, what he looked like or what he did for a living. This is less surprising than it may seem. Their deeds may be the stuff of nightmares but potential serial killers are extremely difficult to spot. They tend to look just like ordinary people, and often have ordinary jobs. It's not so much that they lurk in the shadows as that they blend with the crowd. Twentieth-century London's closest counterpart to Jack the Ripper has remained beyond our view for so long that he never attained the notoriety of his forebear. But we can now state his name with certainty. He is Robert Clive Napper

Robert was born on 25th February 1966. At opposite ends of the UK, two babies were born that day with a macabre shared destiny: in Dundee, a baby girl named Samantha was welcomed into the Bisset family; in southeast London, Robert was born in the suburban town of Erith. As each year's birthday candles passed, both children continued to live their separate lives oblivious of each other. But their paths would one day meet in the most terrifying way, when the boy killed the girl.

Robert was, according to his father Brian, "a lovely little boy" who showed no early childhood indications of the terrible deeds he would commit as an adult. However, his father does not seem to have been the most informed or involved parent. He openly declared that he did not know why his wife, Pauline, had seen fit to take this lovely little boy – as well as Robert's three younger siblings – for psychiatric assessment. Robert returned home, amused, to tell his father, "the psychiatrist thinks I'm mad, Dad." Indeed, this visit may

PHOTOGRAPHS AND FINGERPRINTS

have reinforced young Robert's sense of self and identity as unusual, different and 'mad'.

There are other indications that all was not rosy in the Napper household. His parents' marriage was violent and, after they split, Brian continued to harass his ex-wife. There were reports that Robert's mother was violent towards her children, while her ex-husband described her as promiscuous. Only the family will know the full truth, but such animosity is unlikely to have fostered a sound base from which children could emerge as secure, confident adults.

Brian finally disappeared completely from the family's life when Robert was nine years old. There was also to be another significant tipping point. Before becoming a criminal, this now fatherless boy would first become a victim. When Robert was twelve, in an event which presaged some of the crimes he himself would later commit among the Green Chain's leafy environs, he was confronted by a man as he walked through a local wood. The fact that it was broad daylight did not prevent his attacker raping Robert and sexually assaulting his two companions. Although the offender was caught and sent to jail, Robert had – like those he would victimise years later – now known and experienced the terror of sexual attack. The experience changed him dramatically. He became so withdrawn that he was likened to a robot.

As his father moved to the other side of the world and Robert entered his teenage years, his life became less stable. Unable to cope alone, his mother placed her children in foster care for a period of time. When reunited, she grew increasingly afraid of Robert, leaving him free to bully his siblings viciously – at one point firing an air gun at his younger brother's face. When Pauline Napper finally remarried, Robert's feelings towards his stepfather were clear for all to see: he simply refused to speak to him.

Contrary to his father's claims that there were no signs of childhood disturbance, Robert had undergone years of counselling and professional help by the time he left the family home in his early twenties. He had been diagnosed with paranoid schizophrenia, as well as Asperger's syndrome. In late 1989, when he was twenty-three years old and living locally in a Plumstead bedsit, Robert was briefly hospitalised following an overdose of nonprescription medicine. He gave his visiting mother and brother a blunt explanation for the incident: he was being chased by "some men" after raping a woman.

This shocking admission gave his mother the impetus to permanently cut off all contact with her son. She reported him to the police but, apparently, they could find no record of such an offence. As we now know, the police search parameters were too narrow to turn up a recently reported rape.

Long after his convictions for killing Samantha and Jasmine, Napper's mother admitted that this had been the turning point when he filial bond was irrevocably broken; she destroyed every photograph she had ever possessed of her son. Even at this early stage of his criminal career, she already wished to be rid of him. The photos couldn't simply be locked away in a drawer – they had to be destroyed, as did the memory of him by association.

So did his mother have some special maternal intuition? Did she *know* what he would later become? We cannot know her early gut feelings about her son but, even though some troubling signs were present, Napper did not seem like a

PHOTOGRAPHS AND FINGERPRINTS

monster. Before the 1990s, he certainly did not stand out as a future potential killer.

As the final decade of the twentieth century got underway, Robert blended in with the regular crowds of the southeast London borough of Greenwich. He had trained in catering, later working as a machine operator and a warehouseman in a plastics factory. His family knew of his bullying ways – both his mother and his siblings could testify to his callous behaviour. But out in public, he was just like thousands of others.

Each day, he mundanely passed the hairdressers, the stolid redbrick Barclays bank on the corner, the tired, tile-fronted pubs and the discount furniture shops, maybe stopping off at the mini-market for milk or bread. The waist-high metal barriers which lined the kerb along Plumstead High Street kept people safe, preventing them from stepping into the road in front of the coughing traffic that rushed by. The barriers also penned them in – just near enough to feel a killer brush past, perhaps, though no one would have spotted him at the time.

Robert Napper was just part of a crowd weaving left or right to sidestep oncoming pedestrians as they moved along the busy pavements on their way home. But as the fear in Napper's family home began to subside, now that he had left to make his own way in the world, the coming months and years would see it begin to creep across south London as surely as the Ripper-shielding fog of a century before.

★ ★ ★

The life Claire Tiltman had led could scarcely have been more different from Napper's childhood. Brought up in

Greenhithe, Kent, Claire was a much-loved only child whose parents, Cliff and Lin, had made sure she was always sheltered from any harm the world could inflict. Now, like all parents, they had to adjust to their child's growing independence and accept her going out unaccompanied. But now, as their daughter turned sixteen, it seemed that the biggest worry Cliff and Lin faced was her future career ambitions – Claire hoped to pursue the honourable but dangerous vocation of a firefighter when she left school.

She also lived just a thirty-minute drive from Robert Napper's Plumstead home.

On 18 January 1993, just four days after her sixteenth birthday party, happy grammar schoolgirl Claire set off to visit a friend. Although it was only 6pm it was a dark mid-January night. As she turned off London Road into an alleyway to make her brief midwinter walk even shorter, Claire was suddenly and repeatedly stabbed more than forty times.

Her attacker fled, leaving her clinging to life. Brave Claire continued to fight for forty-five minutes as ambulance crews tried in vain to stabilise her condition at the scene. But she finally succumbed to the stab wounds her killer had rained down on her.

Claire's mother, Lin, passed away in March 2008, fifteen years after she and her husband had been robbed of their precious daughter and all of life's hope and joy. She would never see Claire's killer brought to justice. Having emerged out of the shadows to inflict the most dreadful pain and terror on a young girl, he simply melted back into the early midwinter evening

Unlike teenager Claire, Jean Bradley had at least enjoyed a

PHOTOGRAPHS AND FINGERPRINTS

career. She had travelled the world as an air stewardess and even enjoyed the privilege of being part of the Queen's flight crew. By the time she entered her forties, this attractive blonde woman was a company director who had happily shared her life with the same man for twenty-two years. But, as with Claire, Jean's contented life would come to a brutal end in 1993.

Just two months after Claire left home to visit her friend, Jean was returning home from a day in the West End of London. Home was a four-bedroom detached house in Crowthorne, Berkshire, an affluent town within the London commuter belt. Worldly wise at the age of forty-seven, Jean steered clear of deserted places and had visibly parked her executive car in a safe street near to Acton tube station.

At 7:30 on the evening of 25th March, Jean walked from the station to her car to complete her journey home. But, as she unlocked the vehicle and bent to place her handbag inside, her killer pounced from behind. Like Claire, she was attacked suddenly, without apparent motive, and suffered thirty stab wounds. Like Claire, the emergency services tried to resuscitate Jean, but she too bled to death on a cold pavement.

Her killer escaped, but not before a passing driver leapt from his van to confront the attacker. Showing astonishing courage, for over a mile he chased an extremely dangerous man carrying a large butcher's knife inside a black bin bag. "You've attacked a woman. Now attack a man!" On this occasion, the killer did not melt quite so effortlessly into the midst of ordinary people, but still he finally escaped – and disappeared into a local housing estate.

KILLER IN THE SHADOWS

After Jean Bradley was killed, Alistair Bell quickly saw a link between her death and that of his own beloved wife, Penny, two years earlier. On 6th June 1991, Penny Bell had been killed in the car park of a public swimming pool in Greenford, just three miles away from where Jean would meet her brutal end. Like Jean, Penny had been in what should have been the relative safety of her own luxury car, where she was stabbed fifty times. Also like Jean, she was an attractive, blonde-haired woman in her early forties with a settled relationship and a successful career as a company director.

Police investigating Penny's murder thought at first that she must have known her killer. Penny's husband, Alistair, thought otherwise, and felt sadly vindicated by the death of Jean Bradley. He commented at the time that it seemed "too similar not to be linked to my wife's murder." For there was a killer on the loose who attacked swiftly, without warning, stabbing his victims to death apparently without motive.

The killings did not stop there. Eleven months after Claire Tiltman was stabbed to death, and nine months after Jean Bradley's contented life had ended, Samantha Bisset was murdered at her flat in Plumstead. Samantha was a blonde twenty-seven-year-old whose life had changed completely when she became a mum. Although she had taken on the tough job of being a lone parent, her life now felt complete and she doted on her daughter, Jazmine.

This time, the murder took place indoors. Samantha was stabbed repeatedly just inside the entrance hall to her flat. Unlike Claire and Jean, she was unlikely to have survived for any period of time. Samantha was stabbed eight times, but one blow was delivered with such force that it severed

PHOTOGRAPHS AND FINGERPRINTS

her spinal cord completely. The probability that she died quickly was the only accidental mercy in a crime so vicious and horrific that it left seasoned police officers, accustomed to dealing with the inhuman extremes of human behaviour, stunned.

Before and after this attack, the killer did not emerge from and retreat into invisibility quite so quickly. There were signs that he had been watching Samantha beforehand. A neighbour had earlier spotted a man with "piercing eyes" looking at her flat, and Samantha herself had told her boyfriend, Conrad Ellam, only a week before of a peeping tom who had run off when she spotted him looking through her window. It is possible that this was not the only occasion on which he peeked beneath the gap at the bottom of her window blind to watch her.

Ellam told police that they never made love in the sole bedroom because Jazmine shared it with her mother. Instead, while they saved for a bigger flat together, the couple confined their sex life to the lounge, always waiting until Jazmine had gone to bed.

The killer left Samantha's body on the lounge floor, displayed in the same position in which she had recently made love to her partner. Although Samantha's death was swift, her murderer had the luxury of being alone in private with her body, completely unseen. He had no need to try to act normally because there was no one watching him.

While her devoted mother lay dead in the hall, Jazmine slept unprotected. Conrad Ellam described his girlfriend Samantha as a peaceful and gentle "ex-hippy . . . against smacking kids, so all Jazmine knew was a lovely world where everyone was nice to her." Her mother's killer sexually assaulted Jazmine in her own bed and then suffocated her with the duvet she had been tucked up in earlier that evening. The little girl was four years old.

Leaving Jazmine dead in bed, he now moved Samantha to the privacy of her lounge. While wearing her towelling robe to protect himself from the bloodstains, he carefully mutilated her to the degree that police struggled to determine whether she too had been sexually assaulted – or even whether she had managed to put up any kind of fight. He inflicted a further sixty knife wounds on her body; sawed her open from the neck to the pubic bone; opened her ribcage to display her internal organs; tried, but failed, to dismember her legs; took a part of her lower abdomen away with him as a trophy; propped her hips up on a cushion (just as he'd seen her positioned through the window, with her boyfriend) to show her mutilated genital area prominently, and, finally, covered her with a robe and other items he had taken from her linen cupboard.

It was perhaps a very small mercy that, when Conrad Ellam discovered his girlfriend at her flat the next morning, he knew he could not face lifting the covering on her lower body. The sight was so shocking that the police photographer stayed off work for many months afterwards.

But, thankfully, the man who had destroyed the little Bisset family unit did not vanish completely. Despite the similarities in their mutilation techniques a full century on, this latter-day Jack the Ripper did not dissolve into the crowd forever. Like a London fog of old, the fear eventually lifted when Robert Clive Napper was caught.

PHOTOGRAPHS AND FINGERPRINTS

Napper had left his fingerprints in Samantha's flat, which police had on file from youthful arrests for shoplifting and a conviction for possessing a firearm in 1992, for which he served a brief spell in prison. He had also left in the kitchen the footprint of his baseball boots, a new style that had not yet sold in great numbers. Importantly for the prosecution case, when police came to arrest him he spontaneously denied ever being at Samantha's flat – leaving him unable later to offer an innocent explanation as to how his fingerprints got there.

Although Napper was by then safely behind bars, there was a longer than usual delay in processing the forensic evidence in the Bisset case. The fingerprints taken from the flat to distinguish Samantha's from her murderer's were not of the best quality. Despite fingerprints being unique, even between identical twins, Napper's were a strangely close match to Samantha Bisset's own. Coupled with the odd coincidence that he shared Samantha's birthday, fingerprint experts were initially fooled into thinking that they were looking at Samantha's. But persistent detective work continued, and they eventually linked Napper to a series of 1992 attacks in the locality of southeast London.

★ ★ ★

So why did the police not connect the murders sooner? Certainly there seem to be blindingly obvious links here. One of the most robust findings of police investigations is that offenders don't travel far to commit offences. The police know this only too well, so why didn't anyone put the pieces together? Claire, Jean, Samantha and Jazmine all lived in or around the London suburbs; they all died at the hands of a knife-wielding killer in motiveless attacks during 1993. Napper was a murderous offender who lived nearby. So he's clearly the culprit, isn't he?

It's time to admit that, up to now, we've been giving you selected information. None of the above information is wrong – it's all true. What's also true is this: at no point have we told you that Robert Napper killed all the victims. We think it's a fairly safe bet that you may have reached that conclusion, but you made those connections yourself. We only told you that he killed Samantha and Jazmine – the only killings he was prosecuted for.

When people criticise the police for failing to make 'obvious' links, they've only ever been made privy to part of the story via the media. If this is all we hear, we pretty soon fail to ask whether anything else was available. It's a bit like relying on someone else to do our shopping for us. If they only ever bring home digestive biscuits and bottles of lager, we may soon come to believe that the supermarket doesn't sell Rich Tea/shortbread/chocolate cookies/cider/lemonade or milk. We may even start complaining about what a useless shop it is.

The point is that we need to look beyond what we're given. Instead of drawing conclusions or even passing judgements based on limited information, we always have to ask what else we're not being told, what else is in the big picture that the purveyor of information (whether forensic psychologist or newspaper reporter) is leaving out.

Indeed, knowing what to ask for and knowing that one may not have the whole picture is one of the hallmarks of

PHOTOGRAPHS AND FINGERPRINTS

decision making in criminal investigations. Novices tend to take information at face value and don't know what (if anything) else they need in order to make an informed decision. We've been giving a less than full picture to illustrate how easy it is to make links and draw conclusions from selected evidence, instead of asking what the big picture is and what's missing from it. In other words, what else was going on that prevented or deterred the police from putting these murders together?

We know this much: Napper pleaded guilty to the manslaughter of Samantha and Jazmine on the grounds of diminished responsibility and is, to this day, still detained in the high-security mental hospital, Broadmoor. When we look into why certain killers have or have not been locked up for their dreadful crimes, we also need to remember that the very essence of our justice system can be explained thus: it's not necessarily about what is *true*, it's about what we can *prove*. The sad fact is that Claire's and Jean's cases remain unsolved – there just isn't any evidentiary proof. That is a separate matter from what is *true*. It may not be true that Napper killed other victims; or it may well be true. Let's give you a bit more information and add a little more to the picture.

★ ★ ★

Colin Ash-Smith was a young milkman in his twenties – another ordinary person doing an ordinary job. The only thing that perhaps singled him out from the faceless crowd was the fact that his mum was the mayoress. Otherwise, Colin went about his daily business as part of the local community, joining in with family parties and such when he wasn't working. Community members spoke of his mum's pride in her son; they also told of how the tight-knit Ash-Smith family stuck together to help each other out. When his parents, Diane and Aubrey, needed to support close friends who had been bereaved, for example, Colin remained close at hand.

In 1996, Colin Ash-Smith was given three life sentences following the attempted murder of twenty-one-year-old Charlotte Barnard. Ash-Smith stabbed Charlotte over twenty times. In addition to this crime, he had earlier kidnapped a twenty-seven-year-old woman outside her home, stabbed her in the neck and tried to rape and strangle her. He also forced another woman into a factory yard, slashed her throat and stabbed her sixteen times. It is a sad truth that Robert Napper was not the only criminal with this particular *modus operandi* during the 1990s.

As already stated, it's a reliable statistical fact that offenders don't travel far to commit their crimes. In fact, it is a general rule-of-thumb that the more violent the crime, the less likely it is that the offender will have travelled any distance. Napper may have lived a thirty-minute drive away from Claire Tiltman, but Ash-Smith lived much closer. He attacked Charlotte mere yards from the alleyway where Claire died. The close friends that Colin Ash-Smith's parents helped through their grief were Cliff and Lin Tiltman. The Ash-Smiths had even helped to arrange Claire's funeral, which Colin attended.

Do you still think it was Robert Napper 'whodunit'? Certainly, Claire's parents believed their daughter was killed by Ash-Smith. His mother, however, flatly refused to accept

PHOTOGRAPHS AND FINGERPRINTS

her son's guilt; she was arrested over her admission during a television interview that she had instructed her husband, Aubrey, to dispose of a knife. Aubrey confirmed that he had taken a knife from the house, boiled it clean, broken it into pieces and thrown it away. He eventually served a twelve-month sentence for perverting the course of justice.

Colin Ash-Smith held a self-confessed obsession with Jack the Ripper, so it seems plausible that he modelled himself after the butcher of Whitechapel. He also made claims to one victim that he travelled to London about once a year to find a woman to rape. (This may or may not have been true. The young man was also deluded enough to hold the – very real, to him – belief that he was Superman.) Given the offences he was convicted of, his claims were disturbingly plausible. It is also possible that, as a sex offender capable of extreme violence, he may have killed. But we don't know; much less are we able to prove it. Forensic psychologists, like any other scientists, need proof; so do police, lawyers, judges and juries. If we can't *prove* it, we can't accept it as *true* (even though it may be so).

Nevertheless, psychologists know that it's a part of human nature to look for links between things or people or situations, to try to put things into categories – it's the way we began to make sense of the world as we evolved, in looking for patterns of similarity. We all do it, often so rapidly that the brain doesn't waste much time figuring everything out from scratch. Moreover, we put similar things into categories so frequently that we are scarcely conscious of it. Those children walking along the road who seem to belong with certain adults are put into the category 'family'. Those teenagers who all wear black clothes and makeup and listen to a certain type of music are placed in the category 'goth'. Those people who investigate crime to earn their living are put into the category 'police detective'. Those women who all lived in the same part of the country and died of multiple stab wounds are categorised as serial-killer victims.

We may even come up with a more narrowly defined category: 'victim of Robert Napper', when maybe it should have been 'victim of Colin Ash-Smith'. Maybe our personal biases caused us to make a mistake when we perceived certain similarities. Psychologists even have a term for people finding patterns in events that are actually meaningless – it's called a 'clustering illusion', and police have to be trained to avoid such natural human tendencies. Let's suppose some overzealous detective had managed to build a case against Ash-Smith and saw him convicted of all the crimes against women we've discussed up to now. Robert Napper would still be peering through windows, prior to butchering women in their own living rooms

Obviously, the police do try to look for solid links and they also have to look further afield (just because most offenders live locally to their crimes does not mean that they all do), and investigate suspects who stand out from the ordinary public. Alan Conner was one such person – a drifter suspected by Kent Police of having killed Claire Tiltman, though no definite link could be established. Conner committed suicide a year later, after he had raped and killed Sandra Parkinson, a twenty-two-year-old waitress who lived in Devon.

Some do not stand out at all at the time of an investigation and can only be recognised with hindsight. Peter Tobin did

PHOTOGRAPHS AND FINGERPRINTS

not come to light as a killer until 2007, when he was found guilty of the murder of twenty-three-year-old Angelika Kluk. Angelika was a Polish student whose body was discovered in a Glasgow church where Tobin did odd jobs. It then came to light that other young women had died in the early 1990s, in close proximity to where Tobin was living or working. Fifteen-year-old Vicky Hamilton went missing from West Lothian in February 1991, as she waited for a bus to take her home to Falkirk. Dinah McNichol, aged eighteen, disappeared in August 1991 from Liphook, Hants, after attending a music festival. Only after Tobin had emerged as a killer, following his 2007 conviction, were police able to look back and put the pieces together.[1]

Foresight is akin to doing a jigsaw when you don't have all the pieces; much of the information is just not available at the time. Hindsight is like being given the box lid with the picture on it – we may look back and wonder why police didn't catch someone sooner, but we need to remember that they did not work from the same starting point. This psychological phenomenon, 'hindsight bias', is also called the 'knew-it-all-along effect', or by its Latin term, *vaticinium ex eventu* (foretelling after the event). For example, if we told you that Mark Chapman shot John Lennon and then asked you how confident you would have been in arriving at the same conclusion, you would be likely to generate a more confident answer than if we'd asked you *beforehand*. It is a perfectly normal bias, and none of us are immune from it.

---

1 At the time of writing, the horrors of Josef Fritzel's twenty-four-year incarceration of his daughter and family had recently been discovered. Now that the name and face of the offender are known, another woman has come forward to identify him as her rapist. It will be no surprise at all if there are more.

KILLER IN THE SHADOWS

Once a face and a name – Peter Tobin – was on the lid of the jigsaw box, other pieces fell into place. Police soon unearthed the bodies of Vicky and Dinah in Irvine Drive, Margate, where Tobin had once lived. An ordinary house in a regular street, with an ordinary garden that held the remains of two teenage girls and left their heartbroken families unaware, for sixteen long years, of just what had happened to their daughters. Although painstaking, it was relatively straightforward to work backwards from that point and trace Tobin's history. There were probably even similarities or links between the young women linked to him, but we can only see them with hindsight.

Until Tobin emerged from the crowd and stood out as a killer, it was impossible to make those links. It was not until December 2008 that he was finally convicted for the murder of Vicky Hamilton. Although the police, like everyone else, are not perfect, we would not criticise them for failing to spot links unless we knew a whole lot more about the big picture. It is extremely difficult to look forward when only partial information, or perhaps none at all, is available. It is similarly difficult when a great deal of information is available and you don't know which pieces belong to which jigsaw. In this short chapter, you may even have incorrectly pieced some information together yourself.

Robert Napper was finally locked away on 9th October 1995, for killing Samantha and Jazmine Bisset. Now he too had a face and a name, and the police had a clear picture to work from. It made him resemble nothing less than a modern-day Jack the Ripper. But what could truly be known at this point?

PHOTOGRAPHS AND FINGERPRINTS

We know that people whose first offence causes the death of another tend to be found in the same domestic arena, and the victim is usually a partner or other relative. (This doesn't mean that fatal violence erupts from nowhere. It may just mean that previous assaults went unreported to the authorities.) However, Napper had killed two strangers. It was extremely improbable that this was the first occasion on which he had displayed sexual violence. Much more likely was that his offending behaviour had escalated up to a point of shocking savagery, and the Bisset deaths were the culmination.

Now police could look back to see what else he had done. It transpired that Napper's name was also linked to a notorious unsolved case in the UK. For Laurence Alison, the co-author of this book, this was the case which had occupied innumerable hours, days, weeks and months when he was a student psychologist. Indeed, looking back from this distance, one could say that it amounted to a professional obsession with a man whose identity had remained a stubborn mystery for sixteen years.

Now, finally, he could not only be glimpsed, he also stood out clearly from the crowd. Robert Napper was now identifiable as the man responsible for one of the most infamous and brutal crimes of the late twentieth century. He had killed Rachel Nickell. Unsurprisingly, his crimes against women did not begin there.

CHAPTER TWO

MOTHERS, MURDERS AND THE GREEN CHAIN RAPES

By the time that Napper was carrying out acts of butchery in the home of Samantha and Jazmine Bisset, the police had been through a desperate but unsuccessful struggle to find the man who had stabbed Rachel Nickell to death, while her small son looked on.

Of course, from our perspective, with Napper's name and face clearly visible, the links seem obvious. This was the second time in sixteen months that a young, blonde-haired mother in her twenties had been knifed to death in a south London suburb while her child was present. The killer was evidently a man whose rage was such that it fizzed and spat until its boiling force poured down his arm, into the blade in his hand, and then into his victim, again and again . . .

His rage was so fierce he could not stop to think of the children present. Or perhaps it was no coincidence that both Jazmine and Rachel's little boy, Alex, were present at the scenes of their mothers' deaths

Mercifully, the presence of children during such offences is very rare indeed. Although a frighteningly large number of children witness extreme violence against their mothers every year, these tend to be domestic disputes. This in no way lessens the intensely awful impact of this most extreme crime, but 'stranger murder' is rare and the sexual murder of a stranger rarer still.

The idea of the killer madman who leaps out of the dark has an immensely powerful hold on the imagination, and may make some women scared to go out at night. So they stay home when it's dark, taking care to lock the doors so that *he* can't get in. In truth, the danger is already in the house.

Statistically speaking, women are killed far more often by a husband, boyfriend, ex-husband or ex-boyfriend. At least 2,400 women are killed by an intimate partner each year in the US, and children are present at sixty percent of those murders. With an average of 2.3 children in the home, this means that roughly 3,300 children per year witness their mother's murder. In the UK, between 200 and 250 women are murdered per year, with roughly half of these as the victims of domestic homicide. If we apply the same ratio of 2.3 children in the home in sixty percent of cases, that is roughly 150-170 children per year who will bear the lifelong scars, not only of losing their mother before they grow up, but of witnessing her death in violent circumstances.

However, this figure is drastically reduced in terms of stranger murder. In fact, we struggled to find any specific cases in the UK in the past twenty years. One example is the murder of Lin Russell in Kent, killed in front of her

MOTHERS, MURDERS AND THE GREEN CHAIN RAPES

daughters Megan and Josie. Lin's killer also murdered six-year-old Megan, but nine-year-old Josie survived the ferocious hammer attack. On 9th July 1996, the Russells were unlucky enough to come upon Michael Stone in his car during the family's walk home to Nonington, from the girls' school in Goodnestone.

If it were possible, the horror and violence of such a crime seemed heightened by its taking place in a small corner of England where even the place names were suffused with the peace and stillness of the country. The two little sisters wandered across cornfields and along Cherry Garden Lane, a track that led to their home at Granary Cottage, regaling their mummy with all the excitement of that afternoon's swimming gala. Lucy the dog nosed and sniffed her way along the green verges, with the occasional pause to wag her tail and look back to check on the little trio.

Then Stone caught up with them. He tried, and failed, to get money from Lin, before taking a hammer to her and both of the children; he also killed the family pet. Remarkably, against all odds, Josie survived – though her injuries were so profound that the police initially assumed she was dead. The language areas of her brain were damaged, and it took this resilient child nearly a year to even be able to tell police the details of her appalling story. However, even in this shocking case, there was no apparent sexual motive.

More recently, in 2002, Heather Barnett, a seamstress from Charminster in Dorset, was killed in her own home and horrifically mutilated. Her two children, Terry and Caitlin, then fourteen and eleven respectively, returned home from school to find her with her breasts cut off and, perhaps even more bizarrely, with locks of somebody else's hair carefully placed in her clasped hands.

Perhaps the owner of the hair will be able to provide a clue or even identify the killer? The story told by the few strands of a stranger's hair gathered from Heather's hands revealed that, over the previous three months, its female owner had changed her diet twice and been abroad twice; it even indicated the region of Spain (from Valencia to Almeria) she had visited eleven weeks previously for six days. Likewise, the hair told police that the woman had also spent a week in Tampa, Florida, just a fortnight before her locks were snipped off. These extremely specific details may yet yield a witness who can help police identify the criminal who destroyed Terry and Caitlin Barnett's childhoods.

In the past year of 2008, Sarah Melia, a thirty-three-year-old single mother from Horwich near Bolton, answered the door to a man in a red jacket and was frantically hacked to death, just over the threshold of her home. Sarah was discovered at the foot of the stairs by her fifteen-year-old daughter, Megan, when she arrived home from school. At the same time, her ten-year-old brother, Ethan, had set off home when Mum had failed to appear at the school gates to collect him. He was at least spared the aftermath. Police were at the scene by the time the boy arrived home to learn that he and his sister were motherless, their world changed forever.

Again, there was no apparent sexual motive. Although there are similarities in terms of the bizarre nature of the crime and the horror it will have imprinted on the children (especially those who discovered their mothers' bodies), neither Sarah Melia's nor Heather Barnett's children were present when the murders were actually committed. More often, offenders would see children or pets as distractions, or at least as irrelevant, and would prefer to attack lone women. So there are few cases with which to compare to Napper, either in terms of sexual murders committed in the presence of young children or severe violence and mutilation.

In the UK, the Serious Crime Analysis Section (SCAS) has the task of ensuring the details of all serious crimes are stored in one central database so that the information is accessible to all police forces in the country, details can be traced and links between similar crimes made. The SCAS database is effectively a repository of the worst behaviour in the nation. Even among this enormous dustbin of repugnant deeds, a search turned up only seven cases that fitted the bill. Three of them were committed by Robert Napper

So what can we make of a man whose specific intention was to target mothers? Of course, for him there was a very specific problem. Mums look just like any other woman in the passing crowd. Short of going up and asking them, it is hard to know whether they belong to your target victim category. The only really sure way is to simply select a woman accompanied by children who looks about the right age to be a mother (rather than a grandmother, say).

The reason why mothers were continually targeted by Napper is less clear. Perhaps he was angry with his own mother and used other women as surrogates for his rage. Or perhaps this was a more functional act, the child's presence enabling him to gain control over the victim. More disturbingly, it may be that the presence of frightened children actually elevated his sexually violent euphoria.

KILLER IN THE SHADOWS

This is an upsetting possibility to contemplate, but the fact is that research on human sexuality has persistently demonstrated that individuals can find all kinds of stimuli sexually arousing. These include high heels, nurses' uniforms or, more bizarrely, gasmasks, fur coats and even paperclips. The particular form that these sexual patterns take emerges from what psychologists call 'conditioning'.

Sexual conditioning has been widely researched among animals and humans. We will explore it in more detail later, but essentially, the process works by association – between the relevant psychological and physiological states (i.e. sexual arousal) and various previously neutral images (high heels etc). A wide range of behaviours and feelings can be induced by pairing particular stimuli with particular associations. So, for example, when experimenters present the smell of a particular perfume every time a rat copulates, it results in the rat developing a conditioned arousal response to the scent. After several pairings of copulation and scent, the rat will become aroused merely in the presence of the scent. Similar states can be induced in humans with repeated pairings. Presenting images of nude women alongside some other, previously non-arousing stimuli like paperclips can induce similar conditioning responses, so that the mere presence of paperclips can become arousing.

Psychologists discovered these processes through laboratory experiments dating back to the 1890s – the time of the most famous conditioning study, carried out by Ivan Pavlov, who noticed how dogs salivated *before* the food reached their mouths and began to examine why. (Essentially, it was because they could smell the chilli coating before they

MOTHERS, MURDERS AND THE GREEN CHAIN RAPES

ate it.[2]) He successfully conditioned them to associate food with the sound of a bell so that they salivated when it rang.

Away from the lab, in the real world, conditioning happens in just the same way – as a result of repeated experiences which happen to be paired and thereafter associated with some other stimuli. Some individuals' sexual tendencies may seem baffling to most of us, but the answer to the puzzle will lie in some conditioning experience in their lives. For example, finding gasmasks sexually arousing may seem decidedly odd, but it was not quite so uncommon among some adults in World War II. Couples did not abandon their sex lives completely just because they were forced to spend many nights sleeping in air raid shelters. Indeed, with the realistic possibility that death will come before morning it makes perfect sense for frightened couples to reach for comfort in one another's arms and make love. It may seem ridiculous now, but life or death consequences very quickly cause people to cease worrying about looking absurd. Before long, sexual arousal and the smell of a rubber mask had been repeatedly paired and conditioning had occurred.

Most of these conditioned pairings can be quite benign (particular costumes or lingerie, rituals, sexual games), but when arousal occurs in the presence of others' suffering, individuals can develop sexually sadistic patterns of behaviour. Studies have revealed that rapists are aroused by

---

2 This may seem so natural that we wonder what's to be studied – surely, everyone's mouth waters at the prospect of food that smells good? This is true, but the purpose of salivation is to help break down solid food and so, strictly speaking, it needn't happen when there is no food in the mouth. So what triggers this, and how does the body know how to prepare ahead of time? The answer is conditioned responses, which Pavlov called 'psychic secretion'.

the thought of nonconsensual sex, while comparison samples of men who are not sexually violent tend to show that such images block arousal.

In these sorts of studies it is hard to know whether arousal preferences for nonconsensual activity come first, or whether the actual act of rape conditions an offender towards sexual violence. Attempts have even been made to use conditioning to treat sexual offenders. For example, a Kansas secure facility offers a treatment programme where they present homosexual paedophiles with innocuous images of young boys and urge them to simultaneously inhale from an open jar of ammonia as soon as they experience sexual arousal. Here the aim is aversive conditioning – the pungently acrid smell associates young boys with unpleasantness and pain, and thus, supposedly, arousal will eventually be blocked.

It is true that it can take as little as just one conditioning experience to cause lifelong aversion to a particular stimulus – many of us never again eat a particular food that once made us vomit. We have evolved as the successfully surviving examples of our species by learning quickly not to poison ourselves. However, a permanent dislike for chicken soup because it was once eaten during the morning sickness stage of pregnancy is not an argument for the permanent success of aversion therapy. Thus the Kansas programme for paedophiles remains controversial.

Robert Napper belongs to that rare breed, the sexual sadist. More specifically, he may have been conditioned towards a sexualised response to a child's terror, or to the heightened state of fear that a mother would express when trying to protect her child. Of course, we cannot *know* that this

MOTHERS, MURDERS AND THE GREEN CHAIN RAPES

particular form of sadism was the key to Napper's sexual criminality, as nobody can read a mind to examine another's motivation. But the unusual fact that some of the victims he raped and those he killed were attacked in front of their children cannot be ignored.

* * *

By 1992, at the time of the massive manhunt for Rachel Nickell's killer, police had been trying for four years to pinpoint which of the ordinary-looking men walking around the London Borough of Greenwich was responsible for a series of violent sexual attacks. Until he stepped out from the crowd, he was known only as the 'Green Chain Rapist'. The Green Chain Walk is the name for a loosely connected series of open spaces that follow the southeast London sections of the River Thames. Local residents can enjoy greenery and birdsong while they meander along its series of footpaths. Although tall buildings and bustle are never far away, the Green Chain Walk weaves like a soft ribbon between them.

Julia[3] thought herself lucky to live in a detached house that backed onto part of the Green Chain Walk, more precisely Winns Common in Plumstead. Although, at thirty years of age, Julia's relationship with the father of her children was over, she was proud to be managing well as a single mum. 10th August 1989 began in the same ordinary way for her as for mothers across the entire country. By 8:30 Julia had already made her kids' breakfast and let the cat out of the back door, leaving it open so that it could drift back in along

---

3 Rape victims' names have been changed.

with the fresh summer air, then went upstairs and plugged in her hairdryer. There couldn't have been a more ordinary scene to start the day – save for the man who stood in her bedroom doorway, holding a knife as he quietly watched her dry her hair in her own home.

He ordered her onto the bed but, if the cloth he pressed against her mouth and nose was to silence her, it was unnecessary. Mindful that her family were still downstairs, Julia asked Robert Napper to close the door so that her children couldn't hear Mummy being attacked. He pulled her t-shirt up over her face and tied it across her eyes with a wire. Although he didn't have a full erection, he still managed to rape Julia on her own bed. In the space of a half-hour on that ordinary summer morning, her contented life disappeared completely, making its retreat along with Napper – away through the broken rear fence and across the open land of the Green Chain Walk, an area that would see up to seventy more sex attacks over the next six years.

It is hard to know exactly how many attacks an offender may be responsible for when he never admits guilt and other proof is hard to come by. Sex offences are underreported and, when they are, it is difficult for investigators to link them when there are observable differences. Apart from Napper's final slaughter of Samantha and Jazmine Bisset, the rape of Julia was probably the only attack that took place indoors.

But then, Julia lived to tell the police about the man who stole his way in on the fresh August breeze. She described him as approximately five feet ten inches, of medium build with mousy hair, wearing faded jeans and a brown jacket and looking about nineteen years old – much like thousands of

MOTHERS, MURDERS AND THE GREEN CHAIN RAPES

other young men around London, although Napper was twenty-three by then.

Robert Napper did not stand out from the crowd. Even when DNA from his semen established him as the man who had robbed Julia of the feeling of safety in her own home, he still did not stand out. She could not pick him out from the small group gathered for the ID parade. The mask he had worn while raping her made sure of that.

Napper did not wear a mask when he raped Shelley in March 1992. Neither did he enter her house. Three years on, his behaviour was different. Shelley had got off a bus just south of Plumstead at about 8:40pm, to visit her friend. As the seventeen-year-old girl walked towards the Cordwell estate where her friend lived, she noticed a man on the opposite side of the road. She saw him run towards the row of garages up ahead and thought little of the fact that he had vanished – just another local bloke going about his business.

But as she turned into the alleyway, he sprang from behind and grabbed her arm. Brandishing his knife, he threatened her, "If you want to live, don't make any noise." He dragged Shelley behind the garages, away from the prying eyes of other people. This time his violence levels had increased. He repeatedly punched her face, using the knife to remind her to "shut up if you want to live." He pulled up her top to fondle her breasts and, although he failed to penetrate her, ejaculated onto her after simulating sex while she was pinned beneath him.

He seemed calm as he stood up and fastened his trousers. But by now Napper's violence was so gratuitous that he kicked Shelley eight times in the head before strolling off, leaving his bloodied victim on the ground unconscious. It was just eight days before he would attack another seventeen-year-old.

Any parent will recognise the angry shout of "I'm going out!" followed by a slammed door as typical teenage behaviour after a family row. As Lydia stomped off down Eltham Palace Road, she headed for the soothing breeze of the open fields and woodland nearby. The area was crossed by King John's Walk, part of the Green Chain. From this higher vantage point, she could see right the way across to Canary Wharf.

At this time in the early March evening some of the office windows were dark, their occupants having left to make their second commute of the day; on other floors, the windows still formed belts of light which banded the building. The red lights that edged the four corners of each tower were a supporting act to that at the topmost point of the pyramid, flashing on and off each night to warn passing aircraft of the high-rise buildings. Lydia felt comforted by the solidness of Docklands. All those lives taking place off in the near distance made her problems seem smaller somehow. Feeling calmer now, she had decided to set out for home when Napper suddenly stood in front of her.

This time, he had no concerns about keeping his face hidden. Tugging off his balaclava, he ordered Lydia to her knees, telling her, "I've got this and I'll use it." The knife he held was no longer merely to gain compliance from his terrified victim; he dragged her top up and pushed the tip of the blade into her left breast. He stroked the knife back and forward from her breasts to her neck while he simulated sex as he lay on top of her – once again unable to attain a full enough erection to penetrate her.

MOTHERS, MURDERS AND THE GREEN CHAIN RAPES

Despite this, he spoke as if he were actually having full intercourse while he moved his hips back and forth, repeatedly questioning her, "Can you feel me inside you? Does it feel nice? Are you a virgin?" After he had ejaculated, he moved the knife to the entrance of her vagina and warned her, "You could have got this."

Lydia had hoped to return home with a clearer head that night. In the event, her evening walk ended in a desperate sprint for help as blood seeped through her bra. Two schoolboys helped her to a nearby shop to summon the police.

Two months later, in May 1992, another terrified young woman would run along King John's Walk to escape from Napper. Just like Shelley, Cara had first noticed him up ahead, standing near a dilapidated small building once used as changing rooms for the playing field. Once again, he allowed his victim to overtake him and then sprang from behind. The first that twenty-two-year-old Cara knew of the attack was when her head was wrenched back violently; despite the visceral surge of shock and fear, she was conscious of the roughly scratching fibres of a rope dragging across the skin of her neck. As it tightened, she was jerked back so violently that she could not help but let the handles of her tiny daughter's buggy slip from her hands. The two-year-old was strapped in safely enough, but had to sit alongside the railings and bushes next to the narrow footpath as her mother was repeatedly punched in the face and upper body.

Once Napper had knocked her to the ground he removed Cara's lower clothing, including her underwear. He masturbated near the entrance to her vagina, and then managed penetration by holding onto his soft penis. After he had achieved this he quickly withdrew and ran off. The end of this brutal attack was as unexpected as its onset, but for the young mum life was irrevocably altered. The innocence of a fresh spring day had suddenly changed into a scene of quiet, horror. On this seemingly innocuous May morning, the distraught and bloodied young mother snatched up her clothes and her child, running for the sanctuary of her mother-in-law's nearby house before she allowed herself finally to collapse.

We know the four offences described previously were committed by the same man. The DNA from the semen he left behind disclosed that it was Napper. Three of the women told the police as much, though Julia understandably struggled to pick him out of a line-up. The A-Z map of London found in his flat also told the police that Napper knew where the attacks had taken place – he had marked each spot on the map. There were also many other offences that the police thought Napper had committed, up to seventy sex attacks in the Green Chain area during that period. The trouble was that they only *thought* they knew based on similarities in the offences. DNA techniques were not as advanced as today and, without a significant quantity of material (Napper suffered from erectile difficulties), they could not prove it – at least not beyond a reasonable doubt.

Other factors also prevail upon the likelihood of prosecution and successful conviction. For an offender like Napper – where one extra conviction for rape would not have altered his sentence – consideration will be given as to which cases go forward. Victims may differ in their ability to cope with the ordeal of prosecution and trial, the process of which can stretch out over many months or even years. Police need to respect their wishes and ensure that the process does not re-victimise them all over again.

Thus, it transpired that – despite strong (DNA) evidence of links between the four offences – Napper was only ever convicted of one rape and two attempted rapes.

Despite claims to the contrary, the police *would* make links between the later deaths of Rachel Nickell and the Bissets; indeed, they announced their intention to interview Robert Napper in relation to Rachel's death at the first opportunity – the very day he was sent from court to be detained indefinitely in Broadmoor, as was duly reported in the national press.[4]

The central point is this: we cannot extract the notion that the police failed to make connections from the fact that they did not secure a conviction. Police may well make links between a particular series of offences (and it is a matter of public record that they did so in the Nickell and Bisset cases), but without additional proof these may be as substantial as spun sugar when it comes to prosecution. Any halfway competent defence lawyer can argue away 'mere' behavioural links between different offences – remember our natural human tendency to see patterns of similarity between events even when they aren't there? But investigators must nevertheless continue to attempt to link crimes. Even though behavioural links do not, in isolation, constitute proof, they can help to scaffold a case when combined with other evidence. Besides which, how else would a serial sex offender ever be caught?

4 *Daily Mail*, 10th October 1995.

KILLER IN THE SHADOWS

Although it was never proven in a court of law that Napper committed seventy-plus offences, others in the Green Chain area were certainly similar to those he was convicted of. A teacher who said, "That is the man definitely," when she saw an artist's impression of Napper told the police a familiar story at the end of August 1992. Out walking her dogs at breakfast time, she had first seen him overtake her and then stand rubbing his crotch. He used her own dog's lead, which she had draped around her shoulders as she walked, to drag her by the neck back towards him. He got as far as pinning her to the ground, but then quickly ran away.

The woman explained her lucky escape with the assumption that her dog had bitten the would-be attacker. All these details are similar to Napper's MO, while others are not. The first four victims were young women; the teacher who escaped was forty-seven. Her attacker neither beat her nor ejaculated on her. (Of course, maybe she was correct in thinking she had her dog to thank for the attack being interrupted.) She also noticed his penis had been fully erect when he was rubbing it through his trousers.

As summer turned to autumn that year, another young mum unknowingly passed close to Julia's home. As she guided her baby boy's pram across Winn's Common, she felt extremely nervous about a man sitting on a bench – so much so that she interrupted a courting couple sitting in their car to ask them to ensure she made it to safety. It seems her instincts proved correct, because as soon as she continued along the path the man immediately got up and followed her. The driver shining his headlights made the pursuer stand out from the evening shadows and thus hastily alter his route.

MOTHERS, MURDERS AND THE GREEN CHAIN RAPES

This action may well have saved the young woman's life – though once again, we cannot really *know* this. Certainly, the Senior Investigating Officer charged with catching the Green Chain rapist thought Napper was responsible for these incidents and a whole host of other offences where women reported peeping toms, indecent exposure and sexual assaults during the three years between the first known attack, on Julia, and that on Shelley. Although there were many, many cases that did not result in convictions, one comforting fact is that, after Napper was sent to Broadmoor in 1995 for killing Samantha and Jazmine, the Green Chain rapist abruptly stopped. We also know from psychological research that it is highly unlikely that such an offender will simply change his mind one day and behave differently.

Robert Napper very much fits the avoidant/sadistic sex murderer profile. We shall discuss the development of sex murderers in a later chapter but someone classed as 'avoidant' is – as the label suggests – characterised by a persistent pattern of social inhibition, feelings of inadequacy, extreme sensitivity to negative criticism and avoidance of other people. Describing Napper thus is, of course, easy now that we know he killed Rachel and Samantha. However, it would have been difficult to predict at the time of the first rape although, even then, the offender would be in the category of 'sexual aggressor against females' and, as such, we could draw upon some basic notion of his most likely characteristics.

We might surmise, for example, that the offender would be between twenty-five to thirty years old, most likely around twenty-eight; that he would have had a problematic childhood, potentially with conjugal violence between his father and mother, or parental absence; one or both parents may have been alcoholic, and may well have been violent towards him when he was a child. He would very likely have had problems at school in terms of rebellious and reckless behaviour, and personality problems in adulthood. He might be avoidant and schizoid with few friends. (A 'schizoid' profile will manifest in behaviours such as a lack of interest in relationships, a tendency towards a solitary lifestyle, secretiveness and emotional coldness.) He would be unlikely to be well educated and most likely in a menial job. Marital status would be difficult to predict, but if married there would be violence.

We know many of these things to be true of Napper. His childhood was problematic; his father emigrated in 1978 after a reputedly violent marriage; he was molested by an adult known to the family, and his bullying behaviour was problematic from early on. As an adult, he did not establish friendships easily. His colleagues in his factory job thought him "really boring" and something of a loner; his foreman described him as "really quiet; he kept himself to himself."

This is what makes profilers seem like mind readers – many predictions are very accurate. However, other than age, few of these details would have assisted the enquiry team at the time. The police cannot search databases for folk who had problems as a child or who had violent parents. What they would want to know at the earliest stages was whether the murders of Nickell and Bisset were linked and whether these offences were part of a series. Indeed, one of the first issues for any enquiry team when investigating sex murders is whether the offender has done this before, whether he is

MOTHERS, MURDERS AND THE GREEN CHAIN RAPES

likely to do it again and whether he is likely to escalate. They will ask analysts, profilers and behavioural advisors questions about linking crime, risk assessment and recidivism.

We know that Napper viciously attacked young mothers; this is a fairly consistent aspect of his offending, although his offences escalated from rape to murder. Violence was also a consistent feature, though it too escalated over time. There was always some level of threat or actual violence towards his rape victims, but it became more severe and gratuitous.

This is not to argue that there is such a thing as an acceptable level of violence – we mean 'gratuitous' in the sense that, even from the offender's distorted perspective, it did not aid the commission of the offence. Nobody needed to be knocked unconscious in order to comply. When Napper did this, it was simply violence for violence's sake. He moved from using the knife as a threat, to using the blade to pierce a victim's breast, to the full-scale atrocity of frenzied multiple stabbings to obliterate his murder victims – the final pinnacle being a slow and deliberate dissection of Samantha Bisset's corpse.

With hindsight it is easy to ask, *Why didn't more people link these crimes?* Here we have a man who starts with rape and escalates to murder; he uses a knife and there are children present in several cases. Surely that must be rare? The links between Bisset and Nickell are even more obvious – an attractive blonde victim, murdered in the presence of her young toddler, and mutilated with a knife, all occurring at murder scenes (Wimbledon and Plumstead) within fifteen miles of one another.

In actual fact, all these particular instances did occur to the police. But they needed further evidence, which would only eventually appear in the form of DNA when the technology had caught up. In general though, forensic psychologists need to know whether certain behaviours really are a basis for linking or not. We also need to be able to do something far more practically useful than giving smartarse reasons why something might be true – but there again, equally might not be.

Academics have made significant contributions to many operational areas. Geographical profiling is a major case in point. This is an area which has advanced considerably since the early 1990s and provides some of the most reliable information about offenders. Indeed, it is one of many areas to undergo a radical professional overhaul in the new millennium.

Specialist geo-profilers now work in the National Policing Improvement Agency (NPIA) and lend their expertise to criminal investigations. Given the Green Chain rapes to investigate, and knowing that travelling distance to offences is a reliable foundation from which to begin, today's geo-profilers would break down the 'subtasks' the offender needed to accomplish in order to escape and examine the exit points from the scene of each attack. They would systematically consider the most likely route home, including temporal (time) and topographic (detailed 'lay of the land') patterns that may influence the choice the offender makes in targeting crime scenes.

Relatively simple heuristics ('rules of thumb' that save us time) around geo-profiling have now been scientifically demonstrated. These include the 'centre of gravity' theory: if

MOTHERS, MURDERS AND THE GREEN CHAIN RAPES

you imagine we take a transparent plastic sheet printed with a standard graph (which has the usual 'X axis' running horizontally along the bottom and a 'Y axis' running vertically up the side), we place our see-through graph on top of a map showing the crime scenes; each offence will now have a 'value' on both the X and Y axes. Next we take the X and Y values (the coordinates) of all offences and calculate the average. The average X and Y coordinates of known linked offences form the centre of gravity (imagine the middle point of a circle on the map) which can then be used as a starting point for any search parameters.

Of additional value is the basic finding that offenders tend not to offend in their immediate vicinity (too risky), but, at the same time, don't travel too far away (safe, familiar). As such, the two furthest known linked crimes can be used to demarcate the diameter of the circle with a nearly ninety percent chance that the offender lives within that region.

Different crime types have different 'shapes' that can be overlaid on any map of the area in question and used as a starting point to narrow search parameters. These shapes are influenced by the nature of the target victims (static v. mobile). Thus, a series of burglaries (static targets) tends to occur within a thin wedge shape; serial rapes are more likely to be described within a windscreen wiper shape (i.e. less acutely concentrated); serial murders can be described by a more obtuse, angled chunk of the circle.

However, beyond these simple heuristics, easily taught to the novice, are more detailed, domain-specific types of expert knowledge that relate to the subtleties of temporal factors, base rates, consideration of population density, other behaviours exhibited in the crime, other crimes in the geographical area, and so on. The addresses within a demarcated area can then be crosschecked with other databases – for example, investigators can identify people in the area with relevant previous convictions or even check local hospital records. Police today have a better place to start and a regular team of experts on which they can rely.

These days the geography of the Green Chain rapes would be considered before attempting to delve inside the mind of the perpetrator. Indeed, geography is not the only factor that would take precedent over penetrating the 'mind of a criminal'. Timing of the offences would also be a priority in terms of linking. Thankfully, these types of offences do not occur that often, so if two, three or even four happen within a short period of time in the same vicinity it is more likely that they were committed by the same offender.

So, does this not contradict our warning in Chapter One, to beware of clustering illusions and making links where none exist? In fact it does not. It just means that there are no absolutes, no black and white, just probabilities and shades of grey. The answer is always, "It depends," and investigators must explore carefully the things that it depends upon. To do this, they would consider 'base rate frequencies': the bottom line (the base), and how frequently a particular offence occurs (the rate).

If crime figures showed two rapes in a particular neighbourhood over the last ten years, this would be the base rate for comparison. If reports were received of the abduction of a fifteen-year-old girl who was bundled into a car, sexually assaulted and then raped two weeks ago, a twelve-year-old boy sexually assaulted near the local canal last week and the attempted abduction of a four-year-old girl from a playground today, the close timing would ring alarm bells. The MO (and victim selection) is different in each case, but the timing is stronger cause for linking all three.

Indeed, there is compelling evidence that if an offender is attacking girls and boys of different ages (polymorphic interest) then he is very dangerous indeed. Three cases in a fortnight are completely disproportionate to the base rate of two cases in ten years. The geography and the timing (taking place in the same low-crime neighbourhood) are more significant than the behaviour. Considering only the elements that distinguish the offences (victim type and crime-scene behaviour) would suggest different offenders. However, behaviour is flexible and can change from one situation to the next. Geographical and base-rate information are more reliable. Contemporary investigators are less likely to be sidetracked by intriguing behaviour and will stick more closely to the consistent aspects.

The possible consequence of not linking these offences through a failure to prioritise geography and timing would be to leave a very high-risk polymorphic sex offender free to endanger others. Nonetheless, behaviour matters too; the proportionate significance is shown in the figure below:

KILLER IN THE SHADOWS

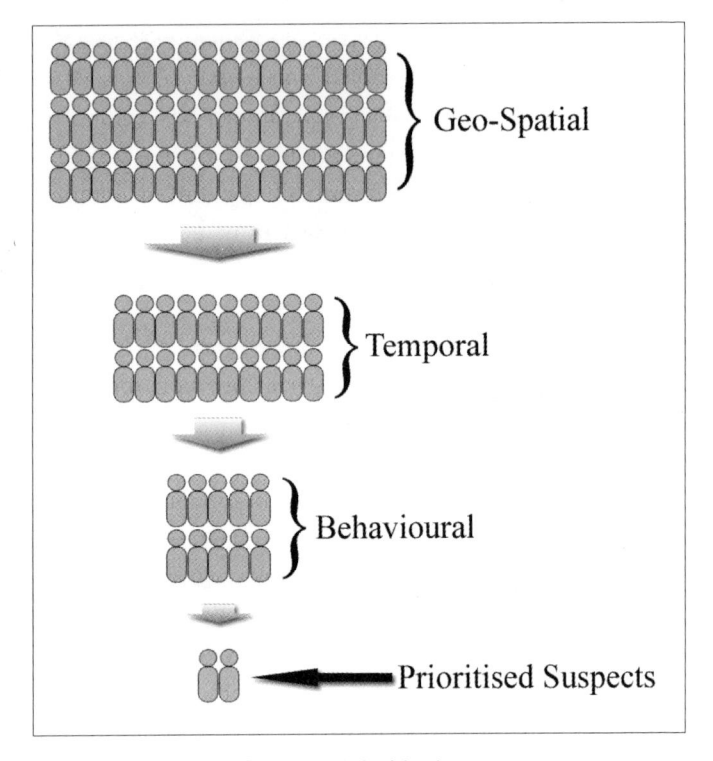

Figure 2.1 Features of Suspect Prioritisation

We need to look again at base rates, to understand the frequency of how often certain types of behaviour occur in rape generally. Behaviour that nearly always occurs (for example, vaginal penetration) is not terribly useful, because if all offenders do this then it is impossible to link one crime to another. If we were using vaginal penetration as a link, then almost all rapes would be linked to a common suspect. However, a very specific behaviour (like threatening a victim to comply and then brandishing a syringe if she struggles) might only occur in two percent of all recorded cases in the UK across a fifteen-year time span. So, if we have two crimes occurring in which the offender has used a syringe, we could quite reasonably assume they are linked. Needless to say, this obvious fact doesn't really require a psychologist.

If, however, we have one offence where a victim is threatened with a syringe and then, one week later in the same park, another rape occurs but no syringe is used, does that mean they are not linked? What if, after the initial threat, victim number two *did* comply? Would that offender need to use the syringe? We need not only to look at what happened, and how common or how rare it is, but also at *why* it might have changed. What else is going on in that situation that could suggest the same offender but, at the same time, explain the change?

This sort of behaviour, by its very nature, is rare. There are only a bundle of cases where there are unusual 'signature'-type behaviours – most rapes are relatively homogenous, in that large numbers of rapists use knives, threaten their victims, and so on. So the variation between one victim and one set of circumstances and the next, plus the relative rarity of unusual behaviour (so to speak), all make linking far more complex. We do need to know exactly *how* rare or common certain behaviours are. If you fill in the following table and indicate how often (in terms of a percentage) you believe these behaviours occur, if you think threatening the victim with a knife applies to nearly all cases then you might give a figure of ninety-five percent; if, however, you believe it hardly ever occurs then you might assign it five percent.

KILLER IN THE SHADOWS

Behaviour	Your estimated percentage frequency
Makes a surprise approach	
Child present during stranger attack	
Uses weapon to control victim (e.g. threatens with a knife)	
Offender reveals details about himself	
Offender kisses victim	
Offender rips clothing	
Blindfold or gag	
Offender kicks or punches victim (more than once)	
Offender apologises to victim	
Blitz attack (sudden violence on initial approach to overpower victim)	

Figure 2.2 Estimated frequencies of behaviours in sexual attacks in stranger rapes

In the next chapter, we shall reveal the answers that have been reliably established by academic statisticians and police data analysts. These figures were not known in 1992, at the time of Rachel Nickell's murder. Since then, many have been undertaking the laborious task of trawling through years of cases on database, so that investigators don't have to guess or make assumptions. But first, let's see how your estimates went ...

CHAPTER THREE
FEARFUL SYMMETRY

Behaviour	Approximate percentage frequency
Makes a surprise approach	35%
Child present during stranger attack	0.05%
Uses weapon to control victim (e.g. threatens with a knife)	22.5%
Offender reveals details about himself	40%
Offender kisses victim	36%
Offender rips clothing	12.3%
Blindfold or gag	3.5%
Offender kicks or punches victim (more than once)	15%
Offender apologises to victim	6.7%
Blitz attack (sudden violence on initial approach to overpower victim)	1%

Figure 3.1 Frequencies of behaviours in sexual attacks in stranger rapes

So, how did your estimates compare? When most people do this exercise, they tend to overestimate the hostile or aggressive forms of behaviour, such as ripping clothing or punching the victim. Rape is, for good reason, seen as a violent offence, which is probably what leads people to assume that serious physical violence is therefore common. It often plays out that way in the heightened dramatic action of movies.

In truth, victims are often so terrified that offenders can gain their compliance without actual violence (though the threat is common enough). In contrast, people tend to underestimate pseudo-intimate behaviour such as kissing although more than a third of rapists behave in this way. In fact, a man who tells his victim things about his own life is associated by very few of us with the type of person who forces sex on another – whereas well over one in three rapists 'chat' about themselves.

The important point is this: if detectives made the assumptions that most people make, then incorrect links, or perhaps no links at all, would be made. Rape, by definition, involves penetration. But knowing that all rapists behave in a particular way is not very useful for making links between offences. Look again at the table, however. If you were the investigator who was told that, say, Shelley had been kicked eight times in the head and Cara was repeatedly punched to the ground, it would be extremely helpful to know that only fifteen percent of offenders behave so violently.

Sex offences are terribly serious crimes, but an investigator would have to encounter 2000 sex offenders before coming across one who would stoop to commit his offence in front of the victim's child. As such, Robert Napper's behaviour was

FEARFUL SYMMETRY

very rare indeed. Such statistics make it easier for police and psychologists to link cases, and are especially useful where the evidence is less compelling in some than in others. It is easier for juries to trust the information when the prosecution can positively quantify just how *unlikely* it is that a particular type of criminal behaviour was committed by anyone other than the defendant. Behavioural consistency across a series of offences is therefore an important investigative tool.

Since the Bisset and Nickell cases, protocols and support frameworks have been developed by UK police forces to collect this sort of information and formally examine potentially linked crimes. Chief among these is the sixty or so-strong set of analytical staff working within the National Policing Improvement Agency's SCAS (Serious Crime Analysis Section) at Bramshill in Hampshire.

SCAS was set up in the wake of serial offences such as Robert Black's abduction and murder of three young children. Although he was suspected of further offences, Black was convicted of the murders of eleven-year-old Susan Blackwell, five-year-old Caroline Hogg and ten-year-old Sarah Harper.

We routinely warn children of such 'stranger danger' because the consequences are so horrific – not because they are common. In fact, this type of child murder by strangers is statistically rare and the figures have not changed in more than thirty years. However, the attendant fear has altered out of all recognition, to the degree that modern children forego the dizzy pleasures of ever playing without adult supervision and are denied all the learning opportunities of such unfettered play (managing risk-taking, problem solving, negotiating conflict, building relationships, developing the imagination, etc).

Instead, children remain within constant sight of parents reluctant to let the wind blow on them, travel nowhere alone and are regarded as in need of chaperones until they are at least as tall as their fathers. The change in our society, in terms of how we rear and protect our children, has been so profound that most people simply refuse to believe children are as safe from 'the bad man who might take them away forever' as Mum and Dad were thirty years ago, when they were little boys and girls with longer hair and wider flares.

(Indeed, a separate book could be written on the prospective collective neurosis visited by contemporary Western adults on their offspring. We do not yet know the impact these constraints are likely to have on the capacity of today's children to develop into psychologically healthy, independent, capable adults. But of course that is not our primary focus here.)

Between five and seven children are killed by adult strangers in the UK each year; if we wish to hark back beyond thirty years, to Granny and Grandpa's halcyon golden age, we find that they were in slightly more danger. They lived in a world without modern forensics, and the corresponding dangers may have been greater either because today's increased likelihood of being caught acts as a deterrent, or else because individuals can now be identified before they become serial offenders. There is also the alternative explanation that a more dangerous world has been made safer by increased vigilance – though it seems, on the face of it, that stable figures are scant reward for such mammoth efforts.

We must also recognise that figures are utterly and

FEARFUL SYMMETRY

insultingly irrelevant to the families of someone who falls prey to such a criminal. For the purposes of detection and linking offences, however, statistics matter. To remind ourselves of what we now know: US figures indicate that less than one percent of all murders are sexual murders; serial murders account for less than two percent of all murders in England and Wales since 1940. When we consider these two aspects in conjunction, the figure is even smaller for serial sexual murders.

Police investigating Robert Black naturally tried to identify whether there were links between the murders of three young girls over a period of four years – given the base rate information (the annual figures given above), it was highly unlikely there was more than one serial sex killer of children operating in the UK at the same time. Add to this the geography and MO – all the girls were taken from the north of the country, over an area spanning Leeds to Scotland, raped, strangled and dumped outdoors in rivers or ditches further south – and police became confident that they were seeking one man for all three murders, plus one attempted abduction in Nottingham where a fifteen-year-old had managed to break free. Black's behaviour was consistent enough for the police to be confident that all offences were committed by the same man.

Occasionally though, all the knowledge, investigative experience and statistical analysis in the world can still prove unsuccessful in finding an offender. Sometimes the improbable, the unlikely, the stroke of luck is the only thing that will close the case. It was just such a coincidence that led to the killer's arrest. He was a man whose name did not appear once among the twenty-two tons of evidence that had filled two entire floors of an office building over the eight years of the investigation. Hector Clark, the deputy chief constable who oversaw it, admitted that none of the 189,000 people involved – from detectives to witnesses to interviewees – had ever put Black in the frame as a possible suspect.

But as luck would have it, when Black attempted his next abduction a local man happened to be outside cutting his front lawn. The gardener had taken little notice as a six-year-old passed his house, just a neighbour's girl playing out in the summer sunshine. He vaguely noticed the blue Ford Transit pull over and the passenger door swing open. But, as he bent to unclog the grass from the mower blades, he could see from his worm's eye view first two and then, strangely, just one pair of legs.

Now his attention had been nudged, he looked up to see where the owner of the second set had disappeared to, perhaps half-expecting to see his small neighbour propped up high in the passenger seat. But little Mandy had vanished. He could still see the owner of the adult legs' upper body bent in the footwell, repeatedly shoving at something under the dashboard. Then the door slammed and the driver drove off. Luckily, the neighbour was unsettled enough to take the van's registration number, leaving his gardening and going straight inside to call the police.

Equally fortuitously, once the man went back outside to tell the police what had happened the van reappeared in the road. He broke off his story to shout an astonished, "That's him!", prompting a police officer to run into the street and force the van to stop. A flurry of activity ensued. As some officers arrested Black, someone else rushed to untie the sleeping bag by the passenger seat. The child looked out red-faced from the lack of air, patently terrified and rendered completely dumb. The man who released her from the bag was shocked into momentary stillness by the most improbable occurrence: the child inside the bag was his own daughter. Even when a strip of Elastoplast had been removed from her mouth, she was still speechless — even though the man who now held her safe in his arms was her own daddy.

It was, thankfully, the last time Black would get away with bundling a young girl into his van — a method he had consistently employed to procure victims. However, just because criminal behaviour like Black's is reasonably consistent, that does not mean it is identical on each occasion. The situation matters too, and the context may alter an offender's MO. For example, Andrei Chikatilo, a serial killer in the former Soviet Union, admitted he was responsible for a murder that the police had completely discounted due to inconsistencies.

The body in question was found completely dismembered. Although Chikatilo mutilated his victims and removed body parts, they tended to be abandoned as bodies that had bits missing — rather than, as in this case, just an assorted collection of pieces of a human being.

However, there was a completely functional explanation. Chikatilo had killed his victim indoors and, having done so, was faced with a disposal problem. He was very likely to be seen by neighbours carting a whole body out of his apartment and down the stairwells. Cutting it into smaller pieces made for easy transportation without raising suspicion. It was of no psychological relevance whatsoever, simply a straightforward practical strategy to help him evade capture. It was entirely due to Chikatilo's confession that this particular case was solved, as everybody on the investigating team believed a different person responsible.

Such a case reinforces how consistency must be used to make links between offences, but also illustrates the difficulties in doing so. We are always in the realms of probabilities, never absolutes; always working on what is likely but not certain; trying to bolster and strengthen those 'possibles' and 'probables' by looking at base rate information.

We only see profilers and detectives cracking the case in less than forty-eight hours in TV and films. In real life, there are hordes of police analysts, statisticians and academics working away in brightly-lit offices, continually updating and refining what is known about criminal behaviour on a worldwide basis. But it would make for a terrible movie pitch: "We open with a bunch of people in an office entering data onto spreadsheets; they maybe have a sandwich and then, after lunch, they conduct statistical tests on the data they entered in the morning." It might even be the dullest film plot ever.[5] But such 'number crunching' is vital to ascertain empirically (i.e. scientifically) how common or how rare particular behaviour is, or which type of behaviour is more consistent than others.

SCAS's remit is to explore possible links between sexual offences and murders, and they continually update an already large dataset (currently over 13,000 cases) which they use to make specific comparisons across discrete variables. Despite

[5] Just because *watching* something would be dull (and thus a bad movie idea) doesn't mean such fascinating work is itself dull, of course. Watching someone drink beer wouldn't make much of a movie either.

FEARFUL SYMMETRY

some of the distinct similarities in Robert Black's MO, the critically defining feature of most offence series is distance and time. We know that very few offenders have unique 'signature behaviours' that allow us to link series offences, and we also know that much behaviour is subject to change in the face of prevailing circumstances. Thus, a burglar will not jemmy open a back window if the front door of an empty house is left open. (In fact, according to latest Home Office figures, from 2007, a quarter of burglary victims are surprisingly helpful in simply leaving the doors unlocked.)

So what types of behaviour are relatively consistent and can help discriminate between one offender and another? Before we answer this, use the map below to consider which man you believe to be the most likely offender. It shows a series of offences (five in total) with the 'X' marking the spot where each offence took place. There is also a face to represent each suspect's home, along with some details about each man.

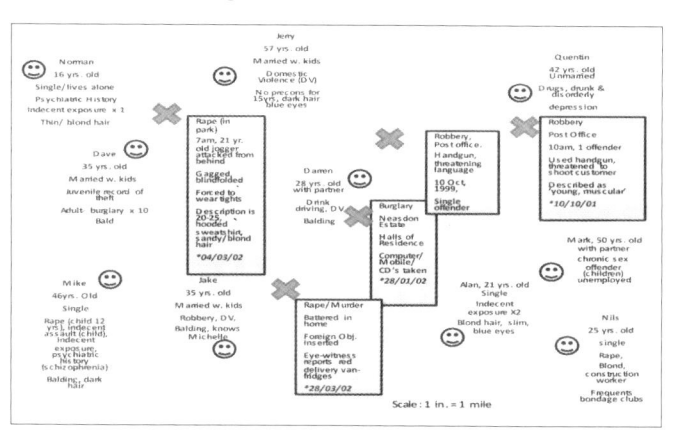

Figure 3.2 Whodunit? (Cross [X] denotes offence location/ crime scene. Face denotes offender's home address.)

KILLER IN THE SHADOWS

Though there would usually be more information than you have been given here, it is still interesting to reflect on your own thoughts and reactions. What often happens when this exercise is run in a psychology class is that students get wrapped up in the details of the offence behaviour. They spend a good deal of time working out whether blindfolds were used, further time thinking about the specific background characteristics of the suspects (for example, the fact that one visits bondage clubs) and also take into account the eyewitness descriptions provided with the map (one describes a blond male, aged between thirty to thirty-five years, of slim build).

Very often then, on the basis of these bits of information, they pick Nils as their number one suspect for the attack in the park. However, this attack occurs in the early hours of the winter months, when it is dark; the victim is attacked from behind and she is blindfolded. One has to seriously question how good the eyewitness information is likely to be. Students also make the leap from bondage fetish to binding, blindfolding and gagging. However, research on most rapists indicates that these actions are rarely fetishistic, but more criminally inclined controlling acts that disable the victim effectively enough to allow the offender to commit the rape.

Finally, students neglect the really key piece of information: the scale on the map. Did you ascribe any priority to it? As stated before, it's a solidly reliable finding that offenders don't travel far. Darren is the man who lives nearest to the crime scenes, but the trouble is that the map scale is probably the least exciting piece of information. But it is perhaps the most important of all, since it gives an indication of how far each

FEARFUL SYMMETRY

offender would have had to travel to commit each offence.

Assuming that the offenders' other relevant geographic anchors are close to where he lives (place of work, family, friends etc), this means that Nils would have to travel over twenty miles to commit the offence. Given that we know nearly ninety percent of rapists do *not* travel further than one and a half miles (Robert Black is almost unique as a UK offender in travelling long distances, and even that may be regarded as incidental in that it was job-related), Nils is *not* the safest bet – at least not according to statistical calculation, since he would have to be the one in ten offender that travels more than one and a half miles. (In fact, only one in a hundred rapists travel more than ten miles.) So why are we so powerfully drawn to Nils?

One plausible explanation is our readiness to see patterns in information (recall the 'clustering illusion'?), to derive inferences from those patterns and weave a narrative structure into how we think about crimes. How often do we, when presented with news about an unknown offender still at large, think about the 'sort' of person that has committed the crime? It is an almost inevitable and understandable natural process. Our lives are driven in part by the stories (or narratives) we create to explain the complex, multifaceted world we live in. We are predisposed to think in terms of who, when, where and why?

We all have a template that is as pre-prepared as a painting-by-numbers kit. This has its positives and negatives. It means that we have a framework which supports our thinking and helps us to organise information in a structured manner. However, it also means we don't begin from a genuinely open-minded place when we try to solve the problem creatively. Instead, we are already confined by the limits of our ready-made kit and we think we must fill in all the blanks in the picture marked, 'Why?' This very naturally leads us to the next stage, the gaps marked, 'Who?'

Detectives will have done the same when they were presented with the Green Chain rapes, the murders of Samantha and Jazmine or that of Rachel. Indeed, it would not be possible to function as a detective if these sorts of narratives weren't drawn upon. The danger comes when the narrative supersedes the evidence but someone continues with their story regardless. Not everyone has the necessary ability to change tack in the face of information that contradicts that storyline.

Nils makes for a good story, but the evidence shows he is not the most likely culprit because most violent offenders do not travel very far from home. So we might have been able to surmise, based on the very first proven attack by Napper, that the (then unknown) man who raped Julia lived very close to the victim's address (as he did). There are countless examples of very serious offences where the offender lived extremely close to the victim; they also often show consistencies in patterns of behaviour that allow for linking.

Such cases include that of Levi Bellfield, a man convicted of attacking three women (a jury was unable to reach a verdict on two further attacks); one victim, eighteen-year-old Kate Sheedy, survived, but two young women, nineteen-year-old student Amelie Delagrange and Marsha McDonnell, aged twenty-two, died. He confined his attacks to a small area in

FEARFUL SYMMETRY

the southwest London suburbs near to his home. Bellfield became known as the 'Bus Stop Stalker', owing to the consistent feature of attacking his victims near where they had just alighted from the bus.

Most of us, at some time, have stood in the darkness waiting. When the glow of fluorescent lights appears out of the distance, the oncoming bus is a welcome prospect. The moving windows of light suggest a comfort we can literally enter as soon as we board, settling into its warmth until journey's end. For Bellfield, lighted vehicles at night illuminated potential victims, placing them in a travelling glass showcase while he followed in his car, deciding which passenger met his preference for blonde-haired young females. And who would, as a result, feel hammer blows rained upon the back of her head.

He was extremely careful in avoiding detection. He moved often and his employment as a wheel clamper allowed him to switch cars regularly without much inconvenience. In this way, he confounded the dogged hours of police work spent searching CCTV footage for a link by sidestepping attempts to pick out the same suspicious car driving through different crime-scene areas.

Police have now linked him to the unsolved murder of thirteen-year-old Millie Dowler; Millie knew Bellfield because, at the time, he was dating her friend's mother. In fact, he was staying at his girlfriend's house – which happened to be just one short mile away from the schoolgirl's home, a mere 100 yards from the place Millie disappeared. Although the offending behaviour is not completely consistent (Millie is not believed to have died from hammer blows to the head), this may have been a case where other factors prevailed. Offenders are based close to their crime scenes.

Ian Huntley too lived close to his victims – on site in the village school where Holly Wells and Jessica Chapman walked to class each day. This case highlights the onus placed on investigators to use behavioural patterns to link offences. The consequent public enquiry[6] roundly criticised the police for not having spotted Huntley's consistent behavioural pattern sooner. His name had previously cropped up in eight separate sexual offence allegations, yet he had managed to clear the vetting process required of all adults who work with or come into contact with children, taking up residence as the caretaker of the school.

Anthony Imiela carried out nine rapes so vicious and was considered so dangerous that police launched the biggest manhunt since the Yorkshire Ripper to catch him. Prosecuting counsel declared that he repeatedly "used exactly the same hunting ground" near to his home in the village of Appledore in Kent, though once again police also had to consider linking behaviour that was not perfectly consistent. Imiela's last known attack occurred in Birmingham when he abducted and attempted to rape a ten-year-old.

Mabel Leyshon met her death aged ninety, the seeming victim of a ritualistic killing by a vampire cult. She had been discovered in her rural home on a small Welsh island with pokers carefully placed at her feet in the shape of a crucifix; an altar had been fashioned out of her mantelpiece, complete with red candles; her heart had been removed and neatly arranged on a silver platter. What first

6 Bichard, M. (2004). *The Bichard Inquiry Report*. London, England: Stationery Office.

seemed like lipstick traces on the rim of a drinking vessel were, on closer inspection, identified as the dried, flaky remnants of the old lady's blood, which the killer had evidently swallowed and savoured, perhaps as the pinnacle of an apparent sacrifice.

This would be the full-blown narrative explanation, where we fill in the blank spaces of 'Why' with especially lurid and macabre details. The far more prosaic answer lay – as is statistically predictable – very close by. She had been murdered by a seventeen-year-old paper boy who lived a few yards down the road. Matthew Hardman was in his first term at art college, favouring ghoulish images in his drawings. For sure, he had told another student of his interest in all things occult, but investigators did not need to focus on the dreadful but ultimately distracting details to find the person responsible.

In all of these cases, the offenders lived a few hundred yards from the attack site. As with other aspects of their lives, offenders are generally lazy and rather impulsive. Violence often erupts as a short-term solution to an immediate problem. Thus, the Peter Sutcliffes of this world are not the criminal masterminds of fiction, the 'Napoleons' of crime that an Ian Brady would like to believe that he is.

People may lump 'criminals' into one big category including the heads of drug-trafficking empires and other dubious underworld business practices, but it is no coincidence that such offences are described as *organised* crime. That is obviously not the type of offending we are discussing here. Sexual predators tend to be violent, impulsive and, albeit rational in some aspects, not especially sophisticated. Even though some may display forensic awareness and take steps to evade capture, they do not tend to inconvenience themselves greatly.

In the same way that we might nip down to the nearest corner shop to pick up the paper, so offenders will expend the least effort necessary to acquire targets. Moreover, in Napper's case – especially the attacks on the first known rape victim, Julia, and on Samantha Bisset – it could well be that both women were the subject of prolonged observation within his local 'comfort zone'. Certainly, Samantha's neighbour spoke of a peeping tom watching the Bisset flat. Such offenders are unlikely to travel large distances to spy on potential victims if they have a ready source at hand. Instead, they 'work' in areas that they are comfortable in, that feel familiar and from whence they believe they can exit quickly if necessary

Researchers have developed different models for the behaviour of offenders in relation to geographical area. One example is that of Kim Rossmo and his colleagues, who proposed types of hunting behaviour depending on the different ways that serial murderers act in selecting their victims. This model proposes four methods of victim selection: the 'hunter', who stays within a hometown/city but travels beyond his immediate home to go out looking for victims in an area he knows (e.g. Levi Bellfield following local buses); the 'trapper' is geographically more static and prefers to lure a victim into his home (such as John Christie, whose victims in the 1950s included a tenant in the same lodgings and her one-year-old child); the 'poacher' operates beyond his own city limits and will use other bases besides home (e.g. Robert Black, who travelled long distances), whereas a 'troller' seizes opportunities in an impromptu manner at any time they occur during the daily routines of his life.

There are other variables in the mix which take account of the 'tracks' or phases of the offence, as well as the method of attack. The unpleasantly theatrical term 'raptor' is used to label those who attack as soon as they encounter a victim, whereas a 'stalker', as the term suggests, follows a victim first, awaiting an opportune moment to attack. These models have strengths, of course, and help us to understand criminal behaviour patterns. But a common difficulty with such typologies is that they tend to reduce the fluid, endlessly adaptable and complex nuances of human behaviour to a terribly restricted menu of choice – A, B, C or D, which fits best?

By this token, Robert Napper was a *hunter*. He frequented the Green Chain area, moving out of his Plumstead flat into a locale he knew well, but nonetheless staying fairly near to his home base to commit rape. When his offending culminated in double murder he chose Samantha and Jazmine Bisset, who also lived locally. And then, in terms of attack method, he was known to have spied on Samantha prior to her death, which would place him firmly in the *stalker* category.

But then what about Rachel Nickell? She was killed twelve miles away from Napper's home, which is a significantly long distance away from his other offences and contradicts the reliably short distance that offenders are supposed to travel in order to commit crime.

This is readily explainable. He was a psychiatric patient at Queen Mary's Hospital on the edge of Wimbledon Common, where Rachel was killed. It makes perfect sense of the opportunity to commit the crime, but it really messes up the neat categorisation offered by the model. Shall we therefore place him in the *troller* category, on the basis that he seized an opportunity which presented itself during the routine of his hospital appointments?

Ultimately, the 'hunter' category may be the most meaningful for Napper – he was just a statistically unusual hunter who travelled further than most. This would be consistent with Napper's known interest in maps and their geography. The rail line in a westerly direction from his house would take him to Wimbledon Common (as well as the sites of a couple of other unsolved murders we will discuss later on).

Excepting the unlikely event that Napper tells us otherwise, we don't know whether he stalked Rachel beforehand – it's plausible, given that she was a regular walker on the common – or whether he simply attacked upon encountering her. With little more than a ten-to-fifteen-minute window between the last sighting of her enjoying a walk with her child and their dog and the discovery of her body, this would surely place him in the raptor category – the attack cannot possibly have been anything other than immediate and swift. It also seems to stretch the definition of the stalker type as someone who supposedly waits for an opportune moment.

To be fair, this particular model does incorporate geography and behaviour in a bid to address the

FEARFUL SYMMETRY

shortcomings of many other models that are even more reductionist, but the problem remains. Human behaviour is complex and will resist being placed into four, eight, sixteen or even thirty-two boxes. What placed Napper in one category for some offences (indoors, say), placed him in another for others, even when the behaviour was in many respects consistent across offences – it was sexual in nature, involving violence and knives, often with young mothers as victims. Notwithstanding our caution about clustering illusions and the limitations of typologies, there is something intriguingly, bizarrely cyclical and symmetrical about Napper's sequence of offences. A casual glance at the matrix below reveals this at once:

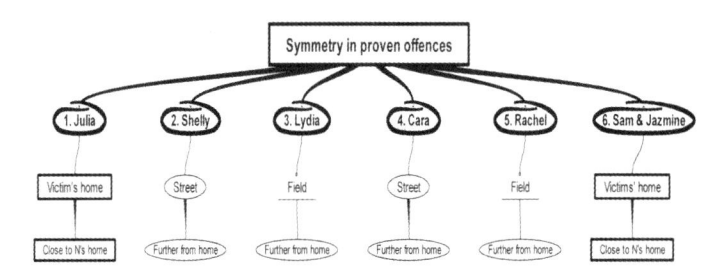

```
                    Symmetry in proven offences
   ┌──────┬──────┬──────┬──────┬──────┬──────────┐
1. Julia 2. Shelly 3. Lydia 4. Cara 5. Rachel 6. Sam & Jazmine
   │      │      │      │      │      │
Victim's  Street  Field  Street  Field  Victims'
 home                                    home
   │      │      │      │      │      │
Close to  Further Further Further Further Close to
N's home  from    from    from    from    N's home
          home    home    home    home
```

Figure 3.3 Symmetry in Napper's proven offences

As we move chronologically from left to right, Napper's offences become more serious. He commits rapes or attempted rapes and finally kills, and kills again. He ended where he began, and thus the far left and far right columns have the same patterns and features. Reading across them all, including the first and last bookend columns, this is how his offences transpired: close to home and inside attack; further

KILLER IN THE SHADOWS

away and outside; further away and outside; further away and outside; close to home and inside attack.

There are also some consistencies throughout most of the offences: use of a knife; children present; forcefully removing victims' clothing. However, there are also many differences: use of a disguise; use of restraints; comment to the victim. Although it is easy to see it now, it would have been extremely difficult at the time to perceive that the key features across the spectrum of offending were a sadistic pleasure in attacking victims with children, threatening or using a knife on them, and ultimately, with both Rachel and Samantha, the destruction of their bodies through evisceration. It should be acknowledged, of course, that the patterns presented here are based on known offences. Things would possibly look different if other alleged offences were definitely tied to Napper. In the meantime, all the behaviours relating to Napper's proven offences are in the diagram below:

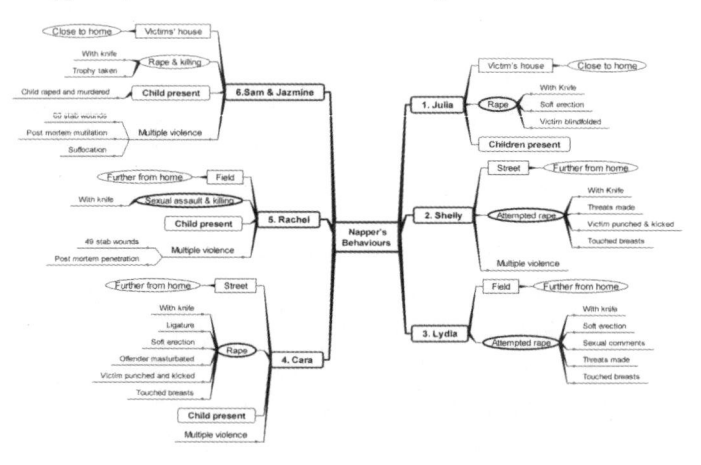

Figure 3.4 Napper's behaviours

FEARFUL SYMMETRY

It is intriguing to speculate as to why Napper spared little Alex but not Jazmine, and why Rachel was killed on the common whereas Samantha was murdered in her own home. In terms of the former, it may simply be that Napper had no time to deal with Alex. It may even be that he was disturbed during the act. Certainly, Alex had a lucky escape – it is hard to imagine that Napper would have intentionally spared him, or felt any remorse at killing either mother or child.

Maybe he knew Rachel as a regular visitor to the common, and stalked her in a similar way to Samantha. Alternatively, perhaps she was a more opportunistic choice. Given Napper's relative specificity in his choice of victims, however, the former does seem more likely. So why did he return so close to home to murder Samantha?

It may be simply that he did not travel very far for any offence. Queen Mary Hospital was just a mile and a half from the site of the murder of Rachel. Moreover, having got away with killing Rachel, he may have felt more comfortable and less concerned about putting distance between himself and the next murder site. The configuration of extreme pre-phase anger, the fact that he had previously watched Samantha through her window and the relative ease of access to her and little Jazmine makes it seem as if his last offence was an inevitability.

Moreover, recent research suggests that sex offenders with paranoid schizophrenia can suffer from loss of normal inhibitory functioning in the less florid phases of full-blown psychosis. As such, their illness can generate more impulsive behaviour. Thus, while Napper's schizophrenia does not fully explain his violence (most schizophrenics are not criminals), it may go some way to explaining a lack of inhibitory control over his violent impulses.

While we have mentioned a range of sexually sadistic offenders throughout these early chapters, the most striking comparison is between the pattern and evolution of Napper's violent development and the most notorious of all serial killers – a man who was operating in 1888, and still remains hidden from public view. In the same way that the 'Jack the Ripper' murders appear to have culminated in the horrific evisceration and disembowelment of Mary Kelly, so Napper's final act of murderous rage, in which he had as much time as he wanted to obliterate Samantha, provided free reign to his sadistic fantasies.

Indeed, the Ripper's last victim suffered a similar level of mutilation to Samantha Bisset, with both breasts removed, disembowelment, a hand cut off and placed in the stomach cavity and her heart removed. Although the Ripper victims and thus the chronology of the case are endlessly disputed by 'Ripperologists' (showing the perennial difficulty in linking crimes), many authors agree that the *most likely* first victim of the Ripper was Annie Chapman, killed at the end of August 1888. Annie was an alcoholic prostitute who had been ejected from her usual lodgings because she could not afford a bed for the night. She got no further than a few hundred yards away before she met her death at the hands of the Ripper; he left her in the street with her skirts up around her waist, her throat slashed and her genitals mutilated.

Subsequent victims, including Elizabeth Stride and Catherine Eddowes, and disputed victims such as Martha Tabram were also brutally hacked apart with a knife.

FEARFUL SYMMETRY

Although a century divides them, Jack the Ripper and Robert Napper are behaviourally linked; both inserted sharp instruments into bodily orifices as a final indignity; in Martha Tabram's case, it was her vagina; in Rachel Nickell's case, her anus was penetrated. When the Ripper stole up behind and effectively lassoed Liz Stride with a silk scarf, he presaged by a century Napper's behaviour. The only difference was that Napper used a rougher ligature to jerk back Cara's head before he raped her. The knife that severed Rachel's windpipe rendered her silent in just the same way that 'Long Liz' was made mute – a knife to the windpipe left both women, 100 years apart, united in abject terror.

It is quite possible (indeed probable) that, prior to the Chapman offence, the Ripper had committed many other crimes, both sexual and acquisitive. Like Napper, the Ripper probably had violent parents or suffered parental neglect; as a youth he may have been regularly in trouble and may well have committed many previous violent or sexual assaults. Thus, all the conspiracy theories about surgeons or members of Royal Masonic societies are (at least statistically, and in terms of the conceptual evolution of violence) extremely unlikely.

The Ripper was probably a much blander suspect, like Napper, than colourful but utterly improbable candidates such as Sir William Gull (Queen Victoria's surgeon). It is not the case that the more extreme the act of violence, the more unusual or unique the person that committed those acts. Napper himself was less than ordinary, his workmates describing him as "quite boring really". In the many years people have had to wonder about the type of person who snuffed out Rachel's young life, and instantly ruined those of her loved ones, their imaginations may have conjured up images of an uncontrollable fiend.

Yet the man walked unnoticed each day through the gates of a plastics factory, just another member of the workforce. We therefore turn next to the dreadful case of Robert Napper and Rachel Nickell.

CHAPTER FOUR
DESOLATED HEARTS

*"I am malicious because I am miserable.
Am I not shunned and hated by all mankind?"*

Mary Shelley, *Frankenstein*

What causes a person to lose all feelings about the sanctity of human life? What allows him to actually enact his violent fantasies on a living, breathing human being? The answer is twofold: he must have disconnected from other humans, and he must have suffered.

The quotation above, from Mary Shelley's famous novel, shows the monster confronting his creator, Victor Frankenstein. He spews out his bitterness at being alone, the only one of his kind. Rejected by all, he warns Frankenstein, "I will revenge my injuries: if I cannot inspire love, I will create fear . . . I will work at your destruction nor finish until I desolate your heart." In fiction, the monster's vengeful cruelty grows out of the pain he himself has suffered. In real life, the roots of Robert Napper's sexual sadism will likewise lie in his personal history. There is nothing special about sexual sadism, other than that it is rare, but it is built on neglect and its aetiology resides in abuse. It has a formulaic shape and structure which explains (but never excuses) violence.

Despite the opening lines of this chapter, life does not always mimic art. The pathway to sexual sadism is a far cry from the fictional portrayal of evil masterminds like Hannibal Lecter, with his diverse interests in art, poetry and music, meticulously plotting his crimes against his next victim and waiting months, even years, to get revenge.

In real life, sadists are often seemingly ordinary members of our communities, keeping their perversions hidden from others, not least because they have little or no contact with the rest of society. The Napper whose workmates found him boring had no significant others. He appeared to have few meaningful connections with individuals at work, siblings, family or friends. Thus the fulcrum of his descent into violence was his isolation.

Indeed, research which compares rapists to sexual murderers shows that one of the key distinctions between these types of offender is that those who kill suffer a greater degree of isolation, in childhood as well as during adult life. This also applies to intimate relationships, where sex murderers are far less likely to have a partner whereas the majority of rapists tend to be married or have one main partner.

Of course, Napper both raped and killed, but such results nonetheless show that those who stop at rape and do not escalate to murder tend to be better connected to other people. Disturbingly, however, rapists and murderers tend to have similar thought patterns. But sexually sadistic murderers lack the social moral compass and social relationships that bind the rest of us to humanity, leaving such individuals to immerse themselves in violent thoughts.

A central component, then, in propelling Napper toward his crimes was the lack of connection to others. Is it that surprising that, when the offender's reality is devoid of contact with others, the more attractive option is fantasy? Tragically, this alienation will also have served as an accelerant to his rage. Both his rage and disconnection had deep roots.

Most frequently, what is lacking is any feeling of love, intimacy or camaraderie – either of a parent to a child, a sibling to a brother, one work colleague to another, or a child to a parent. Our series of unique connections to each other are the precious relationships that we perennially take for granted but, in the most significant moments of our lives (whether relating to birth, death, marriage or spiritual epiphany), they are the things that preserve our humanity and our view of the sanctity of life. Even Frankenstein's crude and misbegotten monster knew that what he lacked was another being with whom he could meaningfully connect, which is why he demanded a bride.

There are countless examples of individuals' expressions of love and affection for others in their last moments of life. Suddenly, these special others come into sharp relief and we realise their special significance as we find ourselves in extreme circumstances. Reflect on the number of individuals who, in their dying moments in the Twin Towers or the plane that crashed in Philadelphia on 9/11, made phone calls to convey a simple message of love. Consider too the many examples of otherwise battle-hardened soldiers who, in moments of extreme suffering or near to death, cried out for their mothers.

Sexual sadists often lack these unique connections. Their violence is borne of an absence of intimacy, a diminished sense of self and a complete lack of understanding of others. Napper's Asperger's syndrome, which impairs the ability to interact socially with others, would have been an extra difficulty in this respect, but it is not the whole story. (If it were, other people with Asperger's would routinely harm others, which is certainly not the case.) Not uncommonly, such an impoverished worldview is formed in childhood and carried over into the teenage years, where a sense of worth needs to develop if one wishes to progress into healthy adulthood.

Sexually sadistic murderers are rarely intellectually malevolent, but are often limited in their understanding of and connection to others, and in their capacity to lead a rich and fulfilling existence. We will consider one such pathway to violence, which is in our view the route that Napper may have travelled down in his escalation from petty theft to violence, to violent rape, murder and mutilation. In his case we believe that the path he took may have included the following elements:

- Parental expectations surrounding the need to grow up quickly, foregoing comfort and support from parents and associated caregivers.
- Feelings of a loss of childhood and the nurturance and love that normally accompanies it.

DESOLATED HEARTS

- Personal experiences of abuse, neglect and violence at the hands of people he may have trusted.
- Perceptions in childhood of parental betrayal.
- Seeing violence as the norm.
- Becoming inured to violence.
- Learning to expect violence as an appropriate response in resolving problems.
- A gradual loss of the normal inhibitions that restrain the majority of the rest of us from enacting violent thoughts.
- Increasing disconnection from others.
- A preference and retreat into fantasy rather than the dull reality that otherwise surrounds him.
- Feelings of hostility, rage and betrayal at the world in general, and toward the archetype of caregivers in particular. In Napper's case, these are women in general and mothers in particular.
- Mental rehearsal of fantasies which incorporate violence and the suffering of others, especially where those imagined others represent the specific archetypes.
- The development of 'mental scripts' that prepare the individual for violent action in the face of relevant stimuli; preparedness to act on violent impulses when relevant opportunities present themselves.
- Violent actions (e.g. rapes).
- Associating these violent acts with feelings of power, sexual arousal and control.
- Association of gratification and pleasure with the distress of victims.
- Increasingly descending into sexually sadistic fantasy, moving further away from any connections with others.

- The development of increasingly specific, mentally rehearsed 'fantasy scripts' that use violence and the suffering of others as a masturbatory aid.
- Increasingly specific arousal to only specific forms of stimuli, in this case the distress of others.
- The development of specific, relatively planned behaviours to facilitate access to victims and satisfy violent scripts.

Although we can never know the thoughts that accompany acts of atrocious violence (even interviews with offenders can prove superficial, with many struggling to articulate what they were thinking and feeling at the time) we can now – with the benefit of knowing about Napper and his crimes – piece together what may have led to the expression of such rage. In particular, we can start to develop an awareness of why he was so focused on individuals who, for him, represented everything he loathed about women – all encapsulated in the archetype of the young mum.

It is important and often revealing to examine such case studies in terms of the thoughts and feelings that precede an individual's behaviour. Thoughts lead to feelings; feelings lead to behaviour; behaviour feeds thoughts. Leading up to and during his offences, Napper will have conducted an internal dialogue that resulted in the very specific behaviour he was prepared to take from fantasy into reality – the stalking, threats, use of a knife, desire to provoke fear and, finally, choosing to interact with other human beings by tearing them apart, exploring their body cavities and reducing them to nothing more than meat.

Although he will have had very specific thoughts and

feelings during the commission of such acts, this does not mean he would be able to articulate them after the act. Indeed, there is some suggestion that he is now so mentally compromised that he would be of little use in offering much insight into his own behaviour over fifteen years ago. We do know that he was not forthcoming in police interviews, and that psychiatrists advised against interviewing him for the Nickell murder in the wake of his conviction for the killing of Sam and Jazmine. Indeed, he initially denied the killing of the Bissets and, for sixteen years, revealed nothing about Rachel. At his 2007 committal for trial on the charge of killing Rachel, when he finally stood before the court and was asked for the first time how he pleaded, he politely stated, "Not guilty, thank you."

The authors were asked by a senior police officer whether Napper would be likely to feel any remorse for his acts, or whether he simply suffered so-called cognitive distortions about his victims. Our answer, based on his crimes and what is known about his background, was, "Probably neither." If Napper were to – or indeed could – answer honestly, our suspicion would be that he would offer a very simple explanation: "I did it because I enjoyed it." Certainly this would fit our view of his crimes as *classically sexually sadistic* – a pairing of his own pleasure at the expense of another's pain and distress. It's a simple but unpleasant correlation: the greater the suffering of the victim, the greater the hedonic response of the offender.

Our abhorrence for such behaviour often leads offenders to attempt to concoct post-hoc justifications or defences for their actions, no matter how hollow they sound. Moreover, offenders often have cognitive deficits which leave them struggling to identify thoughts and feelings. They are often impulsive and lack the ability to be introspective or reflective. In fact, it is often exactly these deficits that are targeted by therapeutic interventions to attempt to change an offender's patterns of behaviour.

However, based on what we know about these sorts of offenders, we can speculate on the thoughts and feelings that may have accompanied Napper leading up to the killing and during the actual offence. Our views are informed by his offending history, the behaviour revealed in the crimes, our own previous work with violent offenders and research on sexual sadism. We would not profess to have known this by examining just one crime scene – nor, indeed, all of the crime scenes.

Part of the power that violent men exert over our consciousness arises from a misguided view that there is something unique or otherworldly about them. Fiction may dramatise their power by representing their inner dialogue as distinct, alien, special, an intellectual malevolence with satanic subliminal power over the unwitting. But the research on violent men suggests otherwise. Moreover, establishing what thoughts accompany violent acts is not enough. Violent thoughts alone do not make us violent.

Vince Egan, a psychologist colleague at the University of Leicester, has conducted several studies of so called 'sensational interests'. These include the extent to which an individual is interested in militarism, vampirism, Satanism, occultism and a bundle of other seemingly fringe interests. Vince has developed a Sensational Interests Questionnaire and has established that many ostensibly normal (i.e. non-forensic) individuals have many diverse and esoteric interests, but have no greater propensity for violence than those without sensational interests.

Although Vince and others have established that sexual murderers do have an unhealthy interest in many such topics and that most mentally rehearse such violent themes, that in and of itself is an insufficient risk factor. More important is an individual's disconnection from others, pro-violent orientation and exposure to violence throughout the individual's lifetime. As we will note later, the degree of violence inflicted on victims directly correlates with the extent of childhood problems, neglect, abuse and isolation.

Nearly all of us have had violent fantasies at some point. Several studies have revealed how a majority of young men have fantasised about murdering someone and a majority of men have fantasies about raping someone – indeed, many women have fantasised about being raped. This must not be conflated with the notion that people would therefore enjoy or welcome such events in real life. They absolutely would not. Thankfully, most of us do not act on such thoughts, not least because of the many social inhibitions that society, parents and peers place on such acts. When an individual actually translates violent fantasies into behaviour, they often have experiences in their background that allow them to ignore or shun such inhibitions. They learn from the violence that they see around them and accept it as the norm.

It is rare for violent men to have had little or no violent experience in their early lives and backgrounds. Some soldiers, in becoming accustomed to violence, come to normalise that behaviour and struggle to adjust back into a world where societal norms prohibit it.

Initially they struggle to inflict damage on other human beings and have to overcome their natural inhibitions. Psychological theory has in fact been instrumental in training them to kill, in gradually acclimatising them to violence. This involved training them under conditions that on each successive occasion more closely approximated reality. First of all, they might be taught to load a gun; then to load and fire at a paper target; then to load and shoot at a dummy; then to shoot at a dummy with a face; then to shoot at a dummy with a face under stressful conditions, over and over again – until the actions became almost unthinking, unfeeling and automatic – pre-existing scripts that, in the face of specific stimuli (the enemy), would become automated.

Vietnam veterans have described their anger and hatred for the government which had complete power to despatch them into, or rescue them from, the bloody environment in which they were forced to operate as soldiers. As individuals they were powerless. Coupled with a fierce sense that 'what is right' had been betrayed, many eventually came to accept their situation while some – like the character Kurtz in Joseph Conrad's 1899 novel *Heart of Darkness* – even relished the horror.

These were formerly ordinary, empathetic people. One described the consequences of trying to introduce his essentially moral self into the arena of war. His reward for showing enough mercy to ask a man in hiding to come out and surrender was to be shot at. His compassion having been summarily rejected, the soldier promptly shot the man dead.

DESOLATED HEARTS

But this action was no longer sufficient. Triggered by the sight of his victim's blood on his hands, the soldier shed his former values and identity completely. He went berserk, dragging the body into an open paddy field and carving it up. When medics tried to call a halt to this mutilation, he fought with them – even though the corpse already resembled "a rag doll that a dog had been playing with".

The 'berserker' cited this incident as instrumental in the transition from his former self as a soldier carrying out his duty into the unrecognisable entity who "really loved fucking killing, couldn't get enough. For every one I killed, I felt better. Made some of the hurt go away . . . I got very hard, cold, merciless." (From *Achilles in Vietnam: Combat Trauma and the Undoing of Character* by J. Shay, p.78, 1994 – see our 'further reading' section.) He was just one more war veteran who went beyond the prescribed training script and developed new habits of cold ruthlessness.

These habits bear some resemblance to the 'scripts' that develop in violent men. Violent offenders have seen, heard and tasted violence throughout their lives and are ready to engage as soon as the requisite opportunities present themselves. This is especially pronounced when an offender has enacted the violence over and over again in his own mind, and where fantasy plays a more important role than merely going through the motions of reality.

Napper's reality included a troubled early childhood, and a rage of great strength was forged in his formative years. By adolescence, his attitude towards his parents will have brimmed with unbridled hatred, and he will have developed a loathing of siblings, peers and the world in general.

'The world' will have become a reified object of hatred — a 'shithole' that has given him nothing but misery and which despised him from the moment he was born. Any individuals who belong to that world are not to be trusted, and are corrupted by hypocrisy and betrayal. Caregivers neglect; siblings are people who just take and refuse to give back. What prohibitions exist, therefore, against shooting an air gun at his brother's face? Against stealing and violence at school?

Why should he listen to the chastisement of a mother who, in his perception, was loose and drunken? From his perspective, she was a hypocrite and his dad was just a bastard who abandoned them, but they were not the only adults to let him down. Why trust anyone in a position of authority when adults — who ought to care for and protect a child — could sexually abuse and bugger you? Other kids didn't like him either; his workmates mostly found him boring. Better then to be alone with one's own fantasies. Fantasies of retribution against a world that left him at the mercy of others.

Research has shown that neglect and isolation are powerful disinhibitors to violence. Animals left in the confines of isolation find it hard to cope once reintroduced to a social milieu, and often attack other animals because they have developed none of the normal prohibitions against aggression. Alone in his hatred of himself and of everything around him, Napper was left to fester in bleak, solitary thoughts that, we now know, almost led to suicide.

Recall how, at the time of his overdose in 1989, he had explained to his mother that his suicide attempt was caused by

DESOLATED HEARTS

fear of being caught for committing rape. It is true that he had recently raped Julia, whose morning hair-drying routine was interrupted by Napper's appearance in her bedroom. However, we also know that by this stage he was delusional and paranoid, his schizophrenia cutting him adrift from reality.

It is impossible, then, to know the truth about his attempted suicide – though it would be interesting to know what turned this internal hatred, these feelings of worthlessness, into an external perspective in which others deserved to die.

With no successful checks and controls as a child on his attitudes to other children, little success in his periods of psychological counselling and continuing hatred towards his parents, Napper progressed beyond the bullying of his siblings to other offences. It would have been a process over time, a process of learning to associate violence with pleasure and of increasing isolation. As previously stated, this isolation is a key distinction between rapists and killers, the tipping point that escalated his offending behaviour from the sexual to the homicidal.

Early on, he may have managed to sustain some semblance of superficial relationships; indeed, workmates suggest Napper shared an occasional chat with female colleagues on leaving the factory gates at the end of a day's work. But, gradually, as his moral anchor loosened, he drifted further and further out to sea until it was near impossible to spot any warning signs as to his own behaviour.

This increasing dangerousness and impulsivity was illustrated in a story by a former workmate who spoke of an occasion when Napper suddenly lunged at the back of a woman walking through the warehouse. The colleague's physical intervention was enough, this time, to restrain Napper, though it is clear his ties to 'normal behaviour' were diminishing.

Paradoxically, though he lived amongst so many others in the biggest city in the UK, he was eventually so distant from other people that he had no use at all for a moral compass. As such, he had to rely on what he had developed thus far – a childish, narcissistic self-focus and a need to satisfy the sexual urges that he was beginning to couple with violent thoughts.

Napper's particular mix of violence and sex was directed at women, and sometimes specifically mothers with children. He was an unusually violent rapist and we need to look further to evaluate what led to knifepoint rape, the sexual assault and killing of a four-year-old child and other brutal acts such as tearing open a mother's ribcage, attempting to cut off her legs and removing part of her womb. What explains this direct and specific form of sexual sadism?

First, let us take the so-called Green Chain rapes. These chart an increasing need to express feelings of betrayal, principally perhaps towards his mother. We know that Napper was the eldest of the children and, in his father's absence, may have been leant on heavily as a proxy for dad and husband. To what extent did the young Robert resent his siblings for this, and then feel that his bullying control over them was a rare opportunity for recompense?

In fact, his inability to see his siblings as children but rather as irritating peers may have reinforced his lack of connection to childhood. His recognition that he would not be nurtured but was expected to be a caregiver himself may have added to his scathing hatred of happy families and the 'fuck-you' inner dialogue running through his mind, as he spotted potential victims going about their business with contented children trotting along beside them.

So his preparedness to act despite children being present may simply have been a lack of recognition, or the refusal to recognise that it was at all relevant. However, the unusual combination of sexual arousal, violence and anger in the presence of children still persists. Sex offenders and many violent men who sexually and physically abuse their own and others' children overestimate a child's independence, treating them in a distorted way as an adult equal, or at least as equally deserving of abuse as adults.

The authors have witnessed such distorted thinking in our interviews with violent men, which emerges often as a product of having no age-appropriate child-adult relationship with their own parents. They may have been expected to grow up too quickly, never experiencing the support and the setting of boundaries that their own parents should have given them, or may have seen conjugal violence between their parents as setting the norm for their own behaviour. Violence begets violence, and in Robert Napper's mind no one – not even the youngest and most innocent – was immune from his wrath.

The only sign that Napper may have felt uncomfortable with his own actions is that, after the sexual abuse of Jazmine Bisset, he pushed her head into the duvet to asphyxiate her – no knife, no mutilation, and no eye-to-eye contact. How different from the pleasure of the knife, the immolation of the adult female form and the awful post-mortem mutilation of Samantha.

Jazmine's death was unusual for Napper, and may hint as to how, on the periphery of his own feelings of self-worth, he did not want to see the face of a four-year-old as he attacked her. The fact that she was left in her own bed and not mutilated reveals that, as horrific as her treatment was, she was not an explicit symbol of his rage.

Alex Hanscombe and the other children present in the rapes were less relevant as victims. Instead, they served as facilitators to Napper's distorted views of motherhood and the way in which he paired the image of 'mother with child' alongside hate, betrayal and sexual sadism. As indicated earlier, arousal can be paired with all kinds of stimuli (from lingerie to gasmasks), but Napper's form of excitement mixed anger with sex, control with sex and sadism with sex. His particular form of sadism appeared to be enhanced by making a mother feel the ultimate fear – the recognition that she could not save her child.

Many of the other offenders mentioned throughout this book used a multitude of methods to elevate their own pleasure by creating fear. But perhaps the most disturbing feature of Napper's monstrous crimes, beyond even the gross mutilation inflicted on Samantha, was the pleasure he took from a mother's inability to protect her child. In our view, this particular form of sadism has its origins in his hatred towards his own mother and the fact that children were present at some of the early rapes. The former explanation has deeply psychoanalytic undertones; the latter is an evidently 'behaviourist' explanation, relating to Napper's ongoing conditioning. Both may have had a role to play.

This may provide some insight into what, at first, seems

inconceivable and alien. When journalists ask what lies behind such madness, the easy answer is to state that Napper was a paranoid schizophrenic. However, this is probably the least significant aspect of his offending pattern – though its psychotic features may have fed it.

Schizophrenia is a mental disorder that includes (most frequently) auditory hallucinations, paranoia and a gradual loss of a sense of self. As mentioned in the last chapter, where schizophrenia and criminality co-exist then the offender nearly always exhibits some form of psychotic breakdown in the offending phase, leading to some loss of the inhibitory controls surrounding violent behaviour as experienced by Napper. However, the overwhelming majority of paranoid schizophrenics are neither criminal nor violent.

In considering Napper as a case study, we can recognise the important impact that biological and social factors have on the evolution of violent behaviour. Moreover, in reconstructing these events we hope to avoid the theatrical glorification of violence and recognise it for what it is – limiting, destructive, often a reflection of powerlessness.

Although Napper may be the closest case history we have to a modern-day Jack the Ripper, we can diminish his grip on our imagination by knowing exactly *who* he is and *how* his escalating pattern of offending emerged. In a sincere attempt to convey the awfulness of the crime, we have, after much consideration, included the italicised section below. It is a bid to portray in narrative form something that approximates to the likely state of Napper's mind at the time.

In truth, of course, we do not know. (It may even be unknowable.) But as we now turn to the day that Rachel

KILLER IN THE SHADOWS

Nickell met Robert Napper, we may make a soberly educated guess.

★ ★ ★

The polo shirts and luridly patterned golf trousers all gathered simultaneously in the car park for a curious event, each of the wearers standing subdued and separate alongside their own particular vehicle. The nearby windmill towered over one end, its arms splayed out, an impassive sentinel witnessing the parade. If any passerby had been in any doubt about the discomforting atmosphere, the police presence confirmed the bleak truth. Where would a gap still remain? Which vehicle would be left with no one standing beside it? That would be the car that told police its owner had just been murdered.

The golfers who used the windmill car park knew before many others that the silver Volvo estate would not be driven back by the same young woman who parked it there. For these people, the summer's morning of Wednesday 15th July 1992 was when a round of golf was halted for a strange, sad identity parade – where the person who mattered was the one missing from the line-up.

For Rachel Nickell, it was the day that Robert Napper briefly entered her life and then ended it. For her partner, André Hanscombe, it was the day he howled "like a wounded animal" in a public phone box when, instead of Rachel picking up the receiver when he called home, a police officer answered instead. For their son, Alex, it was the day his safe and happy life was destroyed before his bewildered eyes, as he saw his mother murdered.

DESOLATED HEARTS

For Rachel's brother, Mark, it was the day he left his office in the City and made a tube journey to the hospital to see Rachel's partner and bruised child, before going to Bedfordshire to secure his parents' home against the press and to inform his grandmother that the family's nightmare had just begun.

For Rachel's parents, Andrew and Monica, it was the day that they enjoyed a boat trip. For they were on a summer holiday in Canada. Such are the vagaries of time that the day their lives irrevocably changed would occur only in retrospect. Until their son completed the last leg of his dreadful odyssey to break the news, they would not know of their only daughter's fate.

Rachel's parents arrived back from their boat trip to find a message from the local sheriff pinned to the door. It merely asked them to get in touch to receive news from home. They realised a fatality was likely if it was serious enough to warrant the involvement of local law enforcement. If it was a family death, they reasoned that the most likely person was Rachel's octogenarian grandmother – two full generations removed from their energetic, twenty-three-year-old daughter.

While her parents were enjoying their summer holiday on another continent, Rachel had awoken that morning at home. Having a two-year-old son meant that she had ahead of her another day of the fatigue and joy that small children foist upon their parents. London offers extensive living space to no one except the extremely wealthy, but rather than keep little Alex confined to their modest Balham flat she took her boy out for exercise in the fresh air several times a week, along with their dog, Molly.

KILLER IN THE SHADOWS

They had ample choice for their outings. Indeed, Rachel's little family was situated close to several famous pieces of common ground in south London. She roamed farther from home these days, eschewing Clapham and Wandsworth Commons for Wimbledon. She didn't mind the extra time for the drive as Alex had enjoyed running around there a week earlier, hunting in the scrubby grass for stray golf balls. Besides, Rachel had recently endured a man indecently exposing himself on common ground nearer home, so she made up her mind that they would take their walks in Wimbledon instead. She felt safer there.

André had left for work at 8:30. He had to put in long hours in his job as a motorcycle dispatch rider in order to support the family. It kept them apart for too long but they were hoping, one day, to have saved enough to be able to leave London and set up home in the French countryside, where Alex would have the freedom to play and grow as tall as maize stalks. This was the future Rachel and André saw for their son. In the meantime, when they got the chance to pull up their duvet together against the world, this was what the young couple dreamed of.

But for now, André would ride his motorbike through the choked streets to earn a living and Rachel would steer her way through south London to give Alex some room to run, some freedom and green space in the suburbs.

So Rachel, Alex and Molly the dog followed out of the flat about fifteen minutes after André had left for work. She did some errands before their walk on the common, but finally pulled into the Windmill car park just before 10am, chose a space and parked up. Rachel sorted out the sundry car seat

DESOLATED HEARTS

belts, buckles and dog leads, then left the silver Volvo behind. She headed off into the summer morning peace of Wimbledon Common with her beloved child and their dog padding alongside beside them.

★ ★ ★

Napper's mental preparation will have begun long before that fateful morning. He will have prepared and rehearsed what he wanted to do to Rachel, stoked his loathing and rage at the thing he most coveted and despised – a beautiful, maternal woman who lavished love on her child. It is this image, this icon that he will have wanted to obliterate, to destroy with his violence and rage.

He may have thought about ways to avoid getting blood on his clothing, believing himself very clever and superior for taking such precautions. He will have savoured the feeling of power that carrying a knife gave him, potent with the threat of violence.

His mind will have run through his previous successful attacks, his grim achievements: the threat to use a knife on Lydia's vagina; the cutting of her breast and the blood seeping out; the visceral thrill of the women begging for him to stop, their eyes filled with terror and the desperately focused desire to live.

The power of such moments will have filled him with self-importance. To hold the life of a young woman as a whim was highly intoxicating, reinforcing a feeling almost of omnipotence.

This godlike power would have been coupled with his burning rage and frustration at the women he coveted. What he wanted was to be desired, their love, their adoration – what he felt from them was, at worst, revulsion and rejection; at best, their indifference to his existence. But he wanted them to see his power, to feel his rage, and most of all to pay – and pay dearly.

KILLER IN THE SHADOWS

On this morning, his rage may have reached its pinnacle – a savage desire for revenge against the women who tormented his thoughts. His paranoia about how they looked down upon him, finding him disgusting and repugnant, will have fed his anger, his self-loathing, and his lust for their blood.

★ ★ ★

What happened to Rachel in the next thirty minutes took hundreds of people many painstaking hours to put together. Detectives, pathologists, other walkers on the common, scene-of-crime officers, nearby residents, forensic scientists, television appeals, child psychologists, friends, family and little Alex himself all had to try their hand at the jigsaw.

Despite their valiant efforts there are still gaps in what happened, and the crucial piece – the name and face of the man who killed Rachel – took sixteen long years to slot into place. Alex's entire childhood had come and gone before anyone could finally declare who stole it from him one July day, a few weeks before his third birthday.

He was trotting along happily with Mummy and Molly, as they pottered from the car park onto the common. If this had continued to be an ordinary walk, people would naturally describe it in vague terms like "they strolled off" or "they wandered along". But investigators need to be much more precise in their use of language, which is why the following will be recognisable as police-speak:

The victim proceeded in a northeasterly direction across Wimbledon Common, accompanied by her two-year-old son and her black mongrel dog. She was dressed in a grey t-shirt, blue jeans, and brown boots. Due to the warm weather, she was carrying her son's blue t-shirt. Her son was dressed in navy-blue tracksuit bottoms and trainers.

The victim's body was discovered in a small wooded section of the common, about twenty to thirty yards away from open parkland and approximately 100 yards from the car park. The last sighting of the victim took place at 10:20am.

The eyewitness could pinpoint this detail so precisely because he was late for an appointment. Had he not stopped his bike to ask someone what time it was, he would likely have ridden past without really registering the very pretty young woman with blonde hair. Then he cycled off to his appointment. The next man to be aware of the pretty young woman was Robert Napper.

★ ★ ★

Napper walked out into the open air and spotted this blissfully oblivious mother, with her apparently perfect life and no worries in the world. But in his distorted mind she was too pretty and seductive to be a mother, wearing the undeserved clothes of a Madonna. Parading around with her child but still wanting men to want her all the time. He may have even felt it was up to him to show her child what such mothers really were – that it would teach the boy a hard lesson that he'd been subjected to as a child. He will certainly have felt that Rachel was deserving of the horrors he was about to inflict upon her. That she was asking for his vengeance.

Napper's own sense of physical self will have been infused with disgust, which is how he will have imagined that women thought of him. After he spotted this happy trio trotting around the foliage, his mixed feelings of disgust at what he saw as the woman's hypocrisy will have blended with his own need for power and revenge against what she embodied. From some distance then, Napper will have stood waiting, lost in his twisted, violent thoughts of possession and destruction.

★ ★ ★

Even now, what followed cannot be stated with complete certainty, as Napper committed the terrible crime without being seen or heard. However, from putting together the various positions and lines of sight occupied by the other witnesses that day, the most likely scenario is this:

Napper saw Rachel coming over the common as she headed for the small wooded section beside the mound, once a dump for soil and rubble excavated to build a nearby road, now grassed over to look scenic. Napper watched her from the top of the mound but, just before Rachel walked by on the left, he slid down the right-hand side and disappeared from view. With the mound between them, neither could see the other – but one of them knew of the other's presence, and her position.

★ ★ ★

An initial sighting will have led to a more determined march up and over the mound, blood now rushing to his head, making his forehead throb and pulse. Pounding with rage and adrenaline, he will have made a beeline for Rachel. "You think you're better than me, but you will not look down on me! I will have you in front of me." In the moment, he suddenly feels truly real, all-powerful – all moral pretence and inhibitions loosened to the point of zero. He can hear his own breath now, and a mixture of distorted thoughts; an urgent need to

DESOLATED HEARTS

speedily press on alongside the mound, ahead of her, the blood pounding in his head.

★ ★ ★

He ran on ahead so he could step out in front of her – just as he had with his rape victims. These were quick, predatory movements as he stalked Rachel to her death. He knew she would reappear at any moment on the footpath. She was about to emerge from the little wood now.

★ ★ ★

He can see her more closely now. No one nearby, no one to stop him. She will try and protect the boy; the dog should prove no problem. What will be his first words to her? Quickly! Think!

★ ★ ★

Rachel came out from the briefly sheltering coolness of the leafy shade. She walked in the warmth of the summer sunshine for another ten yards or so and then never felt warm again.

★ ★ ★

Don't say anything. Hit the boy! In the brambles. Bag. Knife. Grab her!

★ ★ ★

Rachel dropped the t-shirt she had been carrying for Alex. Napper jabbed her in the chest with his knife, then turned her around to walk her back the way she came, into the cover of the wood, jabbing her again in the back to make her move out of public sight.

Such was the conclusion of the pathologist who examined Rachel's cold body and found three relatively light marks, shallow little cuts. They were inconsistent with the savage depth of the forty-six other stab wounds Napper inflicted upon her. Anyone who could use a knife with such fury that imprints of the hilt were left on the skin was not the type of offender to give hesitant jabs, unless he had a reason.

People would wonder how a murder could occur in broad daylight without any of the 500 or so people on or near the common seeing it. The answer was simple. It didn't happen in broad daylight, on the 11,000 acres of open common. They were in sight together for a ten-yard walk lasting mere seconds. Then the killing took place beneath the concealing canopy of the trees.

Napper had dragged Alex and thrown him aside into the brambles. The little boy would tell police officers of the bad man who threw him into the mud. Beneath the trees, Rachel's larynx was penetrated by the knife. It was impossible for her to scream for help, no matter how many people were nearby to hear. Putting arithmetic to a most dreadful use, investigators calculated that it would take a minimum of three minutes to stab someone so many times.

Rachel was last seen alive at 10:20. At 10:35, a retired architect walking his dog came upon the harrowing sight of a blood-drenched Alex clinging to his mother on the ground, sobbing and pleading, "Get up, Mummy!"

His mummy's murderer had left her almost decapitated. Rachel lay with her jeans and underwear pulled down around her ankles, her dilated anus prominently displayed. This arrangement presaged Napper's presentation of

DESOLATED HEARTS

Samantha Bisset, whose hips he carefully propped up on a cushion so that her genital area was on show.

Rachel was also found with a small piece of paper on her forehead. It was a slip notifying her of the new PIN for her bank account, and the care with which it had been placed there seemed to belie the butchery of the attack as a whole. Detectives would puzzle over this curiosity, expecting to eventually learn it was part of a freaky ritual with some oddball symbolism.

As it turned out, the truth was at once far more prosaic and far more upsetting. Alex, in his anguish, had placed the paper on Rachel's forehead as a plaster to help Mummy get better – a child's simple yet powerless hope that he might be able to wake her up.

Just fifteen short minutes earlier, this had been a peaceful space of birdsong where light blinked through branches and leaves whispered into the welcoming coolness of the shade. Now, thickening blood soaked its way into the dry grains of dirt on the floor, rivulets leaking into the tangled tree roots.

It was now a crime scene and a new story began here. The sunlight blinked still, but the leaves whispered to no one of what had taken place.

CHAPTER FIVE
TRACE, IMPLICATE, ELIMINATE

In a murder enquiry, police begin a process of suspect prioritisation. The first suspect on their list in this case was André Hanscombe, Rachel's partner. He was the man who adored Rachel, and wanted to spend the rest of his life with her, which doesn't seem much of a motive. However, contrary to Mark Twain's claim about lies, damned lies and statistics, the statistics on murder don't lie. Women are killed every hour of every day by boyfriends and husbands – many of whom seem to adore them, claim to adore them, or sometimes actually *do* adore them. Many of them also go to elaborate lengths to make it look as though a stranger did it.

In the midst of the awfulness for André, he was at least spared the further injury and pain of a lengthy investigation. He was at work and people could verify his whereabouts, so his alibi was very quickly established.

Police would then begin exploring Rachel's friends and

acquaintances, former boyfriends and so on. Once again, statistically speaking, the danger is most likely to come from the people we know. Thus the police may loosely follow a logical step-by-step process through the probabilities, from most likely to least likely.

The difficulty with starting at the centre and working outwards is that, with each step outwards from the nearest and dearest, there are more people in the pool who need to be investigated. With each concentric circle valuable time is lost, and an increase in suspects means exponential effort and resources. Most people have one partner (though some will have more, often kept secret from wives or husbands), and approximately three to four in their immediate family. If we consider the extended family (aunts, uncles, cousins), then the average pool increases to eighteen people.

What if investigators need to look at friends, acquaintances, colleagues – in other words, all the people that we know? Whoever you are, there are likely to be 150 people in this group. Again, psychologists have found this to be a robust finding as it is thought to be a significant number in evolutionary terms. Apes and monkeys have a social group of about fifty, which is thought to be the maximum size that the species can keep track of and sustain grooming relationships with. Human beings can keep track of three times that number, mainly because we have language to help us. Even though we have evolved to have bigger brains (and no longer partake in apelike grooming to strengthen our social bonds), there is still a maximum group size our brains can keep track of.

(Studies have been conducted to test this in many areas,

from the number of contacts listed in the average address book to the number of people on individual Christmas card lists. Perhaps the interested reader might conduct a similar analysis on Facebook, although a casual glance appears to indicate most folk have between 100 and 150 Facebook 'friends'.)

Once someone is to be investigated, detectives would go through a process they tend to call T, I & E for short – or, to give it its full title, Trace, Implicate or Eliminate (though some refer to the 'I' as standing for 'Interview' or 'Investigate'). TIE can be very resource-intensive. It isn't often difficult to arrange to speak to victims' families, but the necessary follow-up enquiries to corroborate a claim of where a particular person was when an offence occurred can be time-consuming. These days, it may mean checking anything from CCTV or a dated and timed shop receipt to an old-fashioned someone else's say-so.

Even then, the police have to consider whether the colleague who swears you were at work has a vested interest in supporting your story. The ABC of policing is: assume nothing, believe nothing, challenge everything. They must continue until they are absolutely sure that a person really can be fully and properly eliminated from the enquiry. If you think of how long it takes you to travel to different places, or how quickly a day can disappear in just meeting people and gathering information, it gives an idea of how difficult the task can be.

In the first days of the Rachel Nickell enquiry, the team charged with TIE work consisted of a detective inspector leading a team of six detective constables, plus four researchers to carry out background checks. There were regular briefings in the incident room to explore, process and understand the next batch of 100-plus statements they had to read and consider.

Of course, detectives don't follow strictly outwards from the nearest pool in ever increasing circles. They would not robotically check all 150 'people we know'. There would usually be other information to suggest that one person warrants more attention than someone else. After André had been swiftly eliminated, one early suspect who appeared in the frame was a male friend of Rachel's who we shall call Eric. Eric was the full-time 'stay at home' parent of a little boy the same age as Alex. The children had become friends at nursery and so the parents did too. The friendship centred on the children, so Eric and Rachel met occasionally so that their boys could play together.

There were also other signs that suggested he was worth investigating.

Six days after Rachel's murder, André had visited Wimbledon Common to leave a flower at the place of her death. He was accompanied by Alex, who would not leave his daddy's side, and also by the police officers who would not leave father and son to the press pack that intruded into their raw grief.

The police managed to corral the press onto the nearby mound. Thus, reporters and photographers stood and watched the little wood exactly as Napper had six days earlier. The shaded little wood once again offered protection from the public gaze, this time shielding André and Alex from the prying eyes of the press. Their most private moment was hidden, but when they emerged they were met by flashbulbs. One of those shots was later chosen by an editor for the next day's front page. Thus, in a decision quite staggering in its crassness, the sole witness to a brutal murder was displayed, in tabloid size, so that the whole nation – including the killer – knew exactly what he looked like.

Having laid their flower for Rachel they headed back to the car park, André carrying his son. Among the voices that shouted, clamoured and vied for his attention was a more familiar tone. He looked across to see Rachel's friend Eric calling him. Detectives were immediately alerted to his presence.

Why on earth should he have been there that day? Was he perhaps revisiting the scene of the crime? Most alarming of all, Alex suddenly bucked and veered, trying to escape from his father's arms. Why did the child react so? André put his son's restlessness down to tiredness; the little boy was bound to be overwrought. After less than a week, he had returned to the scene of the worst trauma imaginable. Furthermore, their every step had been dogged by a bunch of strangers taking photographs. André thought no more of Alex's reaction, but detectives filed the incident away. The little boy had seemed suddenly terrified.

They reminded André of it some weeks later, when he told them of something Alex had mentioned. André had an understandably urgent wish to make his child's life as full and happy as possible. One day, several weeks after they had left the flower for Rachel, he was asking Alex who he might like to go and play with that week. Daddy suggested the names of different children from the nursery, but Alex seemed clear that he did not want to play with Eric's son. Most of the other children would be accompanied by their mothers, not their fathers, so André wondered whether Alex was simply scared of men in general now. He asked his son, "Are you afraid of Eric?" Alex replied that he was. André had the sudden realisation that Alex might in fact be scared of this particular man rather than just men in general. "Did the man who killed Mummy *look like* Eric?" Alex said he did.

Andre's next question is obvious. Alex had already been quizzed about many of Rachel's friends and acquaintances and had said none of them was the bad man who killed his mummy. Thus, André expected the answer to be no. But it only needed the short word, "Yes," from a three-year-old for the man to be hauled into custody and interviewed again.

The trouble with this type of questioning is that it is leading. Closed questions (which permit only 'yes' or 'no' answers) mean that we don't have free choice over what we say in answer. Consider the everyday example of filling in official forms – tax, bank accounts, mortgages and so on. It is likely that most of us, at some point, have wondered which box to tick because we just don't fit neatly into the categories on offer. Life is too richly complicated to be reduced to 'never', 'sometimes' or 'always', so trying to reduce events to 'yes' or 'no' is harder still. This is why asking open questions is helpful; it gives people a free choice so that they can be as accurate as possible.

Free and accurate answers are not the only advantage of open questions. Interviewers must consider the fact that people's behaviour is affected by the expectations of others. Children and other vulnerable groups are especially prone to answer questions in what is termed a 'socially desirable' manner. Thus they will sometimes say anything – incorrect things, untrue things, even things they don't understand – if they think it is the 'right' answer and will please the questioner.

Open questions give an interviewer an important advantage in this respect, in that the interviewer can check whether the person answering has understood the question properly. Look at how easy it is, with a closed question, to give an answer even though the interviewee hasn't the foggiest idea what the interviewer is on about. If you asked me, "Did you see the clexhem?" I can easily answer, "Yes," if I guess that's what you want to hear. If, however, you asked me, "Can you describe the clexhem?" (an open question), I'm not going to get very far. Even if I don't admit I haven't got a clue what you mean, my answer is going to give the game away because it will be nonsense.

It is extremely important to avoid shaping responses and behaviour, i.e. leading a witness, when investigating an offence. Open and closed questions are only one aspect of it. The problems are often demonstrated by the classic question, "When did you stop beating your wife?"

This presupposes that you *used to* beat your wife. Of course, we could answer in full: "I have never, ever beaten my wife, so it is wrong to ask me when I stopped. I cannot answer, 'yes,' or, 'no,' because the question doesn't apply to me at all."

Unfortunately, we may not get the opportunity to answer in full. Moreover, it requires particular social and cognitive skills. Firstly, you have to be able to articulate all those ideas and explain why the question is not applicable, but some people don't have the vocabulary to do this. Secondly, you would also need to be able to consider the questioner's beliefs and challenge them, and this would be an impossible task for young children.

Young children are not even aware that different people know different things. The ability to distinguish between one's own mental capacity and someone else's is called 'theory of mind', and it typically develops between the ages of four and seven. With no awareness that other people's minds are separate entities which hold different information and beliefs, two- and three-year-olds do not understand that someone can hold a false belief. Thus, very young children have no way to conceive of, let alone to challenge, what the other person in a conversation thinks. "Daddy thinks that I think X, but actually I think Y which means he's wrong, so I think I'll have to persuade him to change his mind and think otherwise," is sophisticated stuff.

Children's developmental milestones are predictable. Although individual children obviously vary considerably, there are lower limits that we can be sure about. One might as well expect a baby of three months old to hold a conversation as to expect a child just turned three years old to have sophisticated ideas about who thinks what. The most intelligent, confident or even cheeky young children take at face value the world that adults present to them. After all, they readily believe in Santa, magic and tooth fairies.

Psychological studies of children as eyewitnesses have shown that they tend to change their answers if a question is repeated. Children are used to questions being framed in a particular way and so they respond in accordance with the

TRACE, IMPLICATE, ELIMINATE

ways they have learned. For example, if a nursery school teacher asks a child to identify a colour and the child answers incorrectly, it is common to repeat the question: "Are you sure? Look again. What colour is this?" Most of us are sensitive to children's needs and so, rather than saying, "You're wrong," we tend to frame things in a way that gives them another chance to get it right. It's kinder that way. The problem is that, for young children, hearing a question repeated is a cue that simply means, "Give a different answer this time because the last answer you gave was wrong."

So Alex was almost bound to give a wrong answer. He was asked closed questions, shaped in a leading manner; he had been asked the same question before, suggesting he must have got the answer wrong last time. Perhaps most influential of all, he was being questioned by the one person in the world he wanted to please most – his daddy.

For children as young as Alex was, it is unthinkable that a parent could be wrong over an important issue. Parents are immensely powerful figures that can, in a child's mind, fix anything. They make food and toys and ice cream and birthday parties appear. They always know the answer to questions. They can magically rub sore knees better. It is extremely improbable that a young child would question a loving parent. Alex would not and could not say, "Now I know what you're thinking because you've asked me this before, but it isn't true. Eric didn't kill Mummy." Nor would a child of that age, no matter how intelligent, have any concept of the implications for the suspect if he replied, "Yes," to his father's question.

André Hanscombe could not have been expected to hold

such knowledge. He was neither a psychologist nor a trained interviewer. It shows the immense difficulty that even professionals face in ensuring they do not lead someone's answers. It also shows the way that we impose meaning on events even when they are only coincidental.

André told the detectives what Alex had said about Eric. In return, the detectives reminded André of the day Alex had tried to escape his father's arms when he spotted Eric in the car park. They put two and two together and made five. In this way, people corroborate each other's narrative 'sense-making' or piecing together of events. This is one way in which we construct the truth, by relying on confirmation from others that things did indeed happen the way we thought they did, and so it is easy to construct an untruth by using the same process.

Eric was taken into custody and asked to account very precisely for his whereabouts on the day of the murder, and to explain the nature of his relationship with Rachel. Had he wanted her? Had he been infatuated with her? By the police interviewer's own admission, Eric was given a "severe verbal battering", subjected to an interrogation that left his solicitor shocked. He admitted nothing more than finding Rachel attractive, as did most people, and was lucky enough to be able to produce an alibi. His partner had stated he was in bed at the time of the murder. She conceded she had been out for part of the time but, given that she had taken their car, it would have been impossible for him to get to the common and back by the time she arrived home.

Sometimes, for innocent suspects, the timing of these things is down to good fortune. We all spend time every day when others cannot verify our whereabouts. We may live alone; we may sleep out of sight of those we live with. Even if we share workspace with others, we may travel solo in a car or where fellow bus or train passengers are strangers and would not recognise us again.

Of course, people are not jailed merely for the lack of an alibi, but definitive proof of alibi is a very valuable thing. It can lay to rest suspicions that may otherwise linger, especially in unresolved cases. Such is the power of having others corroborate our speculative ideas. Eric's wife could have planted a seed in her own mind by wondering if he was attracted to Rachel, whether he was perhaps overfriendly with her. It is much easier to dismiss such thoughts as groundless or disloyal if they are fleeting ideas that no one else shares. It is harder to do so when the police have the same idea and are taking it seriously enough to question your partner about it formally.

Police seized Eric's car and stripped it for a detailed forensic examination. They also began an undercover surveillance operation to trace his movements. He was finally released to recover from the shock of being a murder suspect. Then he and his partner had the enormous task of mending a relationship damaged by the suspicion that he had made advances to another woman, and killed her when she rejected him. In the event, the couple did not get to live happily ever after and they are not together today.

Thus do murder enquiries spread their tendrils into many lives. In Rachel's case the process had only just begun. In the meantime, other leads in the 'people we know' category had halted. And so the police had to broaden the enquiry.

Once they move beyond the category of 'people we know', detectives have to start considering strangers. Obviously, there needs to be some mechanism for prioritising suspects, and it must be more reliable than a hunch or a gut feeling. We know that geography is reliable and the offender is likely to live within a couple of miles of the crime scene. We also know that, domestic murders aside, someone does not wake up one morning a non-criminal and become a murderer by bedtime. Offenders who kill strangers will almost always have a criminal record and police have detailed databases they can use to check criminal pre-convictions.

What is more, very specific behaviour can be tied to particular types of pre-conviction. For example, if a sex offender tears a victim's clothing, they are seventeen times more likely to have a pre-conviction for violence than an offender who didn't tear clothes. Rachel was anally penetrated and offenders who do this to their victims are eight times more likely to have a pre-conviction for a sex offence. These kinds of details help police to narrow down exactly who in the vast Police National Computer (PNC) should be investigated first.

Such findings by academics and crime analysts do not guarantee a solution. If someone analysed the entire PNC looking for statistically significant patterns, it is possible that their findings might apply only to those included in the dataset in the first place. In other words, we know nothing about those people who never get caught. Nevertheless, such behavioural patterns can help to pinpoint a place to begin, how to formulate a list of people to prioritise as suspects, which in turn may help a detective inspector and six detective constables to TIE effectively.

However, just because most offenders are local does not mean they all are. Investigators cannot trust to luck and assume that those who live inconveniently far away are likely to be innocent. Distance alone is no reason not to TIE someone. One such man was a gravedigger who had been working in London at the time of the murder. By means of different pieces of information some twenty gravediggers came into view, some possibly as suspects but certainly as sources of information.

A sniffer dog used immediately after the murder had led police away from the crime scene and across to the common's edge, where a set of railings demarcated Putney Vale Cemetery from the common. The dog led police to where an eyewitness claimed to have seen a man hunched over a stream (actually a drainage ditch), washing his hands in the water just after Rachel was murdered. Alex had likewise told police that, when the "bad man" ran away after the attack, he lay down and "looked into" the water.

Had he been washing blood off his hands? Moreover, the eyewitness's description of this man tallied with Alex's own account. Both said he wore a white shirt with a belt outside, blue trousers, dark shoes and carried a black bag. It was certainly easy to escape unnoticed in that direction if one climbed over the railings to cross the cemetery. Another witness said she had heard someone running behind the railings at the relevant time. The other gravediggers also told police that one of their number left for Europe just twenty-four hours after Rachel's death. These cumulative pieces of information led to the police's decision to TIE Italian gravedigger Henry Lavelle. They were obliged to follow it up all the way to Venice where, only after an interview, could they say they had definitely eliminated him.

This was not the end of the strain on the police budget. A bartender from New Zealand called John Gallagher had to be interviewed and eliminated. A team also travelled to Liverpool on advice from Merseyside Police that they had a man due up on a rape charge in which he had used a knife. He had spent July working in London, fairly near Wimbledon Common.

This incident neatly illustrates the consequences of unwanted press attention. A leak to the newspapers about the Merseyside suspect meant that police were unable to continue with a covert surveillance programme. It also meant that they had to manage public order, given that the news brought more than 200 people out into the streets to air their views on the man they thought was Rachel's killer.

Nearer to the crime scene was Shahaid Chaudry, a known misogynist and racist. He had come to live at a hostel for mental health patients after staff at his previous hostel had moved him on, tired of complaints about his aggressive behaviour towards local females. He would accost white women in the street and subject them to torrents of racial abuse. A fellow patient at his current hostel told police how Chaudry had stormed out in a very irate state on the morning of the murder. He had, the witness said, left at about 9:45am and taken a knife from the kitchen with him.

Neither was he new to seizing knives during episodes of erratic behaviour, once becoming involved in an altercation with a fellow patient and using a weapon to force staff and patients alike to keep their distance from him. Police excluded Chaudry from the enquiry after two staff members indicated that he had been due to transfer hostels yet again on the morning that Rachel was killed, and had been with them at the time in question.

There remained, however, some discrepancy as to the timing of different people's accounts. A third member of staff claimed that the expected transfer was the very thing that had caused Chaudry to become agitated and leave the hostel. This staff member wanted the police to enquire further into the suspect, given that they had not initially been informed of Chaudry's previous history with knives and his aggression towards white women.

As a suspect, he fitted the description of the likely offender offered by Robert Ressler, a former FBI offender profiler. Ressler believed that Rachel's murderer was mentally ill and advised police to check lists of patients from any nearby mental health facilities, hostels or hospitals. Such a trawl would, of course, have netted Robert Napper, a psychiatric patient. However, many other names would also have appeared in that particular net. Deciding which of the big trawl should be put into the keep net – that is, deciding parameters for prioritisation or elimination – is neither an easy nor foolproof process, and we do not seek to offer glib 'if only' comments with the benefit of hindsight.

Two more suspects came into public view only after they had found their way into the newspapers for other reasons. One was the tragic case of Ben Silcock, a twenty-seven-year-old man who suffered from schizophrenia. He had attempted to feed a lion at London Zoo. Unaware of the danger due to his mental illness, he climbed into the cage to offer chicken meat and was savagely mauled. That he ended up in intensive care after the attack was cause enough for many column inches questioning the adequacy of mental health care. Then it was discovered that Silcock had been questioned by the police over Rachel's death, having lived near the murder site and regularly wandered on Wimbledon Common. There had been reason enough to TIE him but, by the time reporters were standing in front of the hospital doors, he had already been eliminated from the Nickell enquiry.

The second man was Roderick Newall, a far less innocent figure than Silcock. Newall found his way into the papers via a combination of elements more resonant of a James Bond film than a real-life crime. Police in the Channel Islands wanted to question him in relation to an alleged double murder. Ex-soldier Newall had sailed away from justice in his luxury yacht but did not count on the Royal Navy. The frigate HMS *Argonaut* intercepted him in the middle of the Atlantic and headed for the coast of Gibraltar, where he would face extradition.

Newall looked every inch the British Army officer, a graduate of the royal military academy at Sandhurst. He was charged with the murder of his own parents, whom he had beaten to death with Chinese rice flails to get his hands on almost a million pounds' inheritance money. His brother was also eventually jailed for helping him dispose of the bodies. Once again, as reporters delved deeper into the background of Roderick Newall, they learned that he too had been in the frame for the murder of Rachel Nickell. In July 1992, he had

Left: Robert Napper as a schoolboy: a killer in the making.

Right: An early police custody shot of Napper, at the time of his arrest for the Bisset murders.

Left: The e-fit that alarmed neighbours of the innocent Colin Stagg.

Right: The e-fit that most closely resembled Napper.

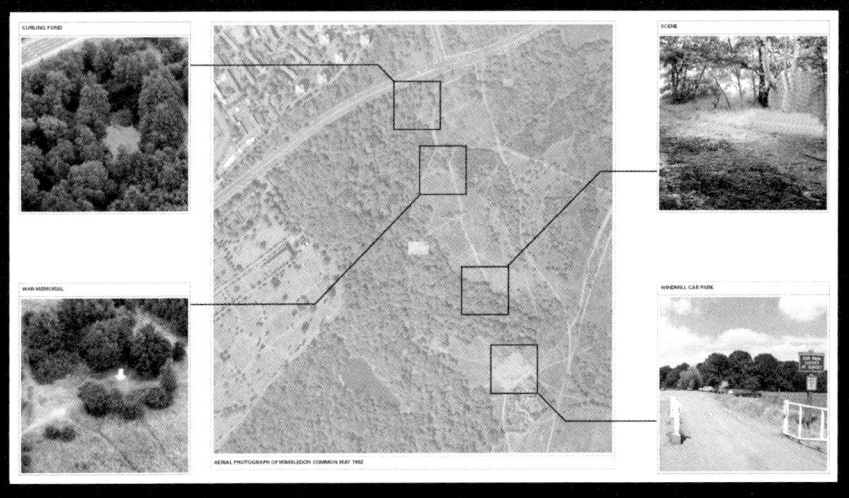

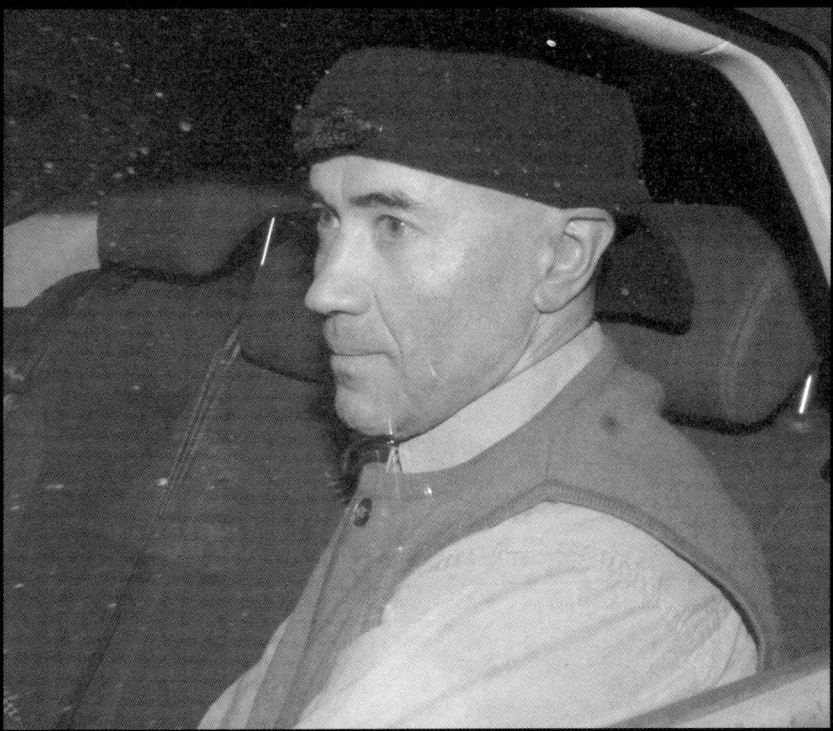

Above: The map of Wimbledon Common released to the press by the Metropolitan Police, showing the site of Rachel Nickell's death.

Below: André Hanscombe on the day that he finally saw justice for Rachel.

In police custody, Napper is forced to answer for the killings of Samantha and Jazmine Bisset – his final victims.

been staying with friends in Mortlake, Surrey, just a few miles from Wimbledon Common. He seemed to have dashed off suspiciously quickly after Rachel had been killed but, like many others, was eventually eliminated.

Another suspect was named in three separate calls to the incident room by two different callers. It looked like a strong lead and the suspect was due to be TIE'd, until it turned out that all three calls came from the same woman. She had invented her different identities, fabricated the nonexistent suspect and lied about where she was calling from. This attention seeker had cost the police £6,000 and a heap of wasted time.

The decision to investigate a suspect further is not always completely clear-cut. How was the information gathered, and from whom? Did it come from one source or many? Is the information reliable? Once it has been decided that a suspect warrants further investigation, how much time should be spent pursuing one individual?

It is patently impossible that everyone should be investigated so parameters obviously must be set somewhere, but in practice they can help or hinder. Corroborating sources can help to confirm that information is reliable. Having one witness who had forgotten her spectacles the day she saw a man over six feet tall in the distance is not likely to be definitive reason to declare an exclusive focus on six-foot men as suspects. However, if a full double-decker bus was parked two feet away from where an offence occurred, and everybody on it said independently that the offender was at least six foot four, then deciding to eliminate men under six feet may seem sensible.

Corroborative sources are, unfortunately, not a guarantee of reliability and can generate 'false positives'. In the 2002 hunt for the 'Washington Sniper' who shot ten people dead and injured three more, police released details of the suspect having a white van. This seemed very reliable as many eyewitnesses had confirmed a white van in the vicinity of a shooting. The police focused on pulling white vans over, checking the drivers as possible suspects, but it eventually transpired that the offenders, John Allen Muhammad and Lee Boyd Malvo, used a blue Chevrolet car. The witnesses did not deliberately mislead police. It was just that white vans were such common vehicles that there was bound to be one somewhere nearby when an attack happened.

Police investigating the Green Chain rapes likewise based an important decision on information corroborated by many. On the say-so of many victims and witnesses, they set their limits for the height of the offender at between five foot five and five foot ten inches. Suspects within these parameters were investigated further, but Robert Napper was too tall.

Hindsight shines a glaring spotlight on the tragic consequences that followed: suspected, investigated and convicted of the Green Chain rapes, Napper wouldn't have been free to go on to commit three murders. But we must remember that is not how things stood at the time. Many pieces of information were missing.

Here is the logical endpoint for anyone who wishes to argue against setting parameters for suspect prioritisation and investigation: taxpayers would have to be happy to shower police with unlimited resources and tolerate everybody being investigated for any and every offence. Until then, prioritisation is necessary. Without the dubious luxury of leaving no stone unturned, the police have to continue trying to turn over the right stone instead. They will not always succeed.

In Rachel's case, some thirty-plus suspects were brought into the enquiry from various sources of information until they were eliminated. Hunting for Rachel's killer, police went to the ends of the earth before they came right back to where they had started. It was there, living on the edge of Wimbledon Common, that they found Colin Stagg.

Stagg appeared in the frame after a televised appeal on the TV programme *Crimewatch*, which led two neighbours to contact the police: firstly, because Stagg walked daily on Wimbledon Common; secondly, because he looked very much like the e-fit police had broadcast. These two things cannot be disputed, but the unintended consequence was that they derailed a man's life.

It was Colin Stagg's misfortune to look like Robert Napper, so Stagg would be hunted while his doppelganger vanished into the crowd for another sixteen months. It was also at this time that police working on the Nickell case asked a man called Paul Britton if he could help with their investigation.

CHAPTER SIX
INNOCENT UNTIL PROFILED GUILTY

At the time Robert Napper was attacking women in London, Paul Britton was the Regional Head of Forensic Psychology in Leicestershire. Treating patients was Britton's day job; in his spare time, he helped police as something of a 'Cracker' figure. Indeed, Britton is said to be the inspiration for the fictional profiler in the TV series *Cracker*, but in truth he is not the only psychologist to lay claim to that accolade. In any case, Britton was certainly not the dishevelled figure depicted by actor Robbie Coltrane. The fictional character Fitz was regularly portrayed on television as rising – bleary-eyed, hair awry and flat out of cash – in the same crumpled clothes in which he had collapsed in a drunken stupor the night before.

By contrast, clean suit, fresh shirt and neat tie were Britton's customary attire. Despite having worked as a policeman for a year early on, there was little in his demeanour to hint at his investigative activities. The nearest he ever came to resembling a 'gumshoe' was a Mac trenchcoat in the style favoured by Chandler-esque detectives, though on Britton the garment looked functional and tidy. He kept his brown hair neatly trimmed, with no attempt to disguise a receding hairline, and sat simple metal-framed glasses on his rounded face. Although his mouth had a determined set, it was offset by softly spoken words which served to enhance his gentle, amenable persona.

Paul Britton would go on to write an autobiographical book entitled *The Jigsaw Man*, published in 1997, detailing the police investigations he worked on and his role in those cases. He is described on the dust jacket as "unassuming", yet simultaneously as someone with "almost mythic status" due to his ability to walk through the minds of criminals. Poetic licence and book promotion aside, these images of a man at once very ordinary and yet possessing seemingly mystical insights into criminal behaviour are not easily reconciled. But, in his persona of ordinariness personified, inoffensive but professional and solidly reliable, Britton was almost bound to elicit faith from the police officers who commissioned his services.

Robert Napper is the ghost in Britton's profiling machine and he haunts *The Jigsaw Man*. As Britton relates the tales of his work on the Green Chain rapes and the Bisset murders, it is the unnamed Napper whose story overlaps. Robert Napper ultimately walks through eight different chapters – just one unidentified offender, yet he inhabits a third of Britton's book. In effect, his criminal activities glided across Britton's radar in three different operations on three separate occasions, but the man never stood out enough to be traced.

INNOCENT UNTIL PROFILED GUILTY

It took a delicate brush and a light dusting of silvery powder from the fingerprint expert to do what profiling could not, and reveal Napper as the intruder in Samantha Bisset's flat.

By 2002, Paul Britton would appear before the British Psychological Society (BPS) accused of professional misconduct over his role in the Rachel Nickell investigation. The chair of the BPS disciplinary committee hearing the case stated that he was dismissing the charges, concluding that the eight-year delay made it impossible to offer Mr Britton a fair hearing. Colin Stagg had brought the complaint after he had been prioritised as a suspect, largely on the basis of an offender profile produced by Britton.

As a consequence, Napper was ignored while the investigation into Stagg expanded, taking on board every new piece of hearsay, garden-fence tittle-tattle and vague possibility. It eventually became so bloated that it was unrecognisable as a murder enquiry. Beginning from a profile of the offender likely to have murdered Rachel, Britton remained involved in the enquiry until Stagg was brought to trial. By the time of the BPS's disciplinary committee statement, Stagg's life had been comprehensively overturned by the failed investigation and he insisted that the lapse of eight years had done little to eradicate its impact. He was, understandably, less than satisfied at the BPS's decision.

Stagg argued that Britton had not conducted his duties in a proper and scientific manner, Britton's lawyers countering that the allegations against their client were "scandalous" and "wholly misconceived". What, then, had Britton done?

He had gone from profiling Rachel's killer as someone with a sexually-deviant personality disorder to confirming

Colin Stagg as fitting that description. (To be absolutely precise, he did not make a formal diagnosis and used the less specific term 'personality disturbance' instead.)

At first glance, this may not seem problematic if it was a reliable claim. It is, after all, fairly routine for such labels to be applied to patients – but Colin Stagg was not Paul Britton's patient; he had undergone no examination nor taken any assessment tests. Indeed, Britton had never met Stagg.

The problem itself is a matter of degree. In principle, a psychologist need not sit facing someone to consider what a particular set of behavioural symptoms might mean. Any fool can listen over the phone to someone complaining of coughing and sneezes and reasonably conclude that their friend is suffering from a cold. Trained professionals too can proffer opinion from a distance. (NHS phonelines are based on that very premise.)

However, for the sake of accuracy there must be limits. As one slips away from what is best practice, there comes a point where you cross the line of acceptability. Can you diagnose someone as suffering from a personality disorder by telepathy? Categorically not. Can you diagnose it by interviewing them and having them undertake standard tests which have been devised scientifically, over many years, for that precise purpose? Yes, most reliably so. In the wide grey area in between, can you diagnose it by reading someone's letters and listening to his phone calls?

Let us first set aside the extremely knotty problem that Stagg was embroiled in a wholly contrived, unnatural situation where he was unlikely to be behaving in any way that approximated to his true self. As an analogy, it is rather

INNOCENT UNTIL PROFILED GUILTY

like asking you to pretend in a role-play that you are three years old, and then accepting everything you say as gospel.

However, for the sake of argument, even from the generous starting point of taking everything at face value, diagnosis *on that basis alone* would certainly not be recommended (though we may allow that the contents hint at problematic behaviours that warrant further examination). This is the essence of the difficulties in Britton's involvement in the hunt for the Wimbledon Common killer. Mr Britton clearly had areas of significant expertise and experience, but limits should be set to prevent a creeping slippage between what constitutes best professional standards and methods of practice that are less reliable, as well as between areas of expertise.

Psychology is a very broad church, and professional psychologists practise and specialise in very different areas. Educational psychologists may assess and treat children with learning difficulties; organisational psychologists may advise companies on how to recruit the best employees or motivate their workforce to maximise profits; neuropsychologists may examine how epilepsy impacts on a patient's daily life in domains such as memory. Different types of psychologist require different training and separate postgraduate qualifications. There may be some overlap: clinical psychologists who specialise in working with children will be cognisant of their developmental needs in an educational setting, even though they are not educational psychologists.

Overall though, 'psychologist' is an umbrella term with subdivisions. The three years of postgraduate study necessary to become a clinical psychologist is separate from the three-year postgraduate course one follows to qualify as an educational psychologist. For sure, all psychologists focus on behaviour, just as all medics focus on mending the body – but we would not want brain surgery performed on us by our dentist.

Within areas of psychological expertise, there is often further specialisation. For example, some clinical psychologists may provide therapy for patients whose quality of life is diminished by debilitating phobias; others may specialise in managing chronic pain or depression. Some investigative psychologists may advise police on the best way to interview uncooperative suspects; others may help investigators with geo-profiling.

When consulted by laypeople for professional advice, psychologists are ethically bound to delimit their area of expertise and explain exactly which competencies they possess. A national database is now held to inform someone who wants to engage the services of a psychologist and the BPS's website provides further helpful information.

We have included a figure here to show some of the types of expert advisor and their roles and tasks. The figure is included merely as a general steer. It is certainly not exhaustive and we must apologise for omissions. Unfortunately, space limits us to a focus on the investigative rather than post-conviction or treatment stages; it likewise restricts us to examples only. There are a multitude of other roles and skills that do not appear such as advocacy in court. Psychiatrists contribute their invaluable expertise in many ways in the forensic arena. Clinical psychologists, in particular, are 'short changed' by the diagram. There is also a good deal of overlap between investigative and forensic psychologists, though many of the latter are more commonly found working with convicted offenders within the secure estate and elsewhere.

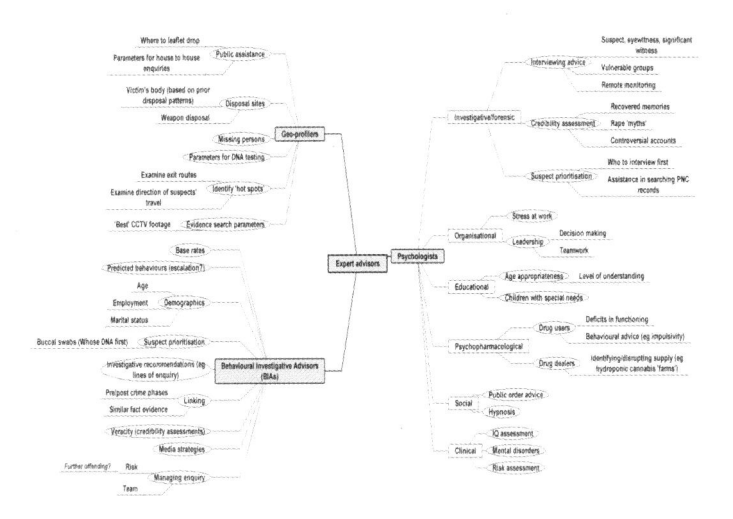

Figure 6.1 Expert Advisors

However, because life does not come neatly packaged, criminal cases often cross the boundaries of a range of areas. Suppose then that an investigative psychologist who specialised in interview techniques was engaged by police to advise on how best to interview a recalcitrant 'no comment' suspect, only to encounter someone who appeared to be low-functioning rather than a hardened criminal who refused to 'cough' to the offence. In such a case, the interview specialist is likely to have more knowledge than a layperson and might consider the possibility of a learning disability; s/he would nevertheless not take it upon him/herself to diagnose a particular disorder, just as a brain surgeon would not transplant a heart just because s/he happened to be in the operating theatre at the time.

Psychologists may refer clients on to someone who specialises in the relevant domain. Alternatively, they may seek advice from colleagues with more knowledge, but in any case professional standards always dictate that the client should be told what is beyond the individual's remit.

Mr Britton claimed that, once he knew about a suspect's sexuality, he would "know immediately that he was likely to have killed Rachel Nickell, without him mentioning it" (*The Jigsaw Man*, p.165). The suspect, Britton asserted, would merely need to walk into his consulting room for this thaumaturgy to occur. It needs to be stated in the plainest possible terms that such a claim is unscientific. In terms of method, claims that the offence of murder can be reliably imputed simply by meeting a suspect (who can remain silent to boot) leave us but a tissue's width away from claiming powers of telepathy.

Paul Britton furnished the Rachel Nickell team with two offender profiles, one detailing seventeen different points to which he expected the offender to conform. He covered, among other things, age and education, type of employment, lifestyle, location, likely pre-convictions and (lack of) car ownership. These days a profiler would not offer such advice without indicating the evidence base for their claims – in other words, they would detail the basis upon which any given claim was made.

Moreover, they would be unlikely to make a claim with such categorical certainty. As we have been at pains to indicate, profiling is a science of probabilities not certainties.

INNOCENT UNTIL PROFILED GUILTY

Today's advisors would reference by name the researchers who had carried out the studies which support the claims they make, or, where such scientific research has not been conducted, they may indicate the other deductive bases which support their claim.

When Mr Britton was advising, the practice was not so rigorous or scientific. He did evidently have substantial knowledge of the area, because many of his claims in the profile are reliable. Even though he did not reference them by name, studies do exist that support much of what he said. Nonetheless, although he was an experienced professional, judgement must still be informed by evidence and some claims seem to have been based merely on his personal opinion. (One example is his negative correlation between car ownership and frenzied fatal stabbings.)

The second profile made claims about the rarity (or otherwise) of particular sexual fantasies. Britton also advised on interview techniques for Colin Stagg. This is an area where the psychologist's role should be strictly confined to identifying any gaps in the interviewer's coverage of events or advising on the best ways to engage with the interviewee, on how to build a rapport perhaps. It is not customary to use what has been gathered from interviews to help devise an undercover operation.

Britton also diagnosed the man as suffering from a supposed personality disturbance, details of which eventually found their way into the public domain via national tabloids and TV news reports. Albeit not the biggest issue Mr Stagg had to contend with, this was not a pleasant experience and it is fairly easy to see how a complainant might equate this with a lack of professionalism or unethical behaviour. (Though many, of course, may disagree. And it is important to note that such a verdict was never reached.) But why did Colin Stagg lodge a complaint of misconduct based on a failure to act 'scientifically'? Why does this matter so much?

In our society, scientists are entrusted with finding the truth. If we don't know the reason for something, we look to the boffins to tell us all the right answers. This is how science works: scientists need empirical (i.e. testable) proof — not faith, not intuition, nor hunches. After scientists have satisfied themselves that something is true, they publish their research for the rest of the academic community to see if others can disprove it. In the world of academia, researchers sometimes spend entire lifetimes trying to prove or to knock down someone else's findings.

The scientific system of having your peers review what you have done and then seeing if someone can replicate it, or disprove it, is as important as quality control in a tyre factory. In any walk of life, if it matters then we need to double-check it. Scientists are as human as anyone else. They may simply make honest mistakes or, worse, may not be trusted to do the honourable thing. This is why it's so important to have a checking system where other academics try to find the flaws in anyone's argument.

In the past, for example, several scientists have gone before the US Congress to state categorically that nicotine is not addictive. We might still have believed that to be true, except for two things: we now know that they all worked for the tobacco industry and independent research scientists had the funding to prove otherwise.

INNOCENT UNTIL PROFILED GUILTY

The quality control that science insists on – having solid published research to back up your claims, and other academics to try to disprove your results – is all crucial in discovering what is true and what is not. So, despite the occasional fun tabloid stories about useless research, the rules of scientific academia are important because, in our culture, we look to the scientists and other experts to determine the truth. Expert advisors have a duty to the public to say when they are remotely unsure. The stakes may be high; expert testimony is known to have swayed juries and caused miscarriages of justice in criminal cases as serious as murder.

So, how did those investigating Rachel Nickell's death come to seek the assistance of an offender profiler? The difficulty for the enquiry team was a lack of evidence. As calendar pages were turned, each new month brought fewer leads. Given the state to which forensic science had developed at that time, there was no useful evidence at the scene, no obvious reason for the attack and – though several suspects appeared – no witness information that pointed to a single individual.

Perhaps because of the media pressure, coupled with the brutality of the crime, the police turned to two profilers to give 'expert opinion' on the likely perpetrator: Robert Ressler, the renowned but retired FBI agent, and Paul Britton. While Mr Ressler got caught up to some degree with the British tabloids, Mr Britton preferred to stay out of the limelight when he advised. Britton had previously claimed some success in high-profile cases and had been used by a number of police constabularies. As noted in his memoirs, however, Britton does not appear to have any systematic basis for his assertions and claims to rely mainly on clinical experience. Concern with his methods would become one of the central features of the case when the enquiry team tried to prepare it for a court hearing.

There are also inconsistencies that ripple through his own accounts of cases he has worked on. For example, Britton puts forward a steady argument for why profiling should be confined to the investigation stage and should not be admissible in court. To support this position, he correctly states that profiling is a matter of probabilities, not absolute certainty. Our criminal justice system, however, demands certainty of proof *beyond reasonable doubt*.

In that environment, profiling makes for an extremely unworthy opponent because it predicts things that are not yet known – therefore it cannot prove anything 'beyond reasonable doubt'. Take our previous example regarding the geographic probability that nearly ninety percent of rapists live within five miles of their crime scene. It does not follow that a suspect who lives within this area and is now facing court is the offender; nor does it mean that a suspect who lives outside this region is not. Such information is simply not useful in court.

Profiling deals in probabilities not certainties and those probabilities do not come close to the reliability that can be ascribed to forensic evidence such as DNA. This doesn't mean that profiling is a useless activity. Offender profiles and behavioural investigative advice were designed to help direct the police towards some things that are more probable than others. Used in that environment, if they adhere to professional standards they can be as useful as a seaworthy boat on water, rather than an old hulk stranded in dock.

INNOCENT UNTIL PROFILED GUILTY

So Mr Britton is quite right that the courtroom is not profiling's natural arena. It can be a very useful psychological tool but it cannot be used to rule something in or out definitively. Unfortunately, he reports that he did exactly that in a case where a suspect being interviewed seemed to have guilty knowledge of a murder. Britton "ruled out the possibility of X being a participant" on the basis that his "psychological analysis" (i.e. his profile) had indicated one offender working alone.

To put it baldly, it really doesn't matter whether a psychological profile has determined that it could only have been the butler in a raccoon hat and a pink apron whodunit. Someone possessing knowledge they shouldn't have needs to be TIE'd properly. Similarly, in the case of the Nickell investigation, Britton advised officers that being happily married with a baby, or enjoying good relationships with women, or even having a job that required some intelligence, were reasons for elimination from the enquiry (*The Jigsaw Man*, p.173).

They categorically are not. They are simply examples of things that didn't match Mr Britton's profile. He may have recognised the parameters in terms of profiling probabilities, not absolutes, but, in practice, it seems those parameters became fuzzy. For reasons that are unclear to us, Mr Britton, by his own account, applied the methods of profiling as if they could absolutely rule a suspect out of an enquiry.

Britton produced one general profile for the Nickell enquiry, detailing the likely characteristics of the killer, and a second profile containing information on his likely sexual preferences, fantasies and so on. He did not, as a scientist should, make reference to the evidence base he used from which he drew his conclusions. However, notwithstanding our argument about the importance of a scientific approach, Britton's methods are of less concern than their effect upon the enquiry. After all, a profile cannot do much harm if a good investigator decides not to rely on it.

Britton relied heavily on the belief that sexual fantasies may help explain offending behaviour, and that a relationship between fantasy material and the commission of an offence can be imputed through examination of a crime scene. He claimed that, as he walked through the area where Rachel was murdered, *an image formed in his mind* of an individual with an "enormously powerful visual fantasy system". He was sure that the offender was a stranger whose sexual predilections involved "exploitation, degradation and the defiling of the woman in his fantasy". This lonely, deviant, sexually dysfunctional 'fantasiser' became the portrait that Britton painted of the offender – an individual who probably hadn't killed before but would have a very high probability of killing again.

The proposed sexual elements of the fantasies played a dominant part in the Nickell enquiry and were a major component of the media interest in the crime. The murder appears to have been widely accepted as a sexually-motivated offence, not only by the press (who chase lurid headlines) but also by the enquiry team and the psychologist, given that considerable attention was paid to this in the fantasy profile. Indeed, Britton suggests that the fantasy profile of the offender was particularly significant because it was so rare.

INNOCENT UNTIL PROFILED GUILTY

He claimed that such an individual would belong to a sexually deviant subgroup (i.e. outside the general population) and would be rare even among that deviant grouping. In other words, the particular configuration was a rarity among rarities. The link that the profile intended to establish was not direct – that is to say, finding a person who met the criteria for the sexual fantasy profile was not automatic proof that he committed the crime. Rather, the argument went like this: identify a suspect who was in the right place at the right time; investigate him further by establishing his sexual fantasies. The proposed sexual fantasies are extremely rare. The chances of two such rare individuals being on Wimbledon Common at the same time are, in Britton's phrase, "vanishingly small". Therefore, he is the likely offender.

This argument is clearly structured and can be followed logically. Britton declared that the offender's sexual fantasies would contain at least some of the features below, as taken from his book. At the time, he was an experienced and senior psychologist who had treated many sex offenders. We may accept without question his significant experience in discovering their fantasies. As an expert in the area, he emphasised that the offender's fantasies would not necessarily contain all the features; neither would his masturbatory fantasies be confined exclusively to the list. Unusually, no contemporaneous records were made of his advice to the investigation squad and no documents kept. The profile's only appearance in written form was on whiteboards that were subsequently erased. With those caveats, his suggested fantasy components are listed below:

1. *Adult woman.*
2. *The woman would be used as a sex object for the gratification of the offender.*
3. *There would be little evidence of intimate relationship building.*
4. *There would be sadistic content; it would involve a knife or knives, physical control and verbal abuse.*
5. *Submission of the female participant.*
6. *It would involve anal and vaginal assault.*
7. *It would involve the female participant exhibiting fear.*
8. *I would expect the elements of sexual frenzy which would culminate in the killing of the female participant.*

The problem with this approach is that the central plank in Britton's profile was the rarity aspect. Concluding that the right offender had been caught depended on the "vanishingly small" chance that two such very rare deviants could possibly be on Wimbledon Common at the same time.

So does this argument stand up? Certainly, Robert Napper's *behaviour* was rare; there is much scientific evidence to support the claim that sex murderers are extremely rare in themselves. It would be unlikely to find two such people on the common together. Unfortunately, the profile focused on the offender's sexual fantasies rather than his real-life murderous behaviour. But what someone does in real life and in their imagination may well be two entirely separate things. When considering the rarity claim we need to consider the sexual fantasies, not the offending behaviour. It is easy to slip from concentrating on the sexual fantasy to the behaviour but it is imperative that there is no elision from one to the other.

INNOCENT UNTIL PROFILED GUILTY

Of course, it's likely that there are people for whom there is little difference between fantasy and reality; indeed, we have argued (and there is support in the literature) that for Napper and other sexually sadistic offenders fantasy is a powerful driver for behaviour. However, imagined actions must be regarded separately from real-life actions and it does not follow that violent fantasy necessarily results in violent behaviour. And it is extremely important to know what really is 'rare' – we constantly underestimate the diversity of sexual behaviour and sexual fantasy. What may seem rare may actually appear with some regularity in large subsections of the population. Britton claimed that 'deviant sexual fantasy' was the thing that set the offender apart, that made him different. But if we focus wholly on sexual *fantasies* and not actual behaviour, is this true? A number of researchers have examined narrative accounts of sexual fantasies. Despite some differences between male and female fantasies, there are common themes that appear to recur across a range of research:

- *Conventional intimate heterosexual imagery with past, present or imaginary lovers who are known to the person.*
- *Sexual power and irresistibility (seduction scenes between mutual partners).*
- *Varied or forbidden sexual imagery (settings, positions, practices, questionable partners).*
- *Submissive-dominant scenes in which physical force or sadomasochistic imagery is implied.*

Some researchers have devised a 'typology', a scientific method whereby similar behaviours are grouped into categories. Obviously, fantasies must be reported in sufficient numbers to determine whether they warrant a category, so these typologies effectively tend to report common sexual fantasies. One such by Arndt and colleagues from 1985 included pretty self-explanatory categories: romance; variety; suffer; dominance; force; same sex; unpopular; macho. It should be noted that the participants in these studies were not sex offenders or people with expressed specialised sexual interests.

In another example, in 1990, Ami Rokach examined the narrative accounts of sexual fantasies of everyday people who took part in her study. This time, the categories are labelled: intimate; exploratory; variation; impersonal; dominance (consensual); dominance (nonconsensual). You can see from these two examples that there is some overlap in the categories: what one researcher labels 'romance', another calls 'intimate'; one prefers the term 'nonconsensual dominance', the other calls it 'force'. We have listed Rokach's framework below to give some idea of the types of behaviours each category includes:

1 Intimate
- Sex with one partner – partner may be a spouse, a friend or a stranger.
- Foreplay – includes kissing, body and genital caressing, mutual masturbation and oral sex.
- Courtship – social rituals engaged in when looking for a mate, e.g. walking through the woods together, dating, candlelight dinners and sending flowers to a loved one.

INNOCENT UNTIL PROFILED GUILTY

2 Exploratory
- Sex with more than one partner – engaging in sex with multiple partners.
- Sex in a unique environment – sex anywhere but in the bedroom, e.g. in a taxi cab or remote exotic location.
- Anal sex (because anal has not gained as wide public acceptance as oral sex it is included in exploratory).
- Homosexual – engaging in sex with a member of the same sex.
- Bisexual – engaging in sex with both sexes.

3 Variation (S/M)
- Sadism – includes beating, whipping, pinching, bondage and verbal abuse.
- Masochism – reception of the abovementioned sadistic acts.

4 Impersonal
- Sex with an idol – includes movie stars, noted athletes and highly esteemed public figures.
- Fetishism – common fetishist objects include rubber, nylons, leather boots, shoes, gloves and underwear.
- Voyeurism – achieving sexual gratification without direct engagement.
- Exhibitionism – achieving sexual gratification by exposing one's genitalia in public.

5 Dominance (consensual)
- Any force or seduction where recipient is enjoying, complying and encouraging the behaviour.

6 Dominance (nonconsensual – rape)
- Suffering or humiliation. The use of aggression and force with no possibility of room for escape or concern for the partner. The main enjoyment for the dominant partner is the suffering of the recipient rather than sex per se.

The interested reader can gain some self-insight into their preferences by scoring themselves across these categories on a five-point scale, where one = 'never fantasises about' while five = 'regularly fantasises about'. That everyday people's sexual fantasies commonly involve dominant or even nonconsensual sex in outdoor locations casts some doubt on the claims of 'rarity' in Britton's sexual fantasy profile. Moreover, we have deliberately chosen as examples studies that pre-date the mid-1990s, to show that these are not new findings. The information was just as available at the time that Britton was working on the Nickell enquiry. A scientific approach should always begin by finding out what other studies have been done in the field.

The consequence of these less-than-accurate conclusions about the prevalence and content of sexual deviancy was the way in which they were used to implicate Colin Stagg. Stagg was not the only person to have fantasised about outdoor sex or sadomasochistic sex. Any psychologist who researches sexual or paraphilic behaviour would know this. One could randomly stick a pin in a map to find people with such fantasies, so it is entirely unsurprising that investigators managed to turn one up living near Wimbledon Common.

Sex murderers may very well have an active and deviant fantasy life; that doesn't mean that all such fantasists are

INNOCENT UNTIL PROFILED GUILTY

therefore sex murderers. The error is this: one cannot flip backward and forward between one generalised truth or fact and claim that, ergo, the reversed statement is also true. For example: *cows are animals with four legs*; when we reverse the statement, it becomes clear that *animals with four legs are cows* does not still hold true. Similarly with *sex murderers are people with active deviant fantasies* (which Mr Britton knew to be true from his work). Reverse the statement and we have *people with active deviant fantasies are sex murderers*. Which is not necessarily true. Many are totally law-abiding citizens who fantasise harmlessly.

Recall Vince Egan's work on sensational interests, where he established that many individuals without any violence in their background were interested in vampirism, occultism, Satanism, militarism and so on. Other fantasists may be archcriminals who defraud and steal as a career and fantasise when they go home at the end of the day, but would nevertheless find a sex murder utterly repugnant. Fantasy is not reality. Ideas are not behaviour (even though they can feed behaviour). You cannot go sifting through someone's fantasies and conclude that you have discovered their behaviour.

Such errors are not the only problem that profiles can cause. One study which showed that early profiles identified the offender in just three percent of cases also showed that eighty-three percent of police officers found profiles to be 'very useful'. How can we explain this disparity?

It is possible that, although they did not lead directly to the offender, they nonetheless helped in some other way, such as suggesting a new line of enquiry the police had not yet thought of. In fact, the study examined these elements too and gave specific figures: officers reported that profiles helped in some way to solve the case approximately fourteen percent of the time and opened up new lines of enquiry in sixteen percent of cases. They are therefore by no means useless, but there is still a yawning gap between the help they actually provide and the proportion of police officers who think they are useful. So why are so many people convinced by such profiles?

There is a psychological phenomenon, well-established by academic research, called the Forer effect (named for the psychologist who studied it) and its close cousin, the Barnum effect. The latter isn't, as one might expect, named after its finder, but derives its name from the circus owner P. T. Barnum whose advertising slogan promised that his extravaganzas contained "a little something for everyone".

This is the essence of the Barnum effect. In certain circumstances, people have a tendency to take vague or bogus information and judge it to be an accurate description. Mediums and fortune tellers of all kinds use Barnum effects to their advantage, but the classic example is astrology. Indeed, the Barnum effect is particularly evident when the information applies to one's own personality. In the astrological horoscope, information which is broad enough to apply to much of the whole world's population comes to be regarded as accurate and even uniquely applicable to oneself. In this example, "The coming month will bring a positive change in the home life of Taureans," the information is vague and general enough to have "a little something for everyone". But people mistake the general for the specific and all too readily conclude that the astrologer has accurately predicted the extended visit of their beloved sister, or the arrival of their new sofa, or the tall, dark stranger who is about to cause them to ditch their current partners (because fate clearly has plans for them to become star-crossed lovers).

In truth, one would be hard pushed not to select some kind of positive event given a whole month from which to choose. Similarly, a profile that indicates the offender is "unlikely to be concerned about others' feelings" can barely help but be accurate. The offender would not be committing a crime if worry about its impact on someone else was a factor.

Positive descriptions can also create a Barnum effect as many people, unsurprisingly enough, are more willing to accept the flattering. ("Geminis are quick witted and intellectual.") The information also has a tendency to seem more accurate if presented by someone of high status – personal validation matters. In addition, people who believe that information has been gathered especially for them are more likely to be susceptible to the Barnum effect. These last two points, in particular, may have implications as to why offender profiles are rated highly and accepted as credible, even in the face of their avowed virtual uselessness in actually helping to solve a case.

While this psychological phenomenon is well known, it doesn't mean that everyone will automatically accept untruths. Indeed, when Paul Britton assisted with a Home Office-commissioned review of the state of offender profiling in the 1980s, he reported many police officers who simply ignored dubious profiles because it was only too obvious that they had the dangerous capacity to mislead an enquiry team.

He actually said of the potential for investigations to be misled by offender profiles, "If this had happened in a murder or rape investigation, then someone else could have died or been attacked" (*The Jigsaw Man*, p.99). This proved to be a tragically accurate prediction.

Even though he could not name him in relation to Rachel's murder, Britton in fact made several accurate predictions about Robert Napper. Reporting to the police, he stated his view of Rachel's killer thus: "It is almost inevitable that this person will kill another young woman at some point in the future as a result of the strong deviancy and aggressive fantasy urges as already described" (*The Jigsaw Man*, p.164).

This was horribly spot-on. As we know, Napper went on to murder Samantha and Jazmine Bisset the following year. But we cannot be selective about profilers' predictions – the 'hits' seem less uncanny when they are laid out alongside the 'misses'. When called to the crime scene containing the bodies of Samantha and Jazmine, Britton was asked directly by police whether Samantha and Jazmine's killer could also be Rachel's. He said no.

Britton acknowledged the links between the cases – young, attractive, blonde mothers stabbed to death in the company of their children. However, he cited two reasons for concluding they were committed by different people:

1) The different amounts of time the offender spent at each murder. There were mere minutes between the last sighting of Rachel alive and the discovery of her body, whereas the mutilation of Samantha could not have been carried out quickly.

INNOCENT UNTIL PROFILED GUILTY

2) Britton saw the children as "the single largest differentiating factor between them", rather than a link, because Jazmine had been killed but Alex had been spared.

Now, with the benefit of hindsight, we can see that the presence of children seems to have actually been a reason to make a link. We also have the benefit of the statistics which tell us that the instance of mothers attacked in front of their children is rare.

In terms of profiling and linking offence behaviours, no matter what information is available, the crucial part lies in the interpretation placed on it. One always has to ask, "What does this behaviour mean?" and decide whether it is significant or not. What Britton saw as a reason for separating two offences, we regard as reason to link them. In our interpretation, the meaningful part was that children were present while their mothers were attacked. This was so in Napper's rapes as well as the murders – recall the rarity of how, among a database of over 13,000 such stranger attacks, only seven were committed in the presence of children. (And Napper is known to have committed three of those seven.)

We have no intention of casting aspersions at Mr Britton for not making a connection on these particular points. We have the omniscient benefit of hindsight and we have the statistics. From the perspective of the time, deciding which behaviours were significant enough to link the offences was extremely difficult. The frenzied murder of Rachel seemed different from the calculated and deliberate dissection of Samantha. A decision had be made as to whether differences in the crime-scene behaviour could be attributed to the individual (conclusion: separate offenders) or the situation (conclusion: same offender, different situation).

The situational context in Napper's murders was different. In Rachel's case he was outdoors in a busy public space; risk of discovery decreased time and increased pressure, so Alex was spared and Rachel was not dissected. In Samantha and Jazmine's case he was indoors in private, where risk of discovery was much lower. This gave him time to mutilate Samantha, but the slow and careful aspects of the crime all took place postmortem; the murder itself was remarkably similar to the blitz attack on Rachel – swift, frenzied multiple stabbings as soon as he encountered her. Maybe, given the time, he would have preferred to stay with Rachel's body after death. On the other hand, maybe the postmortem evisceration of Samantha was part of his escalating behaviour as he moved beyond his first murder.

Spotting patterns is hard. Ascertaining which patterns are meaningful is even more difficult, and so Napper went uncaught for another year and a half after Rachel's death. Having been involved in many cases himself, Laurence Alison, the co-author of this book, can testify as to the complexity of trying to provide meaningful advice in such enquiries and the difficulties in reconstructing behaviours and establishing links (even with the benefit of databases and the research that has followed since 1992). We are still crawling toward understanding and making sense of crime-scene data, and it will be several decades before behavioural profiling can claim to be running alongside other well-established forensic methods.

As Napper went about his daily business and Rachel's

INNOCENT UNTIL PROFILED GUILTY

family were left with the knowledge that her killer was still free, outside of the investigation some things began to change. In 1995, John Stevens, then chair of the ACPO (Association of Chief Police Officers) sub-committee on offender profiling, announced plans to professionalise the system in the wake of the Nickell enquiry. This was the beginning of today's system of Behavioural Investigative Advisors (BIAs). They provide a service nationally to police who need to know (not guess) what particular behaviours might suggest about the location, history or other characteristics of an offender.

These are full-time professionals within the police service, usually with postgraduate degrees in investigative or forensic psychology, trained in scientific methods and the rigours of statistical analysis. They can better avoid some of the psychological pitfalls that may impede an investigator's decision making. Police can still draw BIA help from elsewhere, but these days psychologists are drawn exclusively from an approved list. In practice, these people tend to be academic psychologists, doctors and professors who, by dint of being at the cutting edge of research in the field, possess highly specialised knowledge and expertise. They must first prove their worth to make it onto the list of approved advisors, which is audited each year. But BIAs still deal in probabilities and likelihoods, not certainties. This will always be so because human beings – BIAs and psychologists included – are not mind readers; neither can they 'tune into' an offender's thoughts just by examining a crime scene.

This more scientific approach would have showed that Colin Stagg merely fell into the category of 'man with sexual fantasies'. This did not make him a sex murderer but, back in the early 1990s, when Britton was producing his profile, such lessons had yet to be learned. The profile may well have been a reasonable, or even accurate, description of Robert Napper and his sexual fantasies. Unfortunately, it also described many other people's fantasies. This was not realised by the investigative team charged with finding Rachel's killer, and it was not the only mistake they made. The Nickell investigation was led into completely uncharted waters. And while investigators seemed to find Britton's profile as beguiling as a siren calling, Robert Napper was wandering around, peering through women's windows.

In his place, Colin Stagg was led confused and blinking into the spotlight. Very soon, the media would usher several of his sexual fantasies out into the public gaze. Laurence, our co-author, would analyse those fantasies and find that, contrary to Britton's claim of a disturbed sexually deviant personality, Stagg's imaginings were not so very unusual. More significantly, they did not all belong entirely to him.

CHAPTER SEVEN
STAGG HUNTING

On 17th September 1992, the popular BBC television programme *Crimewatch* showed Colin Stagg's face in their appeal to catch the murderer of Rachel Nickell. Or at least that's what some of his neighbours thought.

What is more, they were convinced enough to pick up the phone to name him, as soon as lines were open in the incident room. Police always have to be wary of cranks who may be seeking attention, and the Nickell case had already turned up one such costly example. The malicious may likewise offer the name of someone they hold a grudge against. On this occasion though, they seemed like good leads because there had been four different callers corroborating each other's information.

It did not require malice to kick-start the investigation into Colin Stagg, just an odd twist of fate. Even in a photograph, Stagg looked remarkably like Robert Napper. When it came to the rather more generic quality of a photofit, he was a dead ringer for the killer.

Police artists had drawn up several photofits from the description of different eyewitnesses on Wimbledon Common. The investigation squad was keen not to use a composite mix of all eyewitness descriptions, which would be a likely route to blandness and inaccuracy – just as mixing many colours of paint together produces nothing more than a shade of muddy brown. Instead, they had decided on two: one from a woman named Jane Harriman, the second drawn from the description given by Amanda Phelan.

Ms Harriman had been walking with her children on Wimbledon Common at the time of Rachel's murder. She had been so unnerved by a strange man behaving suspiciously that she had paid him very close attention.

Many accounts had been gathered from many people about who they saw while they were out on the common, so it is inevitable that some eyewitnesses would have inadvertently been describing someone other than the killer. Amanda Phelan, on the other hand, was unlikely to be one of them.

Ms Phelan echoed the witness testimony of Rachel's son, Alex – and if there was one person the police could be absolutely sure had seen her murderer that day, it was Alex. Each gave matching accounts of the suspect's clothing. Ms Phelan had seen the man leaning down into the stream and washing his hands, just after the time Rachel had been killed. Her account was lent greater significance because it tallied with little Alex's description.

But the reliability of eyewitness accounts is far more

dubious than most people imagine. Storing everything that we encounter visually each day of our lives would entail a massive cognitive load, so our memories are designed to work extremely selectively; anything that passes in the background is unlikely to be processed or stored at all, let alone being available for accurate recall days or weeks later. Indeed, so fallible are our memories it is almost a wonder that eyewitness accounts are given the credence they are within the criminal justice system.

(For those who are interested, a search of video upload websites will yield clips of **experiments** which show just how limited our **visual awareness** is. People frequently do not see things that are incontestably right in front of their eyes – objects as big as other people, gorillas or moonwalking bears, believe it or not.)

Paying attention, however, filters out any superfluous and distracting information while the scene is being processed, storing the memory and recalling it accurately at a later date. Jane Harriman's close scrutiny of the man she saw was therefore a good sign that her description was more reliable than some others. So when it came to the appeal for public help on national TV, the police decided to select only the sharp memories of the two women and forego the various colourful descriptions of others, simply because it wasn't possible to double-check that everybody's was accurate.

There was a small possibility Ms Harriman could have been focusing her attention on the wrong man, of course, so Ms Phelan's account was also used, corroborated by the only witness to the actual murder. The broadcasted e-fits were crisp and clean as could be. They were also successful, insofar as they looked like Robert Napper. Unfortunately, so did Colin Stagg.

A facial resemblance was not the only thing to put Stagg in the frame. He fitted much of the first of Britton's two profiles. He was in his twenties, unemployed and living a solitary lifestyle. The profile also predicted he would possibly be into bodybuilding or martial arts, and would be interested in some form of pornography.

By this point, the reader may be thinking about the Barnum effect and asking, "Is there a 'little something for everyone' in the profile?" Although Stagg fitted it, perhaps many others would too. Predicting an interest in pornography among males in their twenties (when virility and libido peak) is almost redundant in terms of suspect prioritisation. Perhaps only a suspect living a solitary lifestyle in his twenties who did *not* have any interest in pornography might have narrowed things down.

The profile also stated that the offender would live near the common. Stagg lived so near to Wimbledon Common that he walked his dog there every day, and had been in the vicinity on the day of the murder. In fact, he arrived with Brandy just at the time police were cordoning off the scene and was turned away by a police officer. This was how Stagg learned there had been a murder – the constable told him why the common was out of bounds.

Stagg's response was to relate the news to shopkeepers and neighbours he met on the way back home. This became woven into people's narrative of the local suspect; over the coming months, it would be regarded as a suspiciously keen interest in the events. However, the alternative would have been to treat a

STAGG HUNTING

murder that had just occurred in the area he lived in as unworthy of comment – which would be much odder.

Stagg's discussion with the acquaintances he met on his way home was in fact a natural enough response to a shocking event. But from small acorns do mighty oaks grow, and the officer who turned Stagg away from his planned walk duly noted his name for the record. By the time *Crimewatch* viewers phoned in to identify the e-fit, Colin Francis Stagg was already logged in the system.

As Stagg opened the door to the police the following day, he discovered that their arrival coincided with yet another suspicious neighbour, Lillian Avid. She had come to double-check the number on Stagg's front door so she too could phone the incident room and volunteer his name and address.

Naïve enough to think he would be back home within a few hours, he asked police if he could be allowed to drop his dog off with its former owner, his neighbour Rita. In the event, Brandy spent the next few days in police kennels while Stagg, relatively unsupported by the inexperienced duty solicitor he had been assigned, rambled on in day-long interviews about all manner of things that could be interpreted in a suspicious light. When asked, he responded openly and honestly about his preference for nude sunbathing in hot weather. He innocently furnished police with all the details that local people like himself knew, explaining exactly which part of the common was frequented by sunbathers whose practice was tacitly accepted as a harmless way to attain an all-over tan.

When police confronted him with an old complaint from

their files about indecent exposure on the common, Stagg took his solicitor's advice to plead guilty and "get the case out of the way", even though there was little in the way of evidence that could have proven he was the man seen naked several months previously. He wanted only to get back home, and thought that admitting to indecent exposure would see him reunited sooner with his dog. Stagg later described it as the stupidest thing he had ever done, and could only explain his actions in terms of being "tired and frightened".

He was completely unaware of how he should have considered his circumstances. With an ill-judged 'confession' resulting in a conviction for indecent exposure, and a few days' interview under caution for murder, he may have felt quite relieved by that point. But much worse was yet to come.

Released due to the fact that there was little to no evidence against him, Stagg attempted to go back to his rather ordinary life – though suspicion still hung in fat, lingering pockets around the Roehampton estate where he lived. He knew too well – and felt it even more keenly – that many formerly friendly residents were reluctant to shed their doubts. What he did not know, indeed what he cannot have been aware of, was the collaboration that was forming between the Nickell team and Paul Britton.

Of course, by definition, no one can predict the unpredictable. Operation Edzell, as it was named, was so unpredictable that it would take a wild swerve away from standard murder investigations, effectively making history. Perhaps the most remarkable thing about the operation devised to build a case against Colin Stagg was the number of senior people who were consulted to give permission for it to go ahead. From the accounts of those who were involved, maybe the one phrase which echoes resoundingly throughout is, "It had never been done before."

In the absence of forensic evidence, or any other evidence at all that definitively tied Stagg to the Nickell murder, police hoped that he would confess he had killed Rachel or reveal guilty knowledge. When they had interviewed him, however, he steadfastly denied it.

'Belief persistence' is, unfortunately, a fairly common psychological phenomenon. Once people have come to a view on a matter, they are more likely to stick to their opinion than revisit their ideas. One even more specific, problematic phenomenon, well established by many psychological studies, is known as 'confirmation bias'. When someone comes up with a hypothesis (e.g. "I believe that Colin Stagg committed murder"), they have a biased tendency only to look for information that supports or confirms what they already think. To be rational and fair (as well as scientific), one should also look for evidence that disproves what you think, but people tend not to. This bias is certainly not confined to investigators, though it had disastrous outcomes in this particular case; it is a common phenomenon in everyday life.

Police ought to have also looked at features that disconfirmed their hypothesis that Stagg was guilty. For example, there were contradictions in eyewitness testimony with regard to the times of sightings, discrepancies which suggested he was actually at home at the times he said he was.

But instead they stuck to their beliefs, deferring reasonably enough to the expertise of the professional and accepting Britton's argument about the rarity of the offender's sexual fantasies. The police therefore reasoned that all they had to do was elicit from Stagg his own fantasies. If they matched the profile, this would supposedly constitute strong enough evidence for a jury – given the "vanishingly small" chances of two such people being on the common at the same time.

Operation Edzell's first hurdle was to find a way to have Stagg discuss these matters openly. With whom would you share your sexual fantasies? Would you be willing to tell *us*? Would you tell the police? Naturally, the most likely confidante is an intimate partner or possibly a close friend. Operation Edzell set about finding two such people to befriend Stagg.

Two police officers experienced in undercover operations were summoned. The policeman, a prospective pal for Colin, was posted elsewhere at the last minute – and so 'Robert Harris' had a lucky escape from the unsavoury aftermath of Edzell. The operation continued with just the policewoman who was given a role as a potential girlfriend. The team figured that a female officer gave the best chance of success, as Stagg was more likely to spill his most intimate thoughts to her.[7] Thus was the pseudo-girlfriend 'Lizzie James' created as an intimate partner for Colin Stagg.

Lizzie contacted him in the guise of a penfriend – a story made more plausible by pretending to be the friend of a woman named Julie Pines. Some years earlier, Colin had enjoyed a brief correspondence with Julie via a 'lonely hearts' column but she had ended the relationship, unhappy with an overt mention of sex in his letters. Being able to describe Julie as her prudish friend gave Lizzie a helpful explanation for her

---

[7] Incidentally, one type of person *unlikely* to confide in anyone – girlfriend or otherwise – would be a sexually sadistic murderer.

unsolicited self-introduction. The photograph Lizzie enclosed with her letter, revealing her to be a very attractive young blonde-haired woman, also helped.

From the outset, however, not everyone was convinced that Lizzie existed. Stagg later said that his neighbour, Cheryl, had warned him immediately to be wary. Both Cheryl and her partner, Richard, told him that attractive women did not appear out of the blue, promising an energetic and open-minded interest in sex. In fact, Cheryl told him bluntly that she reckoned the police were behind it. Colin's neighbour was a modern-day Cassandra – the ancient soothsayer, cursed and fated always to speak the truth but never to be believed. Her words went unheeded as Colin, now a thirty-year-old virgin, fired up his correspondence with the attractive Lizzie.

The new 'couple' exchanged letters and phone calls, and eventually met. Stagg was comprehensively duped by a 'honey-trap' which would hold him for almost seven months. And, as this entirely contrived relationship wound its mendacious course, he did indeed pour out sexual fantasies to Lizzie.

When the case against Stagg was being prepared for court, the defence employed their own psychologists: our colleague, Professor David Canter, was assisted by the co-author, Professor Laurence Alison (at the time just beginning his career). Laurence analysed the phone calls and letters that Lizzie James and Colin Stagg exchanged. It is worth noting that this is probably a unique professional experience: an entire relationship (albeit a contrived and dishonest one) was on record from first contact to last goodbye. It would be laughable even to contemplate any psychologist attempting to propose such research today, too unethical even to merit serious consideration. In this case though, the data had already been gathered and a man may have gone to prison for life depending on what happened next. In light of the profile, Laurence paid special attention to the sexual fantasy elements of the letters and calls.

The analysis showed that the following themes were predominant in Stagg's fantasies: foreplay; dominant sex (though his preference was consensual); having sex in a unique environment (e.g. outdoors); exhibitionism; sadism. This is not an abnormal profile, since it is neither specific in the sense of a paraphilia (i.e. one of the more unusual sexual practices, which are usually socially unacceptable) nor particularly unusual in terms of previous research on what men find arousing. There was, then, no evidence that the content of Stagg's fantasies was unusual or deviant.

When analysing material in a search for particular themes, researchers' opinions may differ. Suppose the letter writer had expressed his desire to "throw you onto the grass and have the best sex ever"? One researcher may put that in the category 'outdoors' whereas another may assign it to 'dominant' (because of the word 'throw') or both, but scientific analysis cannot afford arbitrary decisions. In accordance with good scientific practice, it is standard to have another person rate the same material.

Therefore, Laurence had another researcher assign the described sexual behaviour to particular categories and count up how many times each fantasy theme appeared. This standard double-check to determine how much consensus there is between different researchers is known as 'inter-rater reliability'. There is the possibility that two people will get the same score by pure chance. Science cannot allow for coincidences, so the statistical tests used are also designed to work out whether the results are a chance occurrence or a genuine agreement.

When all the number crunching is done, a score of 1 would show a perfect correspondence between the raters (extremely rare in practice); a score above 0.5 is accepted as reliable (and one can quantify exactly how reliable); a score below 0.3 is unacceptable and researchers must go back to the drawing board as their system is not working or the raters need retraining. The table below shows the frequencies of particular elements found by Laurence's analysis of the twenty-one letters written by Colin Stagg, as well as phone calls between him and Lizzie James containing sexual fantasy and inter-rater reliability scores.

Fantasy Theme	*Inter-rater reliability*	*Frequency out of 21*	*Percentage frequency*
Intimate	.93	18	86
Exploratory	.81	15	71
Impersonal	.81	13	62
Variation	.90	10	48
Dominance (consensual)	.75	5	24
Dominance (nonconsensual)	.75	5	24

Figure 7.1 Presence of fantasy theme in each of the 21 fantasy letters.

The table demonstrates that Stagg used a range of sexual themes. There are fairly high levels of exploratory behaviour in nearly three quarters of the transactions between him and Lizzie. Despite difficulties in classification of deviance, there is one thing that the majority of individuals who work as sex therapists agree upon: sexual deviancy is *not* characterised by experimentation.

The academic Alex Comfort has pointed out that sexual deviants are not 'trisexuals' (i.e. try anything), but what the old French madames would have called *des specialistes*. For example, the dedicated rubber fetishist is obsessed with, in Comfort's words, "what is, effectively, a rather disabling and isolating hobby" (1987, p.6).[8] The very nature of the variation across the themes in the Britton profile supports the notion that his fantasies are not deviant in the classic sense of the word (i.e. as paraphilic obsessions).

In other words, deviant sexual behaviour is about very specific, extremely specialised activity without which the individual cannot get aroused. It is definitely *not* about variety, but a variety of behaviours were what the profile contained. This is in sharp contrast with what we might expect to see in a sexually sadistic rapist, who may find it difficult to get aroused by anything other than the suffering of others.

Stagg was interested in variety in a pretty 'normal' way. He expressed an interest in sex with multiple partners (mentioned in six of the fantasies), sex in a unique environment (mentioned in thirteen of the fantasies), made homosexual references (five of the fantasies) and also bisexual references (three of the fantasies).

Even where the prominent focus in the exploratory theme involves references to outdoor sex, we should remember that this focus is not exclusive. It is one of a variety of settings, since

---

[8] Comfort, A. (1987). *Imperial Patient: The Memoirs of Nero's Doctor*. NY, USA: Frye & Co. Publishers.

STAGG HUNTING

Stagg chose to write in his fantasy letters about other areas in which sexual activities occur (in the bedroom, in his back garden). A more detailed breakdown of each theme is given in the table below. It shows the specific behaviours, activities and other details that were categorised into each theme:

Fantasy Theme	Presence score is out of 21	Total multi-theme score
INTIMATE	39	
foreplay	14	
sex with one partner	15	
courtship	10	
EXPLORATORY		18
unique environment	9	
more than one partner	4	
bisexual	3	
homosexual	2	
anal	0	
IMPERSONAL		12
exhibitionism	5	
fetishism	4	
voyeurism	3	
VARIATION		7
sadism	7	
masochism	0	
DOMINANCE (consensual)	5	5
DOMINANCE (nonconsensual)	5	5

Figure 7.2 Presence of the elements within themes across the 21 fantasies.

KILLER IN THE SHADOWS

As the table shows, a thorough analysis which examines everything Stagg mentioned (rather than focusing only on the more headline-grabbing items) shows that his most frequent theme is 'intimate'. Certainly, extremely graphic features appeared in his exchanges with Lizzie, in descriptions such as, "I feel the muscles of your cunt . . . I withdraw leaving you exposed, panting against the tree." This was seized upon for the fact that the sex occurs outdoors, with the woman against a tree, but this is selective.

In the very same paragraph, Stagg writes of the "beautiful flush that women get when sexually aroused". Substitute the word 'sexually' with something a little more euphemistic and this last phrase would not be out of place in a Mills and Boon novel. Some of the specifics are, ultimately, distracting. If we can take our attention away from the more salacious sexual details, it transpires that the things Stagg wrote about most were really rather ordinary things like courtship — for example, offering to cook Lizzie dinner. He more often mentioned sex with one partner. He also shared with her his belief that a loving relationship is the way to enhance a couple's sex life — not details that intuitively come to mind when envisaging a disordered sexual sadist.

At the end of the last chapter, we mentioned that one of the most significant factors in the TIE of Colin Stagg was that the fantasies were not all entirely his and his alone. One of the first, most elementary things that students learn when they are very first introduced to the subject is the psychology of learned behaviour. If we want to change or shape someone's behaviour, we need to understand how they acquire it, how and why they come to act as they do. Most people today are familiar with the idea of conditioning and reinforcement, but it is worth revisiting these ideas to focus the mind precisely on the mechanisms which inform so many different aspects of this book.

Robert Napper learned to harm women. Colin Stagg tried very hard to learn how to please his woman. Intentions which seem polar opposites actually involved the same learning mechanisms. None of us is any different. We all acquire extremely different behaviours in the same way.

Recall the process of 'conditioning' and the famous example of Pavlov's dog. Eventually, experiments with rats, pigeons and other species showed that whether a particular behaviour was repeated depended on the consequences that followed it. If behaviour A was followed by a positive consequence, the organism (rat, cat, bird or human) repeated the behaviour. If behaviour A met with no response or a negative consequence, the organism was less likely to repeat the behaviour.

This is known as 'Thorndike's law of effect', named after the man who studied how cats learned to open the door latch of the boxes he put them in. If they opened the door by accident, they got to the food outside the cage. Before long, their 'press paw down on latch' behaviour increased and incorrect responses (e.g. biting at the bars or miaowing) decreased. To use the preferred terminology, we say a particular behaviour has been 'reinforced'.

By the 1930s, an extremely eminent psychologist named Burrhus Frederic Skinner had established in more detail the principles and means of shaping voluntary behaviour (known as 'operant conditioning'). Among other things, he refined the process used by Thorndike. Rather than wait for a cat to escape a 'puzzle box', he invented a more efficient alternative to Thorndike's equipment. His 'Skinner box' contained inbuilt levers or lighted keys which would automatically deliver an instant reward when pressed. A Thorndike cat let itself out of the cage once, and then had to be returned to the box. A pigeon in a Skinner box, on the other hand, could peck all day at the key if and when it chose to. The experimenter thus got to watch the behaviour-reward sequence repeatedly and the process of conditioning happened more rapidly.

In the early days of Skinner's experiment, rats who pressed a lever were positively reinforced by being fed a sugar solution. Rats like sugar – so they repeated the behaviour. Rats who received an electric shock when they pressed the lever were less likely to repeat; they had been punished and the net result was aversion.

But what if there are no consequences to behaviour – neither reinforcement nor punishment? The outcome in this instance is a decrease in the behaviour under investigation. Without any reinforcement, it simply withers away until, eventually, it is extinguished, hence we refer to the behaviour as being 'extinct'. Thus, if you wish to avoid extinction of the behaviour, you need to carry on reinforcing it. However, this is not the whole story.

Interestingly, the surest way to avoid extinction is not to reward everything every time it happens. Instead, you use a method known as 'partial reinforcement'. For example, a human adult – just like many other species – will sit pulling a lever if s/he is rewarded. Rats like sugar and pigeons are

STAGG HUNTING

fond of pellets of grain, but you would probably be better off offering humans money. After the initial learning process has been completed, if you decide to stop giving money in response to the press of a lever then the behaviour will be extinguished.

If you have previously rewarded every pull of the lever, a human being will cotton on pretty quickly that s/he is now wasting her time and stop; this non-reward situation has never happened before, so the message is that there are no more rewards forthcoming. However, if you offer occasional rewards (sometimes money appears and sometimes it doesn't), your human subject will keep on pulling. S/he doesn't know whether the rewards have stopped forever or whether money will appear on the next pull. The lesson s/he has learned is, "If at first you don't succeed, try, try again."

And so intelligent humans while away entire days pulling the levers on one-armed bandits in sprawling behavioural labs like Las Vegas and seaside amusement arcades. Because their slot machine activity has been partially reinforced with occasional wins, the behaviour is extinguished very slowly. Sometimes, they persevere until they are broke in the hope that the next pull will be the one that delivers the jackpot.

If we want to train an organism of any species to perform more complicated tasks, we simply reinforce in stages; the method is known as 'successive approximations'. Initially, we may guide them towards the behaviour we want and reinforce it immediately. If you are training a puppy to sit, you lavish her with praise and offer her a treat the second her backside touches the ground. It doesn't matter whether you push her backside to the floor or just wait for it to occur naturally; as long as it is reinforced the animal will associate the sensation of bottom-on-floor with treats and do it automatically.

If we want to teach a dog to climb a ladder, cross over a plank to another ladder and pick up a paintbrush when he gets there, the principle does not change one iota. There are simply more stages. As soon as the dog walks near the bottom of the ladder, positively reinforce the behaviour. Repeated frequently enough, the animal will associate it with the pleasant consequence and become conditioned to walk over to the ladder. Next, reinforce the placing of a paw on the first rung and so on until pooch is sitting at the top with brush in mouth. Family film audiences have long been entertained by pets that retrieve newspapers, fetch beer from fridges and rescue children from danger. The animals are all trained in the same manner. Our own seemingly dumb pets could do it, though not all of us have the patience to teach our dogs to climb ladders.

Who designed such aspects of Operation Edzell became a matter of some dispute after the investigation. They are beyond resolving now and, in any case, are not our prime concern here. Certainly, Paul Britton advised police against an undercover operation that simply pushed the target suspect "down a slide". He expressly did not want the suspect to be trapped.

Rather, he emphasised that it must be designed so that "a suspect actively climbs a series of ladders whereby he either eliminates or implicates himself by his own choices". Indeed, he stressed that Lizzie James should not lead him on or "put words into his mouth or ideas into his head. Lizzie could only react to the cues he gave" (*The Jigsaw Man*, p.179).

STAGG HUNTING

Britton was unaware that Colin Stagg was the target and found such details irrelevant. The operation was designed simply to elicit fantasies that accorded with his 'deviant sexuality analysis' of the unknown offender – as long as the target climbed the ladder without being forced to do so. But it makes little difference what analogy you use for the operation. Pushing someone up a ladder is no harder than pushing them down a slide. Up or down may matter in the real world – gravity exists in the real world – but as a metaphor for behaviour it makes no difference. There is, however, a more important consideration than the language.

Lizzie was warned not to introduce ideas or themes but to wait for the suspect to do it. She could react but she could not lead. As will be clear from our summation of the mechanisms of operant conditioning, however, proactive force is not required – behaviour can be shaped spontaneously without it. All that is needed is positive reinforcement. Nobody led the rats to the lever; nobody needed to push the puppy's bottom to the floor; nobody needed to instruct dogs or humans to climb ladders. As long as there is a reward when they show the behaviour of their own accord, they will repeat it.

This comparison with simpler species is not intended as any disparagement of Colin Stagg. If our behaviour was positively reinforced by the reward of something we desire, we would all do the same. We may like to think that humans are by far the more sophisticated species, but when it comes to learning the processes are the same.

Thus it didn't matter if the operation had been run impeccably; it was flawed in its conception and the warnings to Lizzie would not provide sufficient protection. Some behaviour might emanate entirely from the suspect's thoughts or ideas; that would be sufficient for him to start climbing ladders. But assuming that he was not led or pushed is applying the most generous gloss possible to proceedings. In actual fact, Mr Stagg was a thirty-year-old virgin and perched on top of the ladder was a very attractive girlfriend who had already indicated that, when it came to sex, she was not prudish like her 'friend', Julie.

Here is a list of some of the things that Lizzie was told would be acceptable responses to Colin Stagg's cues:

- Acknowledge being sexually aroused by coercive activity;
- show her willingness to adopt, indeed, show a preference for a passive role in sexually arousing coercive activity;
- express an interest in the occult;
- indicate her previous enjoyment with other men who shared sexual fantasy that moved from romance to violence;
- be impressed by men who indicate their willingness to achieve their desires in action, even when these clearly conflict with the acceptable range of social behaviour;
- finally reveal her involvement in an occult group practising ritual abuse and her active role in the sexual murder of a young woman.

Thus the trap was set. Colin Stagg was in the Skinner box and he pressed random levers all over the place in hope of reward. With reinforcing responses like those in the list above, the only remarkable occurrence would have been if he had *not* written explicit sexual fantasies. The outcome was sadly predictable. Basic psychology tells us that and who began the process is irrelevant.

The design of Operation Edzell was flawed in other respects. In both conception and implementation, the tiny but crucial letter 'E' was forgotten from TIE (Trace, Implicate or Eliminate). Stagg was traced without difficulty as a suspect in the Nickell enquiry, as a face just like his appeared on national television. Vast, hitherto undreamed of effort was ploughed into implicating him, while the means whereby he might be eliminated was squarely overlooked.

TIE is so much the bread and butter of detective work that the police ought to have been acutely aware of such details. There is, to be fair, some indication that they asked Britton how the suspect might eliminate himself. Britton advised that if a rapport had not been established between weeks two and sixteen of the undercover operation, it should be discontinued. In the event, it proceeded for another two months without any revelation of guilty knowledge. They could reasonably assume that Stagg had eliminated himself, but, unfortunately, zeal overtook caution. The very idea of elimination was forgotten as fast as last year's Christmas cracker, whereas information that hinted at Stagg's guilt was cherry-picked and pored over ('confirmation bias' at work). The operation ran five more weeks beyond the prescribed elimination date, and it was Stagg who refused Lizzie's offer of one last meeting.

It is understandable that police deferred to the professional opinion of Paul Britton. If you knew enough to challenge expert opinion you would have no need of it in the first place. Whether the mechanic who pronounces your car exhaust dangerous, the dentist who recommends a costly brace or the psychologist who predicts certain behaviour is consistent with that of a sex murderer, we sometimes have little option but to trust the experts. Nonetheless, some of us will have learned the hard way that such folk need always to be questioned. The consequences may be too profound if we do not exercise that right.

When Operation Edzell was devised, it was in effect an experiment which predicted the offender would behave in a certain way. Britton came up with a hypothesis that only the true offender would climb a series of ladders. Leaving aside its problematic nature, we should look at another aspect of the design. It is imperative that any scientific experiment makes its hypotheses explicit. It should also be falsifiable and, most helpfully, state which conditions would render it false.

In the Edzell 'experiment', the hypothesis was this: Colin Stagg is the murderer of Rachel Nickell. If true, he would reveal the fantasies that fitted Britton's profile. If false, he would . . . well, what? How could someone disprove such a hypothesis? What behaviour would an innocent man show? What might Stagg do or say or reveal that a sex murderer would not?

Given the profile's prediction that the offender would neither have had nor be able to build or sustain relationships with women, evidence of the suspect showing nurturing behaviour might be one example. Britton claimed he looked for "female agency within sexual relationships" as indicative of someone who was not the killer, but he only searched the sexual fantasy letters. In the context of an undercover operation in a murder enquiry, a more rigorous scientific approach was warranted. All of the related material should have been systematically examined.

When Laurence did so, the most common theme was 'intimate' (see our earlier table). Indeed, Stagg showed a very normal regard for women in his covering letters. He worried about Lizzie's reaction to the accompanying sexual fantasy letters and told her, "I hope you are not offended." He also confided his wishes for the future – "I hope we will have a relationship that will last for a very long time" – and asked Lizzie explicitly to tell him what she wanted, imploring her not to 'dump' him.

Lizzie did not reinforce affection or display nurturing behaviour (remember how non-reinforcement leads to extinction of the behaviour). Rather, she told Colin, "I cannot help but think you are showing restraint . . . I want you to burst. I want to feel you all powerful and overwhelming so that I am completely in your power, defenceless and humiliated." She also told him, "I believe I will only ever feel fulfilled again if I meet a man who has the same history as me" (her 'back story' containing elements of sexual murder and the occult).

Naturally, we too have selected our quotations for the purposes of this chapter, but no one's life depends upon this book. In the operation itself, greater rigour and sounder methods were required. Police should have been apprised of the 'innocent' behaviours. After all, they had a definitive list that would implicate a suspect in terms of the profile itself.

They should likewise have been issued with one that eliminated him, the equivalent of stating the conditions under which the hypothesis would be falsifiable.

Instead, this curious and cold experiment placed a lonely man in a veritable Skinner box for seven months. An attractive but never truly available woman was paraded and dangled before him while he repeatedly scrabbled to press the levers, trying to work out how to win the prize. Any affection he showed as he tried to get closer to the unattainable Lizzie was completely ignored. Any salacious detail, any mention of sexually dominant behaviour, of harm to others, was reinforced by her describing how exhilarating she found such activities.

In the letters, Stagg desperately tries to understand what Lizzie wants and he tells her, "You . . . used to enjoy hurting people. I do not understand . . . please explain as I live a quiet life. If I've disappointed you, please do not dump me . . . I need you, Lizzie. Please, please tell me what it is that you want . . . I still do not know what you want in this relationship, Lizzie, so please darling, tell me."

He goes so far as to invent a story about a murder, trying to placate her and match her own account of her involvement in ritual human sacrifice. He thinks it might finally be the lever that will open the door to her heart, but she dismisses his tale as "just a childish murder". He stops short when it comes to real-life events. Ultimately, when Lizzie tells Colin she wishes he had murdered Rachel Nickell, he simply replies, "I'm terribly sorry but I didn't."

In the final reckoning, despite strong inducements and a powerful scheme to 'shape' his responses by selectively reinforced behaviours, Stagg did not confess. He was repeatedly deceived, tantalised and spied upon while he fell in love with a chimera. It was as cruel a fate as any mythological tale told by the ancients. For his efforts, he was rewarded with a murder charge and the fury of the tabloids.

The man lost over a year of his life in prison on remand awaiting trial, parted from his beloved dog, Brandy, while she was held in police kennels. Finally, he was ushered into a van in 1994, driven beneath black clouds through the September rain from Wandsworth Prison. The van bypassed the press *melée* scrambling for the best pitches from which to click shutters or deliver their piece to camera, vying for the spot that would feature the distinctive façade of the Old Bailey as a backdrop. Colin Stagg was escorted from his holding cell up the staircase into the dock at Number One Court, to appear before Mr Justice Ognall.

The judge decided there would be a delay before the jury could be sworn in. He wanted first to decide on the admissibility of the evidence from the undercover operation. Ognall was the man charged with adhering to the sombre vow that – lest any should forget – was writ large, set in stone above the Old Bailey's entrance: "*Defend the children of the poor and punish the wrongdoer.*" He did not disappoint.

In a ruling which upheld the court's inscribed duty as stoutly as the Portland stone columns that supported the inscription itself, he announced, "If a police operation involves the clear trespass into impropriety the court must stand firm and bar the way."

Indeed, the whole pronouncement on Operation Edzell was scathing. He described it as "a blatant attempt to incriminate a suspect by positive and deceptive conduct of the grossest kind . . . a sustained enterprise to manipulate . . . sometimes subtly, sometimes blatantly, and designed, by deception, to manoeuvre and seduce him to reveal fantasies of an incriminating character, and to, wholly unsuccessfully, admit the offence."

Mr Justice Ognall ultimately declared the operation "reprehensible". In an incisive critique of its design, the judge also commented on the absence of means whereby Stagg might have been eliminated as a suspect. He professed his belief that "it was not merely anticipated, but intended, that there should be, eventually, incriminating evidence from the mouth of the suspect," but it was, he said, "very important . . . that at no stage did [Stagg] ever admit that he was the murderer. Indeed, to the contrary, he repeatedly denied it."

At this stage, the judge could simply have declared evidence gathered by the undercover operation inadmissible. Even the greatest fool could not have remained in any doubt as to his position, but Mr Justice Ognall continued. He indicated the ways in which behaviour had been shaped; he noted the errors made by Stagg in relation to physical details of the murder, errors that pointed to his ignorance of what had truly happened. In short, he made explicit, in the open and very public arena of the courtroom, exactly the kind of 'innocent behaviours' that Britton had failed to make obvious in an operation supposedly designed to eliminate, as well as implicate; behaviours that the investigative team had consequently seen fit to ignore.

In the end no one was triumphant. The prosecution acknowledged that, with the details gleaned from the

STAGG HUNTING

undercover operation deemed inadmissible, they had no case against Stagg and a 'Not Guilty' verdict was recorded. Stagg left a free man, but the tabloids would not release him as a suspect. His life was effectively broken. André and Alex Hanscombe, Andrew and Monica Nickell, along with Rachel's brother Mark, had publicly endured a very intense scraping around in their barely covered wounds. The procedure brought absolutely no relief. Two years on from her savage death, Rachel's killer was still unknown.

Paul Britton was described by the judge as the puppet master of the operation. Certainly his design was flawed but, in truth, such a catalogue of errors could not be laid at the door of any single individual. Britton had expressed concerns about possible entrapment, but finally deferred to others' expertise regarding the legality of the operation. This was entirely reasonable; it was not for him to do the job of lawyers.

The police too bore the brunt of the blame for the failed operation. In particular, Detective Inspector Keith Pedder felt he was singled out for disproportionate approbation, yet the whole sorry £3million enterprise had passed through many hands. The Crown Prosecution Service team largely escaped censure though they had given it the go-ahead, as had senior commanders with vast collective experience.

Indeed, many people beyond those immediately involved in Operation Edzell bear some responsibility for the hunting of Colin Stagg. Claims that the media are mere conduits which report rather than create the news are disingenuous. Various publications fashioned Stagg into a tabloid 'Aunt Sally'. An investigative reporter worthy of the job title might well have turned the course around, and perhaps even traced Robert Napper. After all, he wasn't far away.

Instead, the idlest hacks continued to pick lazily over the carcass of Stagg's life. It was easier to pad along the now well-worn and familiar path to his front door. If they couldn't label him 'murderer', they would settle for 'oddball pagan', or 'unemployed scrounger' – stories that amounted to name calling by the school bullies. Stagg could be relied upon to fill the gap on a quiet news day.

Offender profiling took such a battering in the wake of the Nickell enquiry that it would be more than a decade before it recovered and re-established itself away from the disreputable air that lingered post-Edzell. Undeniably, profiling as it then stood had been killed off. Cracker was dead.

The detectives returned to their offices to lick their wounds after the trouncing by Mr Justice Ognall. 'Lizzie James' sued her employers for the impact Operation Edzell had on her life. Her solicitor pointed to the six-figure sum she received in compensation as testament to the psychiatric injury she had suffered. Still a young woman, her future no longer lay with the police and she was retired from the Met.

Detective Inspector Keith Pedder – every inch the recognisable, stereotypically solid-looking copper, right down to the moustache – also had his police career foreshortened by his involvement in Edzell. He was shunted into an organisational cul-de-sac, where he lasted just fifteen months before stress-related health problems forced him to leave the police service. He was thirty-nine years old.

Silver-haired Superintendent John Bassett had retired. This senior figure – avuncular enough to tolerate his nickname

STAGG HUNTING

'Bertie', after the Liquorice Allsorts mascot – ended an otherwise exemplary career on a low note, berating himself for being "only as good as your last case". In fact, in a case where many ran for cover from the fallout, Bassett stood out. He shouldered some of the backlash squarely and said, "I've got to hold myself responsible for nobody being arrested and charged . . . I think it reflects on me."

In time, many of the other detectives – Mick Wickerson, Neil Giles, Martin Long, Roy Ramm – would move on to other cases. Eventually, a new set of faces arrived to fill the office whiteboards with details of new cases, other murders, different victims, other families destroyed. One thing remained unaltered. Rachel Nickell's killer was still unknown.

The final turning point would have to wait until technology finally heralded change. So let us turn, in the meantime, to the psychology of sex murderers. It is clear that they cannot be uncovered merely by sifting through sexual fantasies. But what *do* we know about them? What does shape such a killer?

CHAPTER EIGHT
SEX MURDERERS

Robert Napper is one of those relatively few people who can break, without compunction, a profound and near-universal taboo that appears across human societies and cultures. It is encapsulated in the ancient commandment: "Thou shalt not kill."

Warfare is the solitary arena in which behaviour otherwise categorised as murder is endorsed. We mentioned in Chapter Four the processes whereby soldiers can overcome their disinclination to kill, but even in this situation only one-to-two percent are considered to cope well with it and a significant number find they are unable to carry out orders. They cannot take another human life.

Following World War II, it emerged that some seventy-five percent of those enlisted into the armed services did not fire their weapons. Although these numbers are disputed and various explanations exist, it is accepted that many simply could not bring themselves to do so. Their life experiences had so strongly conditioned them against inflicting harm that they were unable to fulfil what they knew to be their duty.

The small percentage of human beings who enjoy killing have overcome this widespread aversion to causing the death of another. Napper and his counterparts have not only negated the human instinct to preserve life, they have developed the urge to do the very opposite.

It is a fact that some people — rare though they mercifully are — find satisfaction and pleasure in killing another individual. Most of us are repelled yet somehow fascinated by such behaviour. Much of the interest lies in wondering how and why they are so different from the rest of us. Even more bizarre and rarer still are those who kill for sexual gratification. What do these offenders have in common? How did they come to lose their humanity? What can psychology tell us about those who commit such offences?

In this chapter, we shall look at the features shared by some of the most infamous sex murderers of the past century. By looking at these offenders collectively, we can begin to identify what their formative experiences were, what happened in their lives that helped to shape them and how they eventually became the sort of person who derives sexual gratification from abusing and killing other humans.

Even more specifically than a sexual killer, Napper appears to be a sexual sadist. Baron von Krafft-Ebing defined sadism as "the experience of sexual, pleasurable sensations (including orgasm) produced by acts of cruelty". (Krafft-Ebing was an eminent Austro-German psychiatrist whose seminal work, *Psychopathia Sexualis*, 1886, was instrumental

SEX MURDERERS

in launching the academic study of sexuality. He came to be overshadowed by Freud.) Sadistic offences are defined by the offender's specific intention to seek sexual pleasure from inflicting pain and suffering. Tragically, in most cases of sexual murder there are patterns which emerge in early childhood that appear to generate social isolation, fuel violent sexual fantasies and lead to some of the most brutally savage acts of rape and murder.

Thankfully, this sort of extreme violence is very rare. Figures indicate that in the United States less than one percent of all murders are sexual, and this percentage is even smaller for serial sexual murders. As offenders, however, they grab the imagination like no other. Cinema audiences like to be scared, so the race against time to capture stranger-killers makes for popular movie plots. In real life, because such offenders cause revulsion and terror they will also make press headlines. After reading of particular murderers, people do not forget them in the same way they forget the bank robber or burglar who made last year's news. All these factors can make the incidences of serial or sexual murder seem less rare than they actually are.

Within the current UK prison system, it is estimated that Napper is one amongst only 200 other men who have committed murder[9] with an apparent sadistic sexual motive. Moreover, figures suggest that serial murders have accounted for less than two percent of all murders in England and Wales since 1940. It has even been argued that there are more

---

9 To avoid unwieldy repetition, the term 'murder' is not used with legal precision in this chapter. We use it in the lay sense of someone who commits the crime of killing another. Strictly speaking, Napper was convicted of 'manslaughter by diminished responsibility'.

people studying sexual murder than there are sexual murderers! But the torment for those who have lost someone to this kind of predator is horrific beyond imagining. What constellation of circumstances can create people such as Robert Napper?

In terms of upbringing, most sexual murderers have experienced physical violence prior to age eighteen. Nearly sixty percent of them have alcoholic fathers and in over half of cases both parents are violent towards one another. Domestic violence is, of course, largely unseen, though it can be uncovered through injuries coming to light or even when family members themselves make it public. John Wayne Gacy was one such who revealed the details of the domestic violence that afflicted his childhood, growing up in a middleclass Irish-American family in Chicago. The fear in the home was not public knowledge, but the alcoholism of his violent father was only too apparent. He died of cirrhosis of the liver at Christmas 1969, when his son was twenty-seven years old.

It was not inevitable that son should follow father down the same destructive path. Indeed, Gacy was regarded as a model citizen, known in his community for helping neighbours and organising local events. His community work brought him invitations to events where he got to glad-hand the dignitaries who came to meet deserving locals; the highlight for Gacy was being photographed next to the First Lady, Rosalynn Carter. He worked mostly for the Jaycees, an American non-profit organisation whose volunteer members raise funds and provide services to their communities. Gacy was a prominent member of his local chapter where he was eventually appointed chaplain – an important role, which he was honoured to take. He had so often smeared greasepaint over his face to amuse the children at fundraising events that he became known as Pogo the clown.

The moniker stuck when he admitted to police that the smell in his house emanated from the bodies under the floor. He would go to his execution known as the 'Killer Clown'. Between April 1976 and his confession in December 1978, Gacy had been picking up boys as young as fourteen and young men up to the age of twenty-one – sometimes at bus stations, at other times luring them into his car with offers of marijuana. He kept these young males quiet by stuffing clothes into their mouths; then he sexually assaulted them and choked them to death with a rope, or a board held against their necks.

Gacy liked to keep his victims with him for as long as he possibly could before decomposition set in. Even then he still could not let them go. He kept them nearby beneath his house and garage, storing them at home while he went out to find another to add to his macabre collection. He eventually showed police where the remains of twenty-nine snuffed-out young lives were to be found under his house, and told them he had disposed of another four in the river.

On the other side of the Atlantic, the disturbing nature of these crimes was succinctly distilled into a book title telling the story of a different man. Brian Masters' biography of Dennis Nilsen was called *Killing for Company*, and it sums up perhaps the most sinister aspect of both Nilsen and his American counterpart Gacy – that their loneliness was abated by keeping their victims near. If we can just about comprehend murder, then, by contrast, the necrophilic tendencies of men who want to keep dead bodies close by seem even more unfathomable.

1978, the year that Gacy was caught, was also the year that Nilsen murdered his first victim. Like Gacy, he lured young men to their deaths. He seems to have had sex with their corpses (though he denied this) and then kept their bodies near him for days afterwards in bed. Nilsen's gruesome concept of 'closeness' was finally discovered when the bones of some of the fifteen bodies he boiled down blocked the communal drains at the building he lived in.

The notion of 'killing for company', where the murderer attains a pseudo-relationship without the strains and demands of true interaction, may be a plausible interpretation of these acts. Nilsen, like Gacy, had a violent alcoholic father. Both witnessed dysfunctional intimate relationships and violence in their formative years, while true empathy with another was absent from their family experience – though it is reported that Nilsen was close to his grandfather. (His family's expectation that he view his grandfather's body pre-burial is cited as a traumatic experience that contributed to his developing necrophilia, though many children do so without a problem.)

The family is the most immensely powerful influence on our development as its environment is where we first learn how to form bonds with other human beings. It begins in the very first weeks of life, from the day a baby learns to copy the face s/he sees and first smiles back at a parent, and we continue to depend on it to acquire the necessary skills for building relationships.

SEX MURDERERS

But merely to say that Gacy or Nilsen became scourges of society because their fathers were violent drunks would be preposterously simplistic and naïve. Many experience such childhoods and grow up to become the perfect citizens Gacy only pretended to be. Life is far more complex, but just because it isn't the whole story doesn't mean these were not important factors in making Gacy or Nilsen what they were.

Part of their extreme indifference to the carnage they inflicted on others was 'learned' from their parents' relationships. Indeed, the severity of the crimes for which such offenders are committed is directly related to the severity of violence or neglect they experienced in childhood, even though the details of the crimes may differ.

Robert Napper's victims were female whereas Gacy and Nilsen murdered males. Gacy and Nilsen lured victims into their own lair and kept them there after death, whereas Napper roamed his own locale, stalking and hunting the women he raped or killed, finally abandoning the victims where he had found them. Nonetheless, the gratification gained from sexual assault, rape and murder was common to all. The violence that seems 'natural' to sex murderers is first witnessed in the family and thus becomes normalised. Robert Black, who we mentioned in Chapter Three, experienced the classic childhood of most serial sex murderers. Abandoned by his mother, as a child he was often heavily bruised at the hands of his foster parents and was especially punished for his bedwetting.

These tendrils spread so insidiously that they can choke all humanity out of a family. In an extraordinary example of 'like father like son', Milton Wheeler was jailed in his twenties after killing and sexually mutilating an elderly couple. He followed up this depravity with the rape at knifepoint of a fourteen-year-old and sexual assault of an eighteen-year-old – all on the same day. His own father had been convicted of murdering a seventy-seven-year-old woman by slashing her throat. A life sentence meant he could no longer go on viciously beating his six-year-old son. Unfortunately, Milton's brother stepped straight into their father's shoes. He sexually abused the boy and later grew up to serve his own ten-year sentence for rape. Milton Wheeler's own defence barrister described him as a man who had never "met decency" and acknowledged that it was "not altogether surprising he is what he is".

The poet Wordsworth wrote, "The child is father of the man," and it is true that we are all shaped by our childhood and family experiences. But even the most dysfunctional environments can offer enough opportunities for socialisation so that sex murderers may learn to pass as ordinary folk.

Napper and his counterparts manage to keep their murderous activities veiled over the months and years remarkably well. Just as Napper's colleagues found him "a bit boring really", Andrei Chikatilo (see Chapter Three) also managed parts of his life successfully enough to seem mundane. He hailed from behind the Iron Curtain and Chikatilo's nearest and dearest were as convinced as Gacy's neighbours that he was a model citizen. They knew him only as a gentle, calm husband and father, a former teacher who now held a job as the manager of a machinery supply company. There was, however, a completely monstrous section of his life that he kept entirely separate.

SEX MURDERERS

Investigators found little consistency and no trace of a victim type for Chikatilo. His victims included a thirteen-year-old girl, boys as young as eight and nine, a teenager with Down's syndrome, and women in their thirties and forties. He left bodies near roads, train stations or in woods, sometimes buried but mostly not. They died from hammer blows or multiple stab wounds. Like Napper he mutilated his victims, variously biting off nipples or noses, or cutting off fingers; body parts were discovered jammed inside mouths while other bodily orifices were stuffed with dirt or leaves. He disembowelled some, sodomised others and removed heads or genitals – though common to most of his murders was the laceration of eye sockets, which were sometimes gouged out.

The predatory nature of Chikatilo's offences is very similar to Napper's. Both went out in search of victims and attacked where they found them, rather than luring them into their homes. Both had favourite haunts – for Napper the green spaces and commons near his London bedsit, while Chikatilo so often scoured bus stations that police were deployed there to keep watch for the as-yet unidentified 'Rostov Ripper'.

Chikatilo's mutilation of his victims mirrored Napper's evisceration of Samantha Bisset. Both inserted objects into bodily orifices, a fascination also shared by Robert Black. Chikatilo was like Napper in the way that he discarded his victims. Both left bodies at the crime scene but neither could let go completely. Napper took part of Samantha's abdomen as a trophy, though what he did with his gruesome keepsake is unknown. Chikatilo is less of a mystery in this respect. Rather than store victims under the floor the way Gacy or Nilsen had, he kept them much nearer. He ate them.

The concept of closeness is something we all use to signify someone dear to us whose company we wish to keep, so much so that it has seeped into everyday language. We speak of couples as being 'very close' to indicate the strength of their relationship and say they 'break up' if it ends, perhaps because they 'drifted apart'; if it is a happy family we are discussing, then we call them 'tightly knit'; we say children are 'attached' to their parents. When it comes to loving messages of intimacy and romance, we go further and shift to the internal, telling lovers they'll be 'forever in my heart' or 'always a part of me'.

In fact one, US study[10] found that regular (i.e. non-cannibalistic) people said they would be more likely to eat someone if they found them sexually attractive. We should not be wholly surprised by this finding. After all, much sex play, from kissing to oral sex, involves taking the partner's body parts into one's own mouth – the same place we begin the process of ingesting food. The distinction, of course, is that the consequences of French kissing or the nibbling of lovers' ears are wholly temporary. Despite the metaphorical sexual preferences of non-cannibals, for most of us there are absolute limits.

We speak with disapproval of someone who is 'possessive', but the idea of someone whose concept of closeness is literal – the cannibalisation and ingestion of their victims – is regarded with repulsion. It is also particularly harrowing for victims' families, who are not merely denied the balm of funerary rites but can never rescue, nor retrieve, nor even

---

10 Scher, S. J., Vlasak, M., and White, C. M. (2003). *Cannibalism and Sex: Shared Standards of Social Disgust*. Manuscript under editorial review.

separate their loved one from the killer. However, it is conjecture to suggest that this perverse desire for closeness was the motivation for Chikatilo's cannibalism, for he didn't tell.

When eventually caught, he steadfastly resisted all manner of police interrogations until he was finally interviewed by a psychiatrist named Bukhanovsky. It had been more than six years since Bukhanovsky had come up with a profile of the then unknown offender. He showed Chikatilo this old profile and asked him for his help on how he might develop it – and then he listened. It was thought that Chikatilo responded because this was the first time in his life he had come across anyone who seemed to understand him. He rewarded the psychiatrist's patience with confession after confession, as he told him the dreadful stories of how he had killed thirty-one females and twenty-two males.

His life also unfolded in these stories – he had endured sustained and cruel scolding from his mother because of his bladder weakness, which was a result of hydrocephalus at birth. The neurological damage from this birth trauma was also linked to his involuntary ejaculation in the absence of erections. But a world torn by war was never going to notice a small child's bladder problem. The notion of medical help did not even register.

Mother love in young Andrei's young world consisted of warning the child not to wander far from home, via bedtime tales of an older brother who had been abducted and eaten. This did not describe an imagined world of fairytale ogres. Heroes to vanquish the Nazi occupiers were as yet in short supply and the region was stricken with famine. There are World War II survivors aplenty to corroborate the idea that meat from human bodies, which lay dead in the street, was a horrible necessity if people were to survive. It is not much of a leap to believe some were specifically killed for the purpose, even if the truth of Chikatilo's lost brother was not actually confirmed. This was the world in which he learned his lessons about relationships, about the ways humans treat each other.

Chikatilo survived a harsh childhood in a gruesome world. The lesson of the day was that life was not precious and no attention would be paid to his needs. It follows that any sense of empathy on his part was likewise absent. Again, this is perhaps a partial explanation. Others across various continents have survived appalling wartime experiences and learned to behave humanely. It is possible that the explanation for Chikatilo's sociopathic behaviour lay not exclusively in the environment he grew up in, but rather in his damaged brain and other physiological deficits.

The man himself confirmed that he had used his knife as a substitute for his impotent penis, and that some victims were chosen because he regarded them as socially beneath him. It filled him with rage to think that the homeless vagrants he picked up in train or bus stations were capable of sex whilst he, an educated man with a university degree in Russian literature, a Communist Party member and (in his perception) an upstanding citizen, was not. Neurological damage may have meant he was less able than most to exert control over these angry impulses; psychiatrists commonly find such disinhibition in sex offenders.

Those who survived Robert Napper's attacks also testified to his inability to attain or sustain a full erection, just like Chikatilo. Napper also utilised his knife as an alternative to his penis – one of his rape victims recounted how he had placed it at the entrance of her vagina and told her she was lucky that he hadn't used his blade to penetrate her.

Retrospective studies uncover similar backgrounds behind people like Chikatilo, Nilsen, Gacy and Napper. They have usually been psychologically abused, and may have been abandoned by one or both parents. Napper was sexually abused on the threshold of his teen years, but the father who might have helped him deal with the trauma had abandoned the family to emigrate to the other side of the world.

A small but significant number of sex murderers have been the victims of sexual abuse. Much has been made of the link between being abused as a child and becoming a sex offender as an adult. However, more common in victims of sexual abuse is a burning and corrosive anger that can lead to outbursts of violence.

This knowledge is not particularly new. Dr Karl Berg was a noted psychologist who made a study of the sadistic sexual murderer, Peter Kürten. Kürten was born in 1883 and met his death at the guillotine in 1931, after confessing to seventy-nine offences in Düsseldorf including rape and murder. Like Chikatilo, Kürten led an outwardly respectable married life and had no particular preference in terms of weapons or victims; he attacked middle-aged men, counted two sisters among his victims and killed children as young as five with axes, hammers and knives. He also tortured and masturbated animals. Kürten freely confessed that he gained sexual pleasure from the sight of blood. He also revealed that the number of stab wounds a victim received was directly related to the length of time it took him to ejaculate.

The association between the thrust of the knife and the movements of the penis during intercourse is impossible to ignore.

Kürten had learned at the hands of his abusive father that a man fulfilled his sexual desires without compunction or thought for another. In the single room in which they lived, he had witnessed his father sexually assault his sister and mother enough times to digest that lesson. His father was not deterred by a three-year jail sentence for incest with his thirteen-year-old daughter. Peter emulated his father in serving twenty-seven prison sentences of his own; they wiped out twenty-four years of freedom, but did not rehabilitate this man who first discovered sadistic sexual pleasure in stabbing and torturing sheep and goats with which he had sex. He honed his sadism when he later lived with a masochistic prostitute, thus reinforcing his association of sex with pain and transferring the infliction of such acts from animals to humans.

Although he claimed to have drowned two playmates when he was only nine, Kürten's first proven murder was a precursor of Napper's killing of Jazmine Bissct. Both men had stolen into the supposed safety of a child's bedroom to sexually assault and murder the young girl who lay asleep in the warmth of her bed. Thus the misery of his childhood was delivered unto another generation of innocents. Kürten himself attributed the horror to his own earlier experiences, telling the judge at his trial, "The punishments I have suffered have destroyed all my feelings as a human being. That was why I felt no pity for my victims."

We know then of the likely family environments and

influences that can warp child development, but what of the killers' early behaviour? In childhood, they tend to be prone to daydreams and habitual lying.

Kenneth Bianchi and his cousin, Angelo Buono, were dubbed the 'Hillside Stranglers' when they tortured and killed ten girls and young women in Los Angeles. Bianchi was born of an alcoholic who worked as a prostitute. Though he was granted a more stable environment when he was adopted as a baby, family environment is not the only influence on aberrant behaviour and the damage may already have been done.

Foetal alcohol syndrome (FAS) is a wide-ranging disorder caused by imbibing alcohol during pregnancy. As the name suggests, it affects the development of the foetus and damages the central nervous system. The damage caused to the fragile brain and other vulnerable organs as they develop in the womb is permanent. It usually shows physically in a characteristic fold in the baby's eyelids, a thinner upper lip and a flattened philtrum (the skin between the top lip and the nose), but other manifestations can be of far greater concern. Cognitive functions are limited in various ways by the malformation of brain structures and the neurological damage caused by alcohol. Whatever we may believe about the complexity of someone's personality or character, we are ultimately all reducible in some respect to different parts of our brains and the electrical and chemical messengers that run around them. We only need to think of drug use (legal and illegal) to understand how chemical changes can profoundly alter mood, or even personality.

In FAS, there may be organic damage to a part of the brain called the hippocampus, which plays a role in learning and regulation of emotion; put simply, those affected may not be able to relate to other people and feel emotion or empathy in the same way as others. Impairments may also show as poor memory, weak social skills or difficulty in distinguishing fantasy from reality. Such individuals are more prone to mental illness, which can further complicate the picture. Among mentally ill sex offenders, one study shows that by the time they are convicted of a sex offence and sentenced to prison by a court of law (as opposed to being 'sectioned' by a mental health professional), seventy percent have already been psychiatric inpatients, sometimes with as many as twenty-five admissions. Of course, not all mentally ill sex offenders were damaged by FAS and not everyone diagnosed with FAS becomes mentally ill. Again, we're talking probabilities and likelihoods, not certainties.

FAS can nevertheless underpin many difficulties. It can cause attention deficit problems as well as poor control over impulsive behaviour. The prefrontal cortex, the section of the brain which sits just behind the forehead, is a key player in executive function, i.e. responsible for managing higher order skills that we tend to associate with more mature behaviour. Hence it plays a part in controlling impulsivity, in weighing up consequences and suppressing urges that may be regarded as antisocial. It is the part we rely on to manage the more orderly sections of our life. If we wish to defer gratification by planning ahead – saving for next year's holiday, accepting relative poverty while we study for better career prospects later, leaving the party early because we have work tomorrow – decisions such as these would make the prefrontal cortex light up on the MRI scanner to show it was busy at work.

SEX MURDERERS

It is also linked to more evolutionarily primitive areas of the brain concerned with rage, aggression and sexual impulses. Damage in the prefrontal cortex as an adult, through accident, injury or disease, reduces people's ability to control their behaviour. Upright citizens sometimes become social liabilities overnight due to prefrontal lobe damage. There are cases where formerly loving and faithful wives or husbands have been unable to prevent themselves leaping straight onto the first person they meet if they become aroused. What might make for a mildly amusing stage farce is in reality heartbreaking for family and friends, who have to manage the daily care of loved ones whose personality has been all but lost to indecent and sometimes aggressive behaviour.

When the prefrontal cortex was never able to form properly in the first place, due to alcohol damage in utero, the picture can be bleak with regard to attaining full control over impulses. Indeed, some researchers were first alerted to affected individuals simply because of their hyperactive and unfocused behaviour. Although a physician in Liverpool as long ago as the 1890s had noticed the poorer birth weight and development of babies born to alcoholic mothers, FAS was surprisingly not named as a distinct disorder until the 1970s. Now known in the West to outstrip any other cause of learning disabilities, there was unfortunately no such focus on FAS to explain behavioural problems by the time Kenneth Bianchi was a child in the 1950s.

His adoptive mother raised concerns about Kenneth's lying and daydreaming at an early stage. He was referred for medical intervention by the age of five, such problems commonly showing in early childhood. Naturally, we may look back at most childhoods and retrospectively identify problems of some sort. Indeed, few would be 'normal' if they were entirely problem-free, but trips to medics are more usually of the sprained-wrist-while-falling-off-a-bike type. Likewise, at school, a parental summons to the head teacher's office may result from a playground fight. All children have to learn to manage conflict as they grow up, while most will get it wrong and hit out at some stage. Such occasions are typically infrequent enough to give little concern.

For mentally ill sex offenders, however, the statistics show that eighty percent are sent to special schools, while thirty percent suffer some sort of relevant medical problem such as a prior head injury or epilepsy. The behavioural problems and the involvement of professionals at an early age are of a very different order in sex murderers' childhoods. As a boy, Robert Napper was aggressive at home, a habitual liar who was violent towards his brothers, spied on his sister undressing and bathing, and required psychiatric intervention from childhood onwards.

In Bianchi's case a physician diagnosed *petit mal*, a form of epilepsy, to explain the boy's trances. (Petit mal is characterised not by seizures but by temporary 'absences', where the sufferer will halt and just stare into space.) Like Chikatilo, Bianchi also suffered from childhood incontinence. A psychologist regarded Kenneth's angry, uncontrolled temper tantrums as being caused by excessive dependence on his mother. We do not know whether medics today would make a different diagnosis, but the knowledge that a child's biological mother was an alcoholic prostitute by age seventeen would alert doctors to the probability of alcohol-related damage – a more physiological than psychological explanation. What we do know is that up to fifty percent of individuals over the age of twelve diagnosed with FAS display some form of inappropriate sexual behaviour. However, given that promiscuity is included in the definition of 'inappropriate', many individuals may pose more of a risk to themselves than others.

We also know that Bianchi continued into adulthood as a liar. He lied when he fraudulently claimed to have the qualifications to practise as a psychologist. He lied when he pretended to be a policeman to lure girls into his car, and he lied to an array of psychiatrists after his arrest when he pretended to have multiple personality disorder, claiming it was an alter ego named Steve who was the killer of the ten female victims. Some were fooled, but a detective on the case was unmoved and simply gave the psychiatrist a pithy message: "Tell him the judge will let Kenneth off but Steve gets the chair."

Although the *causes* of behavioural problems are many, the behaviours are similar and nearly a quarter of sex murderers exhibit reckless and dangerous behaviours (e.g. fire-setting, general rebelliousness) during childhood. Napper was a shoplifter and vicious bully by adolescence. Bianchi had been removed from two schools by age eleven. The adolescent Chikatilo was sexually excited by the struggle of a ten-year-old he impetuously grabbed. Kürten was an arsonist and a self-proclaimed killer by age nine, and can also be included among the forty percent of sex murderers who have run away from home in their youth.

The sex murderer Richard Ramirez was another such

individual. As a child he would run away to spend the night in the local cemetery. He found more safety among the gravestones than at home at the hands of his abusive father. In the 'outdoorsy' culture of his home state, Texas, the epileptic Ramirez could not join in the sporting pursuits that embodied masculinity. Thus it is likely that this skinny youngster, who raped and killed at least thirteen people, was excluded from the regular social interaction that helps most people to develop confidence. Indeed, low self-esteem is a very common feature in such offenders. Studies indicate that it is much more common in sexual murderers than rapists, and it appears to be a defining feature alongside social isolation. To some extent, they fit the stereotype of a pathetic loner.

Unsurprisingly, this pattern of poor self-esteem, social isolation, chaotic family environment, parental neglect and sexual or physical violence results in disciplinary problems at school, lower educational standards and few (if any) friends. In early adulthood this very frequently leads to general criminality, and the majority will have convictions for crimes against property or the person (or both). On average, such offenders have at least two previous convictions for property-related crimes and three previous convictions for sexual crimes prior to committing murder. The average age for an official conviction for the first crime (of any sort) is twenty-three years old, although most have started committing such crimes by the age of seventeen.

The single biggest predictor of lethal violence can be ascertained by examining the sum of inappropriate childhood and adolescent behaviours. The more problematic the child in this period, the higher the likelihood of lethal violence as an adult. Unsurprisingly, the sum of inappropriate behaviours is strongly related to the degree of victimisation as a child. Both victimisation and inappropriate childhood behaviours are associated with particular personality disorders. Schizoid personality disorder, for example, manifests in a lack of interest in relationships, tendency towards a solitary lifestyle, secretiveness and emotional coldness.

Any of us may read such a list of symptoms and be reminded of someone we know who is not a very sociable person, or who tends to keep secrets. That does not by any means indicate that someone has a personality disorder. That is a much more serious matter which can effectively prevent sufferers from engaging in or building successful human relationships; their behaviour is so markedly different from what is considered 'normal' that many may not be able to function successfully in society. It may be stable and unchanging across a broad range of situations, regardless of the fact that it may also be culturally inappropriate.

Most of us can quite effectively select our behaviour to match a situation, so if a colleague told us she had just become a grandmother we would smile and show happiness at news of the birth. Even if we don't know the new parents and it won't really have an impact on our own lives, we know to respond emotionally and, moreover, would feel happy for our colleague. Likewise, we would adopt a serious demeanour at a funeral to show respect for the bereaved family. Again, even if we didn't personally know the deceased we would feel moved at others' grief.

Thus the emotional coldness of a schizoid personality

might seem appropriate and even pass for 'normal' behaviour at a funeral, but s/he may not be able to adapt that response to express joy in the 'new baby' situation. In this way, such people may not always stand out from the crowd, though there may sometimes seem to be something odd about them.

Avoidant personality disorder is characterised by a persistent pattern of social inhibition, feelings of inadequacy, extreme sensitivity to negative criticism and avoidance of other people – the stereotypical loner bearing a grudge about some long-ago trivial slight, who appears in so many Hollywood film scripts. Dependent personality disorder manifests as a pervasive psychological dependence on other people. For example, notwithstanding the pain of a love affair gone wrong, most of us learn to accept it eventually because we realise it is culturally inappropriate to become so possessive that we would consider stalking (let alone killing) the ex-partner we cannot let go of.

In short, a vicious circle of parental neglect and violence leads to a troubled childhood; a personality that is disordered; poor educational performance; increasingly remote contact with others and few, if any, intimate contacts; reliance on one's own mind for company (including sexually deviant fantasies); and ultimately, if the configuration is severe enough, lethal violence. Of course, there is no inevitability to individuals suffering abusive backgrounds becoming murderers, but the converse tends to be true: sexual murderers rarely have happy childhoods, supportive parents or effective social relationships, and are rarely socially effective adults.

Interestingly, despite media portrayals, psychotic conditions are extremely rare in sadistic sexual murders. Robert

SEX MURDERERS

Napper's diagnosis as a paranoid schizophrenic is in fact very unusual. Although it may be tempting to view Napper's crimes as the product of delusional states, emerging research suggests that even the grossest acts of violence can be structured by a degree of rationality on the part of the offender. That is to say, even sexual murderers engage in decision-making processes that take into account how to obtain a victim most effectively, and how to avoid being apprehended. Most display enough forensic awareness to know how to escape after the offence. And so, despite all we know of what creates them and how they tick, harnessing that knowledge to assist in tracing this type of offender is still very challenging.

As we have noted, offender profiling remains a controversial area though, as with most scientific research, it is continually evolving. The ideas and explanations that scientific researchers come up with are often called 'models' – they propose ideas or explanations of a particular phenomenon, whether the behaviour of criminals or the behaviour of atoms. Other researchers can then test whether the proposed ideas in the models hold up or not.

The researchers who specialise in the area of offender profiling are no different. Over the years there have been many models proposed; however, many focused principally on *motivational* rather than *behavioural* models, and, as such, were of limited effectiveness. This is because it is nigh on impossible to know what motivated a person to do something without reading the mind. The offenders can always tell us (if indeed they understand it themselves), of course, but would *you* trust what a serial sex murderer says?

Behavioural models were an improvement insofar as behaviour is something we can observe. If someone gets up at 7:30 each day and goes to their workplace between 8am and 6pm, we can note that their behaviour is consistent. Let's suppose we learned that eighty out of a hundred convicted sex offenders behaved in a consistent, routine way with regards to work, we might propose a behavioural model type called 'consistent worker'. Colleagues, neighbours, even strangers at the bus stop can corroborate consistent behaviour – if they see someone at the same time every day – which might be worthy of further enquiry. This would be more help to police hunting an offender than a motivational model that predicts, "He is motivated by revenge." Even if this were true, how would you know this of a colleague, a neighbour or someone at the bus stop? The short answer is that you would not.

Traditional profiling methods have entailed deriving *offender characteristics* – that is, things that we predict about the offender (e.g. age, home-base location, domestic circumstances, mental health issues, pre-convictions, etc) – from *crime scene actions*, the offender's behaviour at the crime scene (e.g. whether the offence was especially hostile, forensically aware, etc).

The common misconception is that lists of characteristics or a 'pen portrait' of a given offender can be generated from a close examination of the crime scene. For this to work, however, two things must be true: the first is that offenders are consistent in the way that they commit crimes (termed the 'consistency assumption'); the second is that particular clusters of crime scene actions are the product of

SEX MURDERERS

demographic and personality-based causes (known as the 'homology assumption').

In plainer English, the homology assumption is making the leap from what someone *does* (action) to what someone *is* (in terms of personality). So a profiler may say something like, "The rape victim was gagged and bound; therefore, the offender is aged between X and Y and he has a bondage fetish" – taking what the offender *did* (bound the victim) and claiming this shows what he *is* (a man of a specific age group with a bondage fetish).

The truth is that there is very little evidence to support the homology assumption. It appears to be the case that the same sorts of actions can be committed by very different people. To use our example above, we know that the use of gags and ligatures in rape is *not* restricted to a certain age of offender. Neither can anyone reliably make the leap from gagging and binding a victim to a bondage fetish. Gagging a victim may have been a purely practical strategy to prevent her screams alerting a would-be rescuer; tying her up prevents her escape.

At the risk of spoiling the plot next time you watch a profiler-type TV programme or movie, it is worth asking yourself, "Can they really know this from the crime scene? Is this the only explanation?" If there are alternative explanations, then the story's hero/heroine may be 'assuming homology' without good reason. Back in the real world, however, there *is* a reasonable degree of evidence to suggest that offenders are relatively consistent from one crime to the next – especially with regard to distances travelled, forensic awareness and specific hostile acts.

It is not only in the world of TV that investigators assume

homology. Despite the lack of research to support it, *modus operandi* (MO) crime-scene information has, for a variety of reasons, been heavily relied upon in profiling work, and the traditional behaviour-demographic typology system is still in place in the US.

This reliance can be disadvantageous, as MO involves an action or set of actions functional to the commission of a crime. An example might be a rapist/burglar who regularly uses a jemmy to open windows (MO) and then attack victims. MO is functionally significant in that it helps the offender to commit the crime, but that does not make it psychologically relevant. As we noted earlier in the book, if a window were left open there would be no need to use the jemmy (and some householders don't even lock their doors).

MO is therefore dependent on context, and as the context changes so too will the behaviour/MO. Just consider a decision as mundane as feeding the family. Parents always have the same goal – don't let the kids go to bed hungry – but, depending on all kinds of factors, our 'feeding behaviour' differs. If we're out and about, we might buy a takeaway or go to a restaurant. At home, we might cook something quick or spend hours making a nutritious and delicious meal. Stop and list how many different influences might underpin different situations and you will get an idea of the influence of context on behaviour. We might spend hours making a healthy meal because: we're at home and we have time today, or we feel guilty about the kids' recent snacking, or we're trying to impress some guests, or we love cooking, or we're leaving for a trip and want the last meal to be memorable, or . . . (carry on yourself!)

The point is this: we cannot assume we know why an

SEX MURDERERS

offender does something, nor should we ignore the influence of situational context on behaviour.

These issues, and the debate over the influence of situation over behaviour, have been considered in depth by our own recent research, wherein we argued that the examination of very specific behaviours as a reliable basis for inferring characteristics of offenders is fraught with difficulty. So, too, is using specific behaviours as a basis for highlighting the similarities between offences (as we saw in Chapter One, the wrong links may be made). The major hurdle is this: longstanding research suggests that human behaviour, including criminal behaviour, is fluid and adaptable. Offenders evolve over time and respond to the environment that they are in. In this very specific context, Robert Napper's offending evolved and escalated from rape to murder.

'Rational choice models' examine offending behaviour at various stages – pre-crime (degree of planning), criminal event (the attack itself) and post-offence phases (behaviour in the aftermath of the attack) – and assume that offenders work toward specific goals. In Napper's case, this would be how to increase and maximise the suffering of the victim and, based on this, the intensity of his sexual arousal.

As such, offenders respond dynamically and rationally to events as they unfold. Thus, decisions about victim selection, offence location, method of attack and so on will be determined by previous efforts, skills, resources, preferences, values, etc. What is notable about Napper is the number of offences that involved attacking women with young children, which was true of women he raped as well as those he killed.

It could be surmised that this was simply a matter of

chance. Certainly, the time of the attacks meant that many women of a specific age were likely to be enjoying a walk in the fresh air with children. It could also have been a practical device that gave him greater control over the women he selected. The most sinister meaning, as we have seen, is that he found the elevated fear and suffering associated with the victim trying to protect her child arousing. Certainly, the latter explanation fits with what we now know about Napper as a sexual sadist. Even in the first known rape he committed, the victim had to desperately plead to close her bedroom door to prevent her children from hearing.

A potentially fruitful line of research therefore involves joint consideration of context (events preceding, during and in the aftermath of the offence) as well as 'rational choice' theories of offender decision-making. Specifically, when researchers have examined violent offending, small but encouraging gains have been made by focusing research agendas on exploring offenders' premeditation, the crime phase itself and the post-crime phase (events leading up to the end of the offence). Recent research has discovered that predicting the risk of a victim being murdered in a violent sexual offence is based on: (i) the offender's feelings of extreme anger prior to the incident; (ii) the offender having no intimate relationship with the targeted victim; (iii) the use of a weapon brought to the scene; (iv) the victim's verbal or physical resistance.

Moreover, in terms of the intensity of the attack, the predictors are: alcohol consumption on the part of the offender; verbal and physical humiliation; physical resistance on the part of the victim. Thus, tragically, the more that victims resist, the higher the likelihood of them being murdered (if the offender has the configuration noted above – i.e. pre-phase anger, a weapon and alcohol consumption).

A group of Canadian academics[11] has summed up the sadistic sexual murderer as follows: drawing on in-depth interviews over several hours with dozens of offenders, they have included the offenders' MO and the characteristics of the murder, and have drawn a distinction between the behaviour during the pre-crime and post crime phases. The table below shows their summary.

Figure 8.1 Proulx, Beauregard and St. Yves' summary of the sadistic sexual murderer

Characteristics of the murder	Pre-crime phase	Modus operandi	Post-crime phase
Mobility	Impressive amounts of unexpressed anger	Ruse and manipulation to approach the victim	Moving of the corpse
High intelligence	Very elaborate sadistic fantasies	Victim unknown to him	Hiding of the corpse
Post-secondary education	Fantasy world more important than reality	Isolated crime scene, chosen in advance, far from his residence	Crime scene reflects control
Preference for work placing him in contact with authority or death	Situational stress	Vehicle used in commission of the crime	Absence of weapons or evidence at the crime scene
Cruelty towards animals	Often murders after a blow to self-esteem	Presence of instruments of torture or of a rape kit	Interest in media coverage of the crime
Enuresis during childhood	'Hunts' his prey	Reflects sadistic fantasies	Possible change of job or city after the crime

11 Proulx, J., Beauregard, E., and St. Yves, M. (2005). *Sexual Murderers: A Comparative Analysis and New Perspectives* (pp.123-141). Sussex, England: Wiley.

KILLER IN THE SHADOWS

Characteristics of the murder	Pre-crime phase	Modus operandi	Post-crime phase
Fire setting	Selection of a specific victim following surveillance	Victim held captive for several hours, with recording of aggression	May volunteer to help during the investigation
Tendency to be isolated	Premeditation of crime	Consumption of alcohol during the crime	Relatively normal behaviour between crimes
Antisocial, narcissistic, schizoid and obsessive-compulsive personality disorders	Consumption of alcohol prior to the crime	Submission of victim demanded	Absence of remorse for his acts
Severe psychopathy		Victim tied up and gagged	Pleasure in describing the horror of his acts
Lack of empathy		Fellatio by victim	Low profile during incarceration
History of breaking and entering		Anal or vaginal penetration of victim	
History of sexual crimes		Possible sexual dysfunction	
Fascination for objects related to police work		Insertion of objects into various body cavities	
Possession of violent pornography and detective magazines		Prolonged and ritualised torture	
Paraphilias: cannibalism, vampirism, necrophilia, fetishism, masochism, transvestism, voyeurism, exhibitionism, obscene telephone calls		Mutilation of genital organs	

SEX MURDERERS

Characteristics of the murder	Pre-crime phase	Modus operandi	Post-crime phase
Sexual sadism		Non-random pattern of wounds on the victim's body	
Serial sexual crimes		Pre-mortem mutilation Death by strangulation Sexual arousal elicited by violent acts committed on the victim, culminating in the murder Dismembering Retention of souvenirs belonging to the victim or taken from her	

The above summary presents a composite picture of most offenders. Naturally, not every individual will display all features but this does not mean the findings should therefore be rejected. Individuals will differ while the mean or median findings for offenders as a whole still hold good.

Although not of direct practical use to investigators trying to apprehend an offender, we do know some things about the inner world of the avoidant sexual sadist. He is plagued by humiliation, suffering, anxiety and anger. He may feel inferior to women, perceive them as rejecting and punishing, and as such retreat from any social contact with them. Anger and the use of drugs (including alcohol) then act as disinhibiting factors, to allow him to attack his victim.

Sadists in particular are more likely than non-sadistic rapists to have a generalised conflict with women and more likely to have deviant sexual fantasies. Sadists are also more likely to select specific types of victims. Non-sadistic rapists often take advantage of opportunities (for example, a teenage girl alone at a bus stop), but a sadistic predator may stalk his victim until he sees a chance to attack, revelling in the cat-and-mouse hunt.

In terms of the pre-crime phase over the two days before the attack, over one third of sadistic sex murderers are suffering perceived rejection, with nearly half suffering a blow to their self-esteem (e.g. loss of a job, being 'knocked back' by a woman and so on). Nearly two thirds have had some form of conflict with a woman and nearly seventy percent are feeling intense anger. Nearly all initiate some planning for the offence and over eighty percent have selected a specific victim. Half will engage in torturing the victim and around forty percent mutilate the corpse, with a slightly smaller percentage having postmortem intercourse. These particularly vicious actions are fuelled by their overwhelming desire to unleash their anger on someone, until the victim is literally obliterated by the force of their rage.

Napper stalked his last victim. Samantha Bisset had earlier complained to her boyfriend about the man who had been peering through her windows; her neighbour had also spotted Napper watching her flat, before he finally carried out his last brutal murders. This pre-crime behaviour was not the only aspect that fitted the features above. His peeping tom activities indicate he selected Samantha. His mutilation of her body testified to his attempts at obliteration. What would end with the slaying of a mother and her child had begun with an assault on a larger family unit, a sex attack on a mum of four. The offence was different, but the mother-as-victim theme was a consistent pattern.

These are the offences which can be proven as having been committed by Napper. It cannot be known how many other mothers he may have chosen as his victims. Napper will not say. Certainly, he is more than capable of keeping his silence, despite his guilt.

He has, after all, managed to do so effortlessly down all the years when people were wondering who had murdered another young mother. Her joyous smile still remains instantly recognisable, sixteen years after Napper ended her life. When forensic technique finally caught up with the fervent wishes and hopes of the bereaved, the investigators and all those touched by her death, Napper was finally called to account for what he had done to Rachel Nickell.

CHAPTER NINE

BROUGHT TO THE LIGHT

"Well you may throw your rock and hide your hand
Workin' in the dark against your fellow man
But as sure as God made black and white
What's down in the dark will be brought to the light."

traditional folk song

Great care was taken with the new investigation into Rachel Nickell's death. The police were not going to get it wrong twice. Ten years after her death, witness statements were once again pored over by the case review team. Other suspects and possibly linked offences were once again considered on the basis of the injuries inflicted on Rachel. Then scientists took an invisible-to-the-eye scrap of material and used modern signal enhancement methods until the DNA was big enough to see; big enough to reveal Robert Napper.

KILLER IN THE SHADOWS

The evidence had lain silently for years on a humble piece of sticky tape. Taking 'tapings' (applying strips of adhesive tape to victims' clothing and exposed parts of the body) has been routine police work since the advent of modern forensics. Any materials present adhere to the sticky tape and can then be examined. Tests can turn up a whole range of interesting findings, from fibres shed by clothing or carpets to paint to human DNA. The tapings taken from Rachel became vitally important to the reopened investigation, but had been too tiny when using the methods of 1992.

What may now seem quaint and old-fashioned was once the cutting edge. Back in 1992, officers had been informed by forensic scientists that the recent innovation of 'genetic fingerprinting' could not offer its miracle solutions to the investigation into Rachel's death. Investigators concluded that the killer had "left nothing behind" of any use. To all intents and purposes, this was true.

Fortunately, even scientific facts change with time. New truths emerge. Thanks to technological advances, it transpired that the offender's DNA, which had been left on Rachel, could now be identified. His genetic marker had been bagged, sealed and stored. It had lain undisturbed for more than a decade, but it was not forgotten.

Time shifts; it creates upheavals as strong as rolling waves churning sand grains at the shoreline. As the future became the present, what was long ago known as the 'white heat of technology' shone on the past that was 1992. Its glare illuminated the serried rows of exhibits, specimens and old case notes. It also illuminated Robert Napper's unique chemistry. What was impossible back then became possible now, as science and technology moved forward into the twenty-first century.

Sir Alec Jeffreys is the British scientist who first realised that the affinity within families penetrates right the way down to their very chemical being. The Oxford-educated biochemist noticed the similarities and differences in the DNA of related individuals. Genetic fingerprinting (now called 'DNA profiling') became as important a breakthrough for investigators as the technique of fingerprinting had been at the beginning of the twentieth century.

Once these techniques had made their way out of the lab and into the forensic field, Colin Pitchfork was the first offender to be convicted of a crime by the one in a billion certainty of DNA evidence. The match between the semen found on the bodies of two murdered teenagers in early 1980s Leicestershire showed unequivocally that the deaths of Lynda Mann and Dawn Ashworth were linked. The same man had killed both girls. It was, however, not until the 1990s that greater strides were made in broadening the application of the technique. Peter Gill and his team at the Forensic Science Service developed DNA profiling further and, in 1995, the National DNA Database (NDNAD) was launched.

The application of the technique is not without its critics. Some countries have shown more reluctance than Britain over the human rights implications of building a comprehensive DNA database of its citizens. In England and Wales, however, anyone who is arrested has their DNA profile stored regardless of whether an arrest leads to conviction. (Scotland restricts storage to convicted criminals.) As a result of this policy, the UK holds the most extensive database in the world, containing the details of between four and five million people.[12] Growing at the rate of 30,000 per month, it will soon contain one in ten of the population.

This will now need review following a December 2008 ruling by the European Court of Human Rights, which found that holding the DNA of innocent people contravenes Article 8, the right to respect for private and family life. One group without criminal convictions which *is* likely to remain on the database is serving police officers. Regular attendance at crime scenes means the professionals need to be distinguished from the offenders. By holding officers' details in the system, quick matches and eliminations can be made. Should they ever decide to cross the tracks and follow a criminal career instead, they may begin with a certain disadvantage!

Many uncaught offenders have good reason to fear new DNA testing methods, and police may yet capture many who have long since believed they got away with old crimes. However, new technology brings its own new difficulties. Low template and low copy DNA testing – where results can be extracted from tiny quantities of DNA material – is now so sensitive that contamination becomes a growing problem.

Given that profiles can be produced from samples small enough to be known as 'touch DNA' (e.g. a fingerprint), police have to take ever greater precautions. The whole

---

12 The US database is regarded by some as the largest, with around five million samples, but figures inevitably fluctuate depending on rate of growth from year to year. The US and UK databases are of similar size in absolute terms; in the context of the population size of the two countries, the UK's is vastly more extensive.

process from pre-crime scene to test site, plus everything in between and everyone involved in the investigation, must be clean. Scenes of crimes officers and crime scene investigators must be trained to collect evidence correctly, with 'Scenesafe' kits (including DNA-free swabs and containers) and sterile vehicles now on the equipment lists of modern police forces.

Lab personnel likewise need careful training and strict routines – from masks and double rubber gloves to ultraviolet irradiation of lab benches. Microscopic contamination lurks everywhere. Even someone's DNA from the plastics factory which makes the bags can be an accidental contaminant, and so suppliers need to be included on the DNA database.

This may seem clean and thorough enough, but then one Robert Napper also worked in a plastics factory. Supply companies and their staff therefore need to be vetted. The list is extensive and national standards are being devised to ensure that no police force can risk compromising justice by using a cheaper company with lower standards.

Forensic science has transformed criminal investigations but no system is foolproof. Each new development brings its own downside, so there will always be a need for review if we are to ensure that the potential for error is reduced to a minimum. In the reopened Nickell case, forensic scientists and police alike showed careful thoroughness combined with steady persistence. The police commissioned an independent scientific analysis company, LCG Forensics, who had previously helped bring the killers of Damilola Taylor to justice, to carry out new tests. Under the leadership of a scientist named Roy Green, no fewer than twenty analysts worked to re-examine what had been found on Rachel.

They discovered that Robert Napper had indeed been in physical contact with Rachel Nickell the day she died. The DNA lifted from her clothing said so. It was, concluded Green and his team, 1.4 million times more likely that this DNA belonged to Napper than to someone unrelated to him. If that were not close enough to certainty, they also revealed that tiny flecks of red paint retrieved from combings of Alex's hair matched Napper's toolbox.

Even then, the new investigation team did not rely on such impressive odds. Every eventuality was accounted for. There were concerns that a future Napper defence team might challenge the legitimacy of having acquired his DNA without proper consent. Similarly, Napper's psychiatrists had reputedly long been reluctant to permit interviews with such a mentally compromised man. A judgement was sought as to whether the case being built involved any breach of his human rights. It took two years before prosecutors felt confident that a defence team would not be able to rely on such legislation to derail any future trial. Only then could police press on with the decision to confront Napper about his long-kept secret.

In 2006, the new team of officers spent two days interviewing him. Police finally charged him on 28th November 2007. It had been well over fifteen years since 15th July 1992, when he had spotted Rachel on Wimbledon Common and ultimately murdered her. He would still be denying it on 24th January of the following year, when he entered an official plea of 'Not Guilty'.

It was a case where much had diverged from the routine,

BROUGHT TO THE LIGHT

from the expected, and it continued thus until the very end. For centuries, it has been a cornerstone of our justice system that defendants must know their accusers. They must always be brought to court and appear in person to face justice, and be given the opportunity to cross-examine their accusers. Napper made legal history in that he was allowed to enter his plea in court via video link from Broadmoor hospital, where he has been detained since his conviction in 1995 for killing Samantha and Jazmine.

Back in 1994, when the case against Colin Stagg collapsed, Rachel's father, Andrew, emerged from court after the 'Not Guilty' verdict, accompanied by his wife, Monica. The forlorn parents faced the gathered press outside the Old Bailey. Misled by the massive hunt for Stagg into believing that their daughter's murderer had escaped on some impenetrable legal technicality, her father declared that the scales of justice were out of kilter. He believed they had swung too far towards protecting the rights of the accused, at the expense of victims and their families, and asked, "Where's the justice?"

It was certainly slow in coming. It took precisely sixteen years, twenty-two weeks and two days to arrive.

On a clear winter morning in London on 18th December 2008, the attention of passers-by was momentarily drawn towards the flurry of police vehicles and blue flashing lights that escorted Napper to court. Napper himself was still hidden behind the darkened windows of a police van. It drew up to the heavy wooden gates of the Old Bailey at 8:50am and was promptly swallowed by the gates that opened and swung shut behind the vehicle. Just after 10:30, Robert Clive

Napper finally emerged into full and open public view of Court Number One. Shod in white trainers, he climbed the steps into the same dock where Colin Stagg had faced trial fourteen years earlier.

A black patterned tie rested on Napper's slight pot belly. His dark-blue checked shirt served to accentuate the glaring pallor of his doughy skin. His now balding head was not much like the dated police photographs, just a tuft now remaining in the centre above his forehead. He displayed the unctuous humility of Uriah Heep, limply pink hands clasped before him as he stood, round-shouldered and with head bowed.

Later on in the proceedings, we would see his head rise and track the movements of the court official who walked across his path en route to place a microphone in the witness box. Napper's gaze followed each step of the young, blonde-haired woman who passed within two feet of him. So keenly did he watch her that the burly guards who flanked him would provide a very real reassurance for those gathered in court.

But for now, at the start of proceedings, his head remained bowed. Only his eyes looked up as he answered Mr Justice Griffiths Williams: "Not guilty to murder, but guilty to diminished responsibility." He quickly corrected himself and named the offence. Still hesitating over the appropriate form of words, Robert Clive Napper said, "Guilty to manslaughter by diminished responsibility."

Two forensic psychiatrists testified to his dual conditions of paranoid schizophrenia and Asperger's syndrome. Professor Don Grubin, Napper's former psychiatrist, confirmed that Napper's psychosis had been evident as far back as 1989, when he was admitted to hospital following an overdose, and continuing records showed that he would have been mentally compromised at the time of Rachel's death.

Dr Natalie Pyszora, his current doctor at Broadmoor, told the court about his grandiose delusions. She explained that Napper believed he had a master's degree in mathematics and that someone was distorting time by rearranging the calendar. His grandiosity was evident in his certainty that he was a multimillionaire; he hailed, he claimed, from a family listed in *Who's Who*, his wealth apparently deposited in a bank in Sidcup. He also possessed telepathic powers.

Given the gross violence of his crimes, it was a desperately tragic irony that he was convinced he was a winner of the Nobel Prize for Peace. He had, he thought, been 'kneecapped' by the IRA and had his fingers blown off while defusing a bomb. Shown the irrefutable completeness of his hands, he had explained how his fingers had re-grown because he inhaled "sparkle fumes". The doctors presented a stark picture of a man leagues away from reality, but the limited extracts of the psychiatrists' reports did not explain the distinct thinking patterns of Robert Napper, or why he did what he did.

Very many people with Asperger's syndrome lead truly peaceful lives. It is a condition on the spectrum of autistic disorders, some of which cause more serious impairments than Asperger's. Some individuals with autism do not develop language skills, but people with Asperger's show no language impairments and possess better cognitive skills than many other people with an autistic disorder. The essential defining trait they share is that their social interaction is poor.

Thus they will have limited understanding or empathy with another person's feelings. Also distinctive (and common to different types of autism) is the tendency to show restricted and repetitive behaviours. But before we make a crude leap toward concluding that this wholly explains Napper's repeated and obsessive stalking of women (repetitive behaviour) and callous disregard for their suffering (lack of empathy), we should consider another concrete (albeit clichéd) example of the behaviour of someone with Asperger's.

Imagine chatting with someone who tells you in great detail about his model train collection and how he follows the same daily routine of carefully logging their numbers and engine types. He doesn't seem to be aware that you are bored by his conversation, nor does he give you a chance to speak, instead continuing with his monologue. This too would indicate restrictive, repetitive behaviour and a lack of empathy, manifested in his inability to pick up the social cues that you have no interest in trains.

This is far more representative of the behaviour of someone with Asperger's, though our simplistic example should not minimise the real difficulties the disorder can cause. For instance, disruption to set routines can cause intense anxiety for sufferers, so there tends to be more depression among this group than in the rest of the population. Similarly, problems with self-care mean that some individuals cannot manage independently as adults. They may continue to live at home with parents or require permanent support from other carers.

However, although the disorder causes problems, impaired social skills should certainly not be automatically equated with violent behaviour. Indeed, such a narrowed field of interest can be a definite strength in other areas. A leading academic in the field, Simon Baron-Cohen, notes the advantages of a precise eye for detail in fields such as maths, engineering, science and computers. Therefore, the fact that Napper has Asperger's syndrome is just a very small piece in the puzzle of his behaviour.

Similarly, the most threatening aspect of paranoid schizophrenia, contrary to popular misconception, is a burden borne by the patients themselves. The condition can be terrifying for sufferers, who may hear voices in the complete absence of a speaker and wake up each day with the unshakeable belief that someone genuinely intends to do them harm – even kill them.

Schizophrenia is not, as popular misconception once again has it, a 'split personality'. Rather, it is characterised by the auditory hallucinations and delusions which are the symptoms of the sufferer's different 'reality'. This loss of contact with reality is what is properly meant by 'psychosis'. A sufferer deluded enough to genuinely believe s/he is an angel sent from God to protect and bestow love on the world could accurately be described as psychotic, even though such a delusion is entirely benign. Most people do not associate the term with someone who behaves in a gentle, kindly or benevolent manner, which illustrates how the term has become wrongly synonymous with violence.

Napper, of course, *was* madly violent, but most sufferers, even those unfortunate enough to have a dual diagnosis do not – as Napper has admitted he did – go out with the specific intent of finding a woman for sex and then stabbing her to death.

Robert Napper, unlike you or I, cannot be held fully responsible for his actions. But the Old Bailey is a court of law, not a forum for reviewing every detail of a defendant's mental health. So we are limited to knowing what was legally relevant: the twin labels of paranoid schizophrenia and Asperger's syndrome met a legal standard for diminished responsibility.

However, the details which made his behaviour so distinct from non-offending individuals with similar mental health problems remain undisclosed. Perhaps the most significant word in his plea was 'diminished', which means to make smaller. It is not synonymous with 'completely absent' or 'no responsibility whatsoever'.

It is interesting to reflect on the more rational features of events disclosed in court. The crown prosecutor, Victor Temple QC, made sure the court heard how, notwithstanding his mental condition, Napper's intent had been crystal clear. He put it to Dr. Pyszora that when her patient set off for Wimbledon Common, he had known full well he was going to 'get' a woman for sex. In response, the psychiatrist confirmed Napper had admitted as much.

Speaking through his barrister, Napper then submitted specific denials of two particular behaviours: he had not, he claimed, dragged two-year-old Alex's face along the ground to get him away from his mother (such an action was consistent with the child's facial injuries). Neither, he said, had he inserted anything into Rachel's anus, as indicated by the extent of the postmortem dilation. Robert Napper discriminated amongst the litany of shocking behaviour, successfully choosing the two most heinous acts that would surely cause most revulsion, and gave an outright denial of both.

Perhaps to offer the family a modicum of balm during this ordeal, the judge did not refer again to the sexual assault on Rachel – though his final words contained reference to Napper's other denial. He was clearly unconvinced by the retreat from responsibility for one of the worst aspects of the killing, and for dragging the face of a terrified little boy over rough ground away from his dying mother. Regarding the latter act, Mr Justice Griffith Williams looked directly at Napper and said simply, "I judge that you did."

He went on to imply that Napper was not so disordered that he had been unable to plan his escape. The judge told him, "That he [Alex] was not killed as you were later to kill Jazmine Bisset is almost certainly explained by your anxiety not to be caught by staying too long." He finally told Robert Clive Napper, "You are, on any view, an extremely dangerous man," and instructed the three guards who had accompanied him throughout, "Take him down."

In court, Napper had apologised via his barrister to Rachel's family, and also to Colin Stagg. But, lest we forget, he is a man who has not admitted to any offence unless and until there is incontrovertible evidence that he did it. He denied killing Rachel until the very last. The Green Chain rapes – of which he admitted four and was convicted of three (one rape and two attempted) – are thought to form a series of forty, or even seventy, perhaps even more than a hundred offences.

With reports that police are set to interview him on other unsolved murders from the early 1990s (recall the deaths of Penny Bell, Claire Tiltman and Jean Bradley, with whose

KILLER IN THE SHADOWS

dreadful stories we began this book), it seems unlikely that Napper will rush to cooperate fully with any new investigation. But if we pause for a moment to consider these other offences, it is clear that they need to be reexamined. We provide a timeline and a map of the known offences, as well as the murders of Penny, Claire and Jean, in the figures 9.1 and 9.2 below:

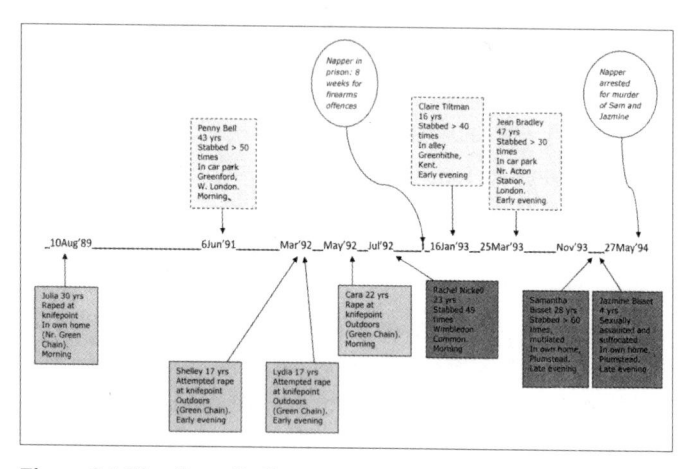

Figure 9.1 Timeline of offences (Napper convicted of offences *below* line; unsolved cases *above* line)

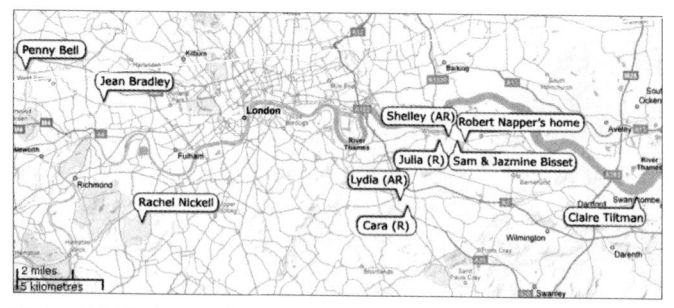

Figure 9.2 Knife attacks against women in early 1990s.

BROUGHT TO THE LIGHT

1. **Julia – 10th August 1989** Green Chain rape. Aged thirty, knife threat. Her house backed onto Winns Common, Plumstead (children present).
2. **Penny Bell – 6th June 1991** Aged forty-three, killed; stabbed fifty times. Found in her parked car, Greenford, west London.
3. **Shelley – March 1992** Green Chain (attempted) rape. Aged seventeen, knife threat, kicked unconscious. Plumstead (near the Cordwell Estate).
4. **Lydia – March 1992** Green Chain (attempted) rape. Aged seventeen, knife used on breast. King John's Walk.
5. **Cara – May 1992** Green Chain rape. Aged twenty-two, rope around neck, knife used. King John's Walk (child present).
6. **Rachel Nickell – 15th July 1992** Aged twenty-three, killed; stabbed forty-nine times. Wimbledon Common (child present).
7. **Claire Tiltman – 18th January 1993** Aged sixteen, killed; stabbed forty times. Greenhithe, Kent.
8. **Jean Bradley – 25th March 1993** Aged forty-seven, killed; stabbed forty times. Near Acton tube station, west London.
9. **Samantha and Jazmine Bisset – 3rd November 1993** Aged twenty-seven and four respectively, killed. Sam stabbed sixty times and mutilated; Jazmine sexually assaulted and suffocated. Plumstead (child present and killed).

As we indicated earlier, the most useful linking features are a knowledge of base rates (how often a given offence or behaviour occurs), temporal patterns (how often an offence occurs within a given timeframe) and distance (how far any given offence occurs from another offence). If base rates are low (e.g. an offence such as frenzied knife killing is rare), if several attacks occur within a short timeframe and are not too far from each other, they should be considered as potentially linked.

If we take the sequence as a whole – the known offences (below line of Figure 9.1 above) and the unsolved offences in question (above line, Figure 9.1) – we have five murders involving multiple stabbings within a three-year time period. As the map shows, all occurred within the outer London boroughs, with the exception of Claire Tiltman – but even that offence is less than a thirty-minute drive. (Greenhithe was, in 1993, less than forty minutes on the train from Plumstead station – which in itself was less than a five-minute walk from Napper's home and place of work.)

None of the offences would have been more than an hour away in total from Napper's home or workplace. In fact the killings of Penny Bell, Jean Bradley and Rachel Nickell are all near stations well connected on a route in a westerly direction from Plumstead. Each offence was committed less than a five-minute walk from the respective connected stations.

It may be tempting to exclude Penny Bell and Jean Bradley based on age, with both women being in their forties. Indeed, it may be even more tempting to exclude all three unsolved cases due to apparent lack of sexual motive: they were all stabbings but there was no obvious sexual element. In this respect, they were unlike Napper's proven offences. But none

BROUGHT TO THE LIGHT

of these reasons to exclude outweighs the reasons to include.

We know, for example, that the Green Chain rapes included victims in their forties and not all the attacks were 'successful' – Napper regularly had erectile problems. We also know that Napper attacked women as young as seventeen. Another, more legitimate reason to exclude them would be distance – rapists and murderers rarely travel very far. Travelling over five miles is unusual, and serial murders (in the UK at least) which take the offender over an hour to travel to are rarer still.

However, we do know that Napper killed Rachel Nickell. We also know that Jean Bradley and Penny Bell were killed within a relatively narrow geographic angle (picture a 'slice of pie' shape with Napper's home as the apex). If we likewise take Napper's home and connect that to the murders of Penny, Jean and Rachel, they were all committed in a westerly direction along connected rail lines.

Further, if we take the sequence of fatal stabbings in chronological order, then the offences mirror how serial killers tend to select victims: first by committing the first offence in one direction (e.g. northerly), then moving the next offence in a different direction (e.g. southerly), then the third in the west, only returning north after a further offence. In other words, they use in sequence all points of the compass far more reliably than, for example, burglars, who tend to have a very acute attack angle (resembling a very thin slice of pie).

Rapists' angles of attack (or 'pie slices') are fatter; they tend to move at a broader angle from the apex of their home. Murderers take a very large piece, with their farthest apart offences creating an oblique angle from the apex of their home-base. In this regard, Claire Tiltman is something of an exception – she is in a different direction, on a different rail line and in a county outside London. Napper would have needed a more evident reason to make a decision to select a different path and direction on the off-chance of coming across Claire.

Maps were certainly important to Napper – he collected them and marked down on an A-Z some of the victims he attacked. If the deaths of Penny Bell, Jean Bradley and Claire Tiltman[13] are linked, our view is that there was an intentional distancing between the offences and a conscious use of the geography of the area, potentially with Plumstead railway station as the fulcrum of these ventures outward. It was a stone's throw away, and may have been a clear starting point for accessing all these murders. Indeed, it was geographically connected to the rapes as well as the attack on the Bissets, being less than an eight-minute walk from the home that they were murdered in.

Finally, the pattern of an offender increasing in violent attacks and then retreating closer and closer to home is also quite common in serial murders. The arc of the attacks – finally culminating with the killing of the nearby Bissets – fits this pattern well. But, as mentioned earlier, it seems unlikely that Napper will admit any further offences unless there is forensic evidence. Indeed, he has said as much.

However, today's forensic science is a powerful tool, and as

---

13 We are limiting the discussion to potential links to Napper here – but recall that Colin Ash-Smith lived much closer to Claire, had convictions within a similar timeframe and also had personal connections.

BROUGHT TO THE LIGHT

technology continues its inexorable march forward, Robert Napper may yet be forced to stand in a dock once more. Certainly, in the case of Rachel Nickell, time and science caught up with him.

★ ★ ★

On the day the Old Bailey saw Robert Napper convicted of killing Rachel, our raised position in the public gallery upstairs offered a bird's-eye vantage point denied to most. As his pale dome retreated down the steps below the eye level of most people in the courtroom, we had a final glimpse of Napper. He puffed out his pallid cheeks to their fullest extent and then exhaled visibly – a very drawn-out sigh, as if the court appearance had been testing for him. Or perhaps it was a long sigh of relief because he was not going to prison but returning instead to Broadmoor, from which it is judged "highly unlikely" that he will ever leave.

As he disappeared finally from view, we were left wondering what other secrets he may still be keeping. With this latest conviction, all those wounded by Rachel's murder could finally claim to have belatedly received the justice denied them over a decade ago. Albeit too late for Rachel, Samantha and Jazmine, Napper's crimes were brought into the light and his depraved behaviour was put under scrutiny. He was eventually forced from the crowd and made to stand out of the shadows.

CHAPTER TEN

AUTOPSIES

Au-top-sy (ô'top'se) n.
1. *Dissection and examination of a dead body to determine the cause of death.*
2. *An eyewitness observation.*
3. *Any critical analysis.*
[from Greek autos, self + opsis, sight: the act of seeing with one's own eyes].

COLLINS ENGLISH DICTIONARY

Today we have lost sight of the fuller meaning of the word 'autopsy'. We hold onto only the first definition above: the dissection and examination of a dead body. Maybe this is because it is the most vivid. The others seem perhaps a little dry by comparison.

If crime films and TV series are anything to go by, the close examination of death in violent circumstances seems an endlessly rich seam to be mined for dramatic purposes. It requires deliberate focus to pull our eyes away from the intriguing combination of death and drama, but we must pay attention to the other meanings of 'autopsy'. Away from the prurient fascination with murky fantasies, fatal crimes and sex murderers, there is a critical analysis that demands to be undertaken.

As this book nears its end, we shall turn to the aftermath of Robert Napper's crimes. In this chapter, we focus on the professionals: an autopsy of the weaknesses in forensic psychology back then, the improvements today and the challenges that remain. Let us bear witness to and examine what happened after Napper's final offences – the killings of two young women and a little girl.

By September 1994, Colin Stagg had been found not guilty of Rachel Nickell's murder. The fallout persisted much longer than the media scrum gathered outside the Old Bailey. Away from the cameras, boom microphones and on-the-spot reports, the Stagg case had a profound impact. Its negative influence seeped into the professional relationships between the police service and psychologists. In the immediate aftermath of Operation Edzell, the consequences were dire. Trust had been eroded; bitterness and blame led the police service to disengage from academic and clinical departments.

For several years, many Senior Investigating Officers would bristle at the thought of some 'expert' interfering in their enquiry. Psychological contributions were met with a mix of hostility and resentment. A colleague who travelled to assist police in North Wales reported that he didn't have to struggle hard to figure out that officers were referring to him when he overheard, amongst the flurry of Welsh, the word 'wanker'.

AUTOPSIES

Adding to this incendiary environment were the many positive but utterly unrealistic portrayals of brilliant profilers assisting dull police officers in solving crimes. These included the preposterous *Silence of the Lambs*, in which a novitiate agent, Clarice Starling, gets inside the mind of a brutal serial killer by daring to brave an interaction with the sinister Dr Hannibal Lecter. Starling's trial by fire concludes with her walking around in the dark whilst a serial killer predates her, watching her through the eerie green haze of night-vision goggles. She of course prevails in the last moments of the movie and, by virtue of her 'relationship' with Lecter, has delved into the depths of offenders' minds and come out the other side an expert in serial murder (though a bizarre consequence of this new knowledge appears to be an implicit romantic attachment to Hannibal).

The UK's counterpart to Starling was Robbie Coltrane's belligerent, hard-drinking, hard-gambling Fitz in *Cracker* – a clinical psychologist (oh, the irony!) whose eagerness to back Wayne's World in the 2.30 at Haydock never interfered with his ability to assist the police in all manner of ways. He provided them with anything from attendance at office meetings to crime scene investigations, from off-the-cuff pen-portraits of the offender's characteristics to actually interviewing suspects! This included the dramatic conceit of shouting at suspects, belittling them and playing psychological cat-and-mouse games to make them confess.

These 1990s archetypes provided contemporary echoes of Sir Arthur Conan Doyle's Sherlock Holmes, the cocaine-using private detective with a mercurial mind and nigh-on precognitive abilities. Holmes, too, could see clues where the police could not, and he too was difficult, troubled and eccentric. (In fact, the real mystery was why Dr Watson ever tolerated such a dreadful narcissist.) However, the attributes of Conan Doyle's greatest invention have more to do with narrative structure and the audience's needs rather than real life.

The authors of detective stories have to make the reader admire the hero. This is a straightforward enough task; simply make him clever and extraordinarily able (or unflappable, or wisecracking, or . . .). In Holmes' case, he has the answer the moment the client seeks his help. Like Poirot and Fitz and other protagonists of the detective genre, Holmes immediately and effortlessly knows 'whodunit'. Unfortunately, this may make the reader feel inferior by comparison, and no one is entertained by being made to feel stupid. We, the reader/viewer, may not be that clever but we can stand alongside Watson. He serves to guide us through the story and questions Holmes on our behalf. There is no shame in ranking ourselves besides him – he is, after all, a learned doctor (just as Poirot's less able sidekick, Hastings, is a captain, not a 'lowly' ranking private).

The audience also needs some reward for their efforts to solve the mystery; they need to feel they're not always lagging behind. Enter the 'dumb copper' next to whom everyone can feel smug, probably chosen because people don't get many chances to undercut authority figures in real life. Audience and hero alike join together when it comes to condescending to the police. Hercule Poirot had Detective Chief Inspector Japp of Scotland Yard to look down on. For Holmes, Inspector Lestrade served as the archetype of 'plod' – the

AUTOPSIES

pedestrian thinker, who ran his conclusions by the book but had little room for innovation, creativity or the sparks of insight that defined Holmes. Conan Doyle had Holmes sneer at Lestrade's inability to pick up on the subtlety of clues and, on more than one occasion, took delight in first asking for Lestrade's interpretation of a crime scene, only to subsequently provide his own inevitably correct assessment.

However, we must remember that these constructions deliver only what whodunit readers require. Wandering around advising on every aspect of a crime is fine, as long as it's only 'on telly' or confined to the covers of a novel. Ultimately, fictional ideas should not leak into the real world. It serves no one to conflate the real with the imaginary. There is no place for star billing in police investigations.

Back in the real world of the early 1990s, the police were reeling from the collapse of the case against Stagg and psychologists had an uphill battle to convince the service they still had something to contribute. In 1992 there had been no formal regulation of profilers and no audit trails. There were no recommendations agreed by any central body on the nature, extent or formulation of any given contribution and no quality assurance at all. This promoted a framework in which the grand personalities in the field of offender profiling (or squeaky wheels, depending on your perspective) got all the oil. Much of the contact between profiler and police was largely driven by strength of personality, or by whoever popped up regularly in newspapers and popular books or on TV.

The knock-on effect of these talking heads – alongside their absurd fictional counterparts – was, and to some extent still is, manifold. As noted, it probably inflamed the already problematic relationship between police and psychologists, promoted completely unrealistic views of what was possible to students wishing to study investigative psychology and provided, on the one hand, a distorted picture of the ineptitude of the police and, on the other, an inflated view of the capability of psychologists.

In our view, psychologists at the time did little to rectify this, although David Canter was instrumental in advocating a scientific approach and developed a course at the University of Surrey to address the need to bring science into the domain. The course now thrives at the University of Liverpool under a different director, and the discipline has moved beyond 'profiling' to a broad range of investigative contributions, including police interviewing, decision-making, risk assessment and critical incident management.

Now, several other researchers in academic departments in the US, Canada, Australia, and, of course, the UK have moved this field forward by considerable leaps. Although there are still some (probably healthy) pockets of tension, much of the previous unhelpful animosity between so-called 'statistical' and 'clinical'/'deductive' and 'inductive' approaches – which was probably more about personal opinion than academic rigour – has now abated. Forensic and investigative psychology and its application to crime investigation has changed a great deal since the crimes of Robert Napper.

However, fifteen years ago this field was barely developed and was poorly understood. The limits of what was possible were unknown, the cautionary words of an infant science

AUTOPSIES

appealing far less than the media's simplistic portrayal of grand claims and fictional heroes. But even in such uncharted waters, it was not advisable to take fiction as a reference point. We needed to remind ourselves that Conan Doyle was a man who wrote fiction, not fact. And he was a man who believed in fairies, supporting the view that photographs taken by two little girls of fairies in their back garden were probably genuine.

Thus, despite our love of the 'brilliant eccentric' archetype and our need to believe in it, the idea of a singular figure that can do everything necessary to solve crime is as unrealistic as expecting to see fairies at the bottom of your garden. Crime investigation is enormously complex, brings in its wake considerable responsibilities and must be supported by many people, often across many agencies and sometimes across different boroughs. Unlike the hapless Japp in the Poirot stories, detective chief inspectors are not stupid; neither do the many other demands of the job stop while they devote all their time to a single case.

In the real world, it can sometimes feel like whatever you do is wrong and there are rarely optimal solutions within the quagmire of complexity. A particularly apposite quotation comes from Deputy Chief Constable Simon Parr, who ran the response, in 2005, to the accidental explosion at the Buncefield oil depot near Hemel Hempstead. The initial blast was loud enough to be heard in France and was followed by the biggest fire in peacetime Europe. With 2000 people evacuated, mile after mile of shattered windows and roofs, significant stretches of motorway closed completely, a raging fire and a pall of smoke covering much of the South of

England, DCC Parr commented that critical incidents "were about consequence choosing rather than decision making".

Buncefield was not a criminal investigation, of course, but the decision-making (or consequence-choosing) factors are common to any types of police work where the stakes are high, entailing life-or-death consequences should things go wrong.

For example, protecting firefighters until the fire had passed its most ferocious stage might mean exposing a greater area of residents, animals and land to acrid, damaging smoke for longer periods. Choose your consequence: who to put in danger? Should you pick life-threatening danger right now for the few or lesser danger for the many (which may, in any case, lead to unforeseen chronic problems in the future, or road deaths from poor visibility)? Sometimes even the best expert only gets to choose the least bad option. Choices made or decisions deferred can have profound effects, sometimes with unintended consequences.

Sometimes – unlike Buncefield – the situations do not look the least bit dramatic and the consequences are not apparent. If the decision had been made to make a search of the flat of a local 'odd type' a number one priority, if a decision had been made to scrutinise with a fine-tooth comb every item found there for possible links with other offences, Napper might have been caught sooner. Not making these decisions had profound unintended consequences. Had officers been briefed that the man whose flat they were to search might be the Green Chain rapist, they would have undoubtedly made different decisions. However, a call from a local printer saying he had had a bloke asking for paper with

AUTOPSIES

the Met Police logo would not make the task the number one priority in the borough. Real life is complex.

Fictional portrayals have to reduce complexity to one or two protagonists so that the reader can engage with the characters. However, the crimes of Napper affected many people – working outwards from victims in concentric circles, there were the families, the witnesses, the suspects, the investigators, the experts, the legal services, the media, the local communities. The Rachel Nickell enquiry, as with any critical incident, incorporated elements of high emotion, bereavement, violence, professional gambles, accountability, trust, confidence and blame.

Since then, the talking heads have abated somewhat and psychologists have had to (quite rightly) eat humble pie and recognise their place as very small cogs in very large machines. Over the last fifteen years, by virtue of hard work, diligence, academic endeavour, humility and integrity – as well as results – many folk have foregone widescale public recognition in favour of making a real contribution, keeping out of the limelight and on top of their particular specialism.

There is, of course, a role for psychologists to play in the media – it provides a tempered view of what is possible (and thus acts as a form of education); it can contribute to keeping student numbers healthy and stimulate interest in the area. In some instances, contact and working relationships with the media can assist in enquiries, though it needs a steady hand at the helm to negotiate through all the formal channels.

However, commentary on live enquiries where the psychologists in question know little or nothing about the case at hand, and have had no involvement in it, *is* potentially dangerous. Nevertheless, there are still a gaggle of psychologists willing to make bold statements every time a major case hits headlines. The police service is quite right to be wary of the psychologist who spends more time in front of the camera than getting on with the business of research.

Many other positive developments have occurred since 1992. Now there are formal procedures for the recognition of expertise and an approved list of advisors who are subject to peer review and scrutiny. Moreover, as noted, there is a dedicated team of fulltime advisors at the National Policing Improvement Agency (NPIA), many of whom have an academic or police background, or both. They have various systems which assist them in recognising the limits of what is and what is not possible, as well as a far more involved and detailed understanding of policy and procedure relevant to the business end of crime investigation.

Many of these names will not be known by the general public, though they are the key players in providing the overwhelming bulk of behavioural advisor contributions in the UK. They have internal peer reviews, keep abreast of the academic literature and are governed centrally. Moreover, other advisors on the list are regularly consulted for domain-specific knowledge about other relevant areas. It is rare for any single advisor to work exclusively on a single case – a rather different example of the dangers of isolation.

Laurence was recently asked to advise on a murder enquiry. No fewer than four people assisted him in this task and he took further advice from NPIA, a clinical psychologist and two senior police officers. Likewise, it is not uncommon to

AUTOPSIES

receive a phone call from other advisors on the list who will crosscheck information and invite others' views. We are reliant on each other and it would be quite inappropriate to suggest that any one person has all the expertise required to make a meaningful contribution in any complex case.

This network provides a wealth of expertise and tacit experiential knowledge that is constantly expanding. As yet, its actual shape and size has not been well identified and hence there still remain naysayers. Just this year, a flurry of articles questioned the use of *any* form of profiling advice – stating that not only should it never be used in court, but that it should not be used as an investigative tool until such a time as it has demonstrated its scientific worth. Although it is important to challenge psychological contributions to crime investigation (indeed, the early part of Laurence's career was largely devoted to that explicit aim), there are concerns that some of the current research inaccurately represents what contemporary 'profilers' do[14] and that the wrong questions are being asked about its value.

For example, a series of articles have bounced back and forth regarding the role and contribution of geo-profiling. On one side, researchers have vouched for geo-profiling expert decision systems, complex geo-profiling training and the need to develop this skill on the back of real investigative experience. On the other, a series of articles has demonstrated that, with very limited training about some very basic ideas in geo-profiling, undergraduate students can outperform these decision support systems in tasks where they are given a series

---

14 It is worth noting that much of this research is not based in the UK and may reflect differences between national and overseas profiling.

of crime locations and asked to use an 'X' to mark the spot where the offender is most likely to be living.

Similarly, Laurence's early research indicated that you could provide vague and ambiguous 'profiling' information to crime investigators and convince them of its worth through the use of the Barnum effects and personal validation we mentioned in earlier chapters. These are interesting debates and remind us of the need to be wary. Questions such as, "Do you need to spend lots of money on decision support tools when you can train students to do the same thing in half an hour?" and, "Do you need profilers if you can convince detectives that any old bunkum helps describe who they should be looking for?" are important questions to ask. Academics should not pursue their work in isolation from the other professionals or organisations involved in developing this area.

Although we have advocated that researchers conduct their critical analyses ('autopsies') away from the camera, they cannot afford to be located in the uppermost spire of academia's ivory towers. It is very much an applied field and worthwhile research must examine what practitioners do, rather than what academics (psychologists or otherwise) imagine they might do. Personal contact and experience with the police and behavioural investigative advisors teaches greater humility, greater appreciation of complexity and better understanding of relevant gaps in our (academic) knowledge about what the police service might benefit from.

It has also highlighted how some recent questions have oversimplified the debate. Principally, and in relation to gaps in our knowledge, the fact is that we don't actually have a clear

AUTOPSIES

picture (yet) of exactly what contemporary geo-profilers, profilers or behavioural investigative advisors actually *do*. Researchers (ourselves included) have assumed, for example, that geo-profilers use expert decision support systems to point to specific crime locations when they are given a series of offences to study. But is this assumption correct?

One particularly insightful recent masters student named Susanne Knabe was fortunate enough to be given access to Neil Trainor and his fellow geo-profilers. Her objective was to establish what they do and whether there was any domain-specific knowledge peculiar to these professionals. Armed with some skills in identifying expertise, she established that the 'X marks the spot' decision system analysis was actually a very small component of their contribution. In fact, forty percent of the cases that the geo-profilers dealt with were not series analyses but single offences, and in only twenty percent of cases did geoprofilers use the decision support system at all.

As well as examining crime locations, geo-profilers examined exit and entry routes, local topographic features, temporal elements and base rates of crimes within particular socio-demographic areas. Looking at the value of marking 'X' on the map seriously underestimates the range of work they undertake.

Because it adopted a pragmatic approach and began in the workplace, the recent study made explicit the nature of the geo-profilers' contribution. It demonstrated that these individuals did indeed possess domain-specific knowledge beyond that of experienced detectives, let alone students. The results also indicated that geo-profilers gave advice with greater precision and with greater potential to generate specific lines of enquiry. So, interesting though the debate is as to whether geo-profiling systems outperform students, we have to ask if we have a clear appreciation of the range of contributions these various advisors make.

The geoprofilers' work is just one example of where, in recent times, academics have usefully come together with those who work in the field. Some useful academic articles have also started to appear which have begun to categorise the contributions of various specialists and experts. Although better late than never, in our view this is a point that academic psychologists should have perhaps started from in the 1990s. Putting things in the right categories is a fundamental first step to understanding what is happening in a whole complex area.

Things have improved since 1992, although, crucially, the fact that things have moved on significantly may be of little consolation to the families of Napper's victims. There is no doubt that mistakes will continue to be made – you simply cannot deal with high risks and yet always avoid disasters. This is why, for example, it is foolhardy to invest exclusively in the prevention of terrorism without also enhancing the resilience of the relevant law enforcement agencies to deal with an attack, for this very simple reason: it will happen again.

In the meantime, cops and behavioural advisors retain their gallows humour but, though they may find it hard to admit, many are deeply moved by and emotionally connected to their jobs. Many strive for excellence and are prepared to take criticism on the chin. So, while the media will continue

AUTOPSIES

to point fingers at events such as the Stockwell shooting, the London bombings and even historic cases such as that of Stagg, it is a shame that not a single article gives praise where it is due.

Were there, for example, any column inches devoted to the bravery of the officer who sat next to Jean Charles de Menezes at Stockwell, fully believing that he might detonate a bomb on the underground? We should be able to acknowledge and recognise such acts as courageous, without feeling that to utter the statement somehow tarnishes the respect due to the victim of a tragically wrongful shooting or his family.

It does not hold that, if one deserves our recognition and our sympathy, then another individual must *ipso facto* be denied it. It is not a case of either/or, black/white, goodie/baddie. Real life is complicated. Many officers tried, with the best of intentions, to choose the least disastrous consequences. The wrong decision was made. The results were grave: a man lost his life and his family was devastated, and we must strive to get it right next time. But it does not diminish the tragedy nor imply disrespect to acknowledge the other aspects. We all rely on people willing to run towards suspected suicide bombers on our behalf.

Similarly, there was little recognition of officers who went into the pitch darkness and sixty-degree heat of the underground on 7/7/05, and worked double shifts for hour after hour, crawling beneath and between train carriages to recover the maimed so that loved ones could be reunited with their families. No one gave up until the job was achieved. Even though, in fifty-two cases, the only reunion was a funeral, each and every police and rescue worker made sure that everybody went home.

And, of course, at the close of 2008 the media were asking, "What went wrong *vis a vis* Stagg?" Blame was almost the single issue that the press latched onto when Napper was convicted of killing Rachel. There were no media reports of a successful prosecution. The determined efforts of a new enquiry team which painstakingly built a new case over four years went without comment.

Today's story is one of police securing an admission of guilt from a man who is resolute in his determination never to admit anything unless there is absolute proof. It is one where forensic science has brought impressive and intriguing advances that made the proof irrefutable: tiny flecks of red paint which had been combed from little Alex's hair could be matched to Napper's toolbox, with lab workers even proving that the metal of the miniscule fragments adhering to the paint were damaged in the same way as the toolbox.

Today's story was ignored in favour of the fiasco that was the Colin Stagg enquiry, a fourteen-year-old news piece. By contrast, Andrew Nickell was gracious enough to acknowledge that – despite the dreadful mistake of the Stagg prosecution – the police had always tried their best. Even though, fifteen years ago, their best fell far short of acceptable, Mr Nickell displayed a magnanimity that the press seems unable to show.

We analyse debriefs of many operations and investigations by different forces. Time and again we learn of dedication, hard work and the many heroic acts that always seem to remain unsung. Such deeds are forsaken by a media that prefers to ask: "What lessons will be learned?" "Surely their

AUTOPSIES

position is untenable?" "When will s/he be sacked?" All are variations on the same *J'accuse* theme. We may well ask in return, "Who's to blame?" for the unimaginative regularity with which the media adopt the same angle for every story. This is not journalism at its probing, incisive best. It is lazy.

Of course, it is right when we – scientists, the public, the media – speak out when we see problems and errors, especially when they have such a massive impact on our lives. Outrageously poor practice deserves to be condemned outright, if that is what a case merits. We simply note that when we look for public acknowledgement or praise of the police service when deserved, it is absent.

Likewise, hindsight bias should not be allowed to generate misconceived stories of 'blunders'. Let us recap here on many of those reported in the wake of Napper's conviction. We need also to consider carefully what we shall call the 'Instead Rule'. Corresponding with each criticism, ask what we might have expected someone to do *instead*. It can be a helpful way of judging whether alternative courses of action might reasonably or realistically have been expected.

Firstly, in autumn 1989, when Napper's mother phoned to report her son's confession of rape, police failed to turn up the record of his first known attack (in Julia's home, August 1989) because they did not search more widely. They restricted their search to reports of rapes *on* Plumstead Common instead of *near* the common. Napper's mother reported that the attack had – according to her son – taken place *on* the common. However, she also advised police that her son frequently made up stories. The police 'blunder' was to act on the information given to them by Napper's mother, Pauline.

Let us apply the Instead Rule here. The police would have had to assume: i) Napper's mother was wrong about the location; ii) and also wrong about her son's tendency to lie. Thus, we are saying that *instead* of accepting the word of a mother (enough of an 'upright citizen' to report her own son) they should have assumed her report was wrong. This is another example of the profound and unintended consequences of decisions not made, but we ought not to be swayed by hindsight bias.

We cannot pluck selected information out of its context – the details of which we do not fully know. How many other tasks did the receiving officers have that day? What factors might then have made this one stand out as a top priority? Remove the hindsight bias and consider that they did not, and could not, know Napper would go on to commit serial rapes and become a killer.

They had one piece of information on a busy day, one member of the public claiming, "My son says he committed a rape on Plumstead Common, but he's a habitual liar." It is easy to see how someone would follow it up without being exhaustively thorough, because they believed there was unlikely to be any substance to the report. We do not know if Napper's mother told the police that her son had mental health problems, maybe even that he was delusional, but this would have been further reason to disbelieve the report.

Secondly, when Napper appeared as a person of interest in the Green Chain rapes, detectives ruled him out because, at six foot two, he was too tall. One victim had described the attacker as six foot three but others concurred he was below five foot ten, and police accepted the majority as accurate.

AUTOPSIES

In truth, the victims' descriptions were not so wrong – in person Napper is so round-shouldered that he looks much shorter than his actual height. In this instance, the police should presumably have assumed *instead* that most descriptions of Napper's height were wrong and one person was right. (But at the time, how could they have known to choose the one person who was accurate?)

Thus the Instead Rule leads to: Everyone must be investigated (*instead* of setting parameters). As we argue elsewhere, if parameters are not set somewhere then everyone is a potential suspect, so we would need a far wider tolerance of investigations. Imagine you are a five foot four male. Would you accept being taken in for questioning on suspicion of being a six foot two rapist?

In essence, the errors in these instances seem to amount to accepting at face value what people with no reason to lie had told them. The ABC of policing – assume nothing, believe nothing, challenge everything – is wise advice, but resources are finite in the real world and there are always competing demands.

In another reported blunder, a police search of Napper's home turned up an A-Z map, on which he had marked spots that corresponded to the sexual attacks on women. This seems to be a glaring oversight, but let us go back to a time before the story of Napper was known. The search had been generated because he tried to obtain notepaper headed with the Metropolitan Police logo and a suspicious printer alerted police. A crossbow and an unlicensed handgun were found in his flat, for which firearms offences Napper later served an eight-week jail term. In this context, these weapons would likely seem a more significant discovery than a map with spots marked on it. But would police notepaper, a gun, a crossbow and a dotted map (and who knows what else) make you think, 'knife attacks on women'?

Again, we cannot allow hindsight to make us selective about the information available at the time. Sometimes *too much* information is available and the relevant pieces only become clear with hindsight. We do not know how many other odd items (besides a map) were turned up in the search of a whole flat belonging to a mentally ill man. Perhaps the A–Z map did not stand out. As the authors have not examined it, we do not know whether all of the spots marked upon it related to the offences we now know to be relevant. We cannot use hindsight to select only partial information.

Suppose the map did stand out. It may have made you think, firstly, that the spots referred to the locations of offences, but you would then have to know where all the other crimes took place to be able to understand their significance. In reality, if you were not part of the team investigating a series of sexual attacks on women, you may have been unlikely to know the specific location of each offence. They would just be marks on a map. You might adjudge that they meant something, but you would be hard pushed to know exactly *what*. We may believe that an officer ought to have had more initiative and contacted the various teams investigating the offences – but how many would that amount to, and what other tasks at that time were of greater priority than a possibly meaningless map? (We do not even know which individual found it.)

Let us hypothesise the details: if an experienced officer

AUTOPSIES

who had long served in the Royal Borough of Greenwich, where Napper was resident, readily found the map which showed the locations of the Green Chain rapes (and nothing else) and did not put two and two together, then s/he made a blunder that cost lives. If, on the other hand, novice officers new to the borough – and therefore unfamiliar with local events – attended one search of a chaotic flat filled with oddities and found a map littered with crosses, notes and jottings, then their response was perfectly understandable and acceptable. Likely the truth lies somewhere between the two extremes, but it serves to illustrate the effects of hindsight bias and the propensity to cast blame.

In another example, a member of the public reported a man spying on the home of a young, blonde-haired woman. Police found Napper walking nearby and let him go after questioning him. But how many other people were out walking? Should everyone near the scene of a reported incident be taken in for questioning? The officer noted that Napper was odd, a possible rapist – but constables' notebooks will contain many jottings about odd characters that come to nothing; when responding to a call, everyone seems suspicious.

The errors in terms of the map and the peeping tom behaviour amount to not paying enough attention to significant pieces of information. But back then, police were faced with many different pieces of information. We can pick out the relevant ones so readily only because we already know the answers. We have the benefit of hindsight.

The links between the offences Napper was convicted of are as clear as broad daylight – with hindsight. We now know

KILLER IN THE SHADOWS

beyond a reasonable doubt that he targeted young mothers with young children. We know his offences were sexually violent and that the violence escalated over time. This is because we have been told what the pattern of offending behaviour was over seven linked offences. This is just like being told there are seven definitely linked stars forming the pattern of a plough – anyone can look up at the night sky and find it.

But that is not the position police were in. They did not know what (if indeed any) pattern might exist. Indeed, *was there* a pattern? Or was there more than one pattern? Since Napper's conviction, Paul Britton has been keen to state that he told police "their man" would already be in the system somewhere.[15] All they had to do was to go and find him. Just like we could tell you to go and find a pattern in the sky.

But the question is always, "What were they looking at then?" not "What are we looking at now?"

Figures 10.1 and 10.2 below illustrate the difference between hindsight and foresight. By borrowing the shape of

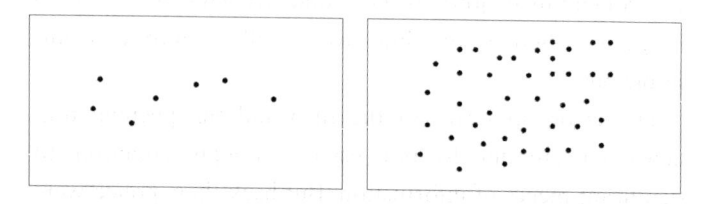

Left: Figure 10.1 Hindsight condition (What we see now).
Right: Figure 10.2 Foresight condition (What they saw then).

---

15 Mr Britton has also appeared on television news reports claiming that he told police emphatically there were links between the killings of Rachel and the Bissets. This latter-day claim directly contradicts the account given in his book (*The Jigsaw Man*, p.265).

AUTOPSIES

astronomical constellation 'the Plough', Figure 10.1 shows the effect of reaching judgement on the basis of selecting partial information. With hindsight, we know of seven proven offences and therefore the shape indicates links very clearly. Figure 10.2 shows the foresight condition. It illustrates what investigators saw; this is the bigger picture, showing all the information. The Plough is still there in exactly the same position it occupies in Figure 10.1, but it is not nearly so easy to spot. (In fact, there is another pattern contained in Figure 10.2. Can you spot it easily?[16]).

If, taking into account the mass of detail at the time, the pertinent point was still discernible, then practice was poor and the criticism is just. Criticism is vital for improving practice but using hindsight to criticise is unfair. There can, however, be no doubt that things went very wrong in the investigation into Rachel Nickell's death.

In 1992, Napper was one of dozens of men scheduled to undergo voluntary blood testing as part of routine TIE work. Two members of the public had named him, including a neighbour who thought he could well be the Green Chain rapist. But Napper twice failed to report to Eltham police station for his blood test, and nobody followed him up.

There were also two more weapons discoveries: his fingerprints were on a gun found inside a biscuit tin buried on a common; he was also conclusively linked to a hunting knife discovered very near to the site where Rachel was murdered. He was not questioned about either weapon. *Instead* of letting it go unchecked, the police should have

---

16 The killer's initials, RN, occupy the top right-hand corner of the diagram. Any other patterns you found were unintentional and are therefore clustering illusions.

gone back to make sure that Napper took his blood test and interviewed him for an explanation as to how his fingerprints were found on buried weapons.

Applying the Instead Rule here throws up entirely reasonable courses of action. Demanding jobs and finite resources notwithstanding, difficulties in making links aside, this required only good, old-fashioned, thorough police work. Errors like this should not happen. They were straightforward mistakes, errors of omission that had profound consequences. The undercover operation, on the other hand, was different. Its complexity, the fact that the errors were sustained and ratified by many different overseers, makes it, in our view, the most indefensible aspect.

Napper spent too long in the shadows, but much has been learned from those mistakes and we cannot afford to let the legacy of the case plunge us into the hopeless darkness of his world. After the catastrophe that was Operation Edzell, Rachel's killer remained uncaught, and although murder investigations are never officially closed until the offender is brought to justice, in practice they are wound down and other cases take priority. This does not mean that the case file lays undisturbed. Back then, as now, murder cases would be reviewed regularly. In a bid to have fresh eyes look at the investigation, different forces could look again at an unsolved case. However, it took the failed investigation into the murder of Stephen Lawrence to highlight the shortcomings in practice.

The Lawrence case – where practice was shockingly poor on just about every front – became a landmark for police reform. Lord Macpherson, who chaired the public enquiry, reported (among many other findings, including the famous

AUTOPSIES

statement that the police were 'institutionally racist') that the case review of Stephen's murder had not judged the *quality* of the first investigation. If they had done so thoroughly, the many errors would have become clear.

It was also deemed unacceptable to allow police forces to adopt their own individual approaches to case reviews, as some of the methods were clearly perfunctory. At worst, someone might just take down the file, note there had been no new evidence and replace it until the next round of cold-case reviews. Macpherson insisted that such reviews should be a systematic series of stages.

Coupled with the same type of failure to review thoroughly across other forces – without which failure the Yorkshire Ripper might have been caught before he reached his appalling total of thirteen victims – Her Majesty's Inspectorate of Constabulary (HMIC) took up the baton. They eventually examined the procedures used across the police service as a whole, starting with the Met – whose investigators had failed to bring to court the killers of both Rachel Nickell and Stephen Lawrence.

Today, the expectations for cold-case review – among many other policy and procedural standards – are set down by ACPO in the *Murder Investigation Manual*. The decision-making of earlier investigative officers is examined regularly, which helps to keep the investigative mindset as open as possible. These days, senior officers are also taught about psychological biases that may compromise decision-making. Thus, any 'confirmation bias' (recall Chapter Seven – looking only at evidence that supports your hypothesis and ignoring evidence that disconfirms it) can be weeded out.

'Clustering illusions' (see Chapter One – finding patterns where no meaningful pattern exists) can be spotted and procedural errors highlighted. The senior investigating officer who originally had the case may review it informally, but is expected to report to the Head of Criminal Investigation. Peer review is a particularly important part of the process, but reviewing decision-making supplements review of new evidence; it does not replace it.

The changes over the last decade and a half have been many. Many improvements have been made and many aspects of the failed Nickell case would not occur today. But – until humans are perfect – different mistakes will inevitably be made and we must ensure that "Lessons will be learned" is more than a media soundbite. The process of improvement is ongoing.

As the new millennium got into its stride, police reviewing the Nickell case eventually found new evidence against Napper, though, as we have seen, it was actually very old evidence – time changes perspectives, though the then infant science of DNA left many years between her death and Robert Napper's conviction. The consequences of this were both widespread and profound, for the people he attacked and the families who loved them. Now, as we turn to their stories, we shall leave Napper himself locked away.

CHAPTER ELEVEN
PIPS IN THE HEART

Rachel's partner, André Hanscombe, relates in his own book[17] the story of how they told their son Alex one day to be careful around Molly the dog. Molly was newly returned from a visit to the vet, where they had successfully removed seeds of some description that she managed to get stuck inside her ear; they had most likely become lodged there while scratching and nosing around in the undergrowth of the common. The dog was not seriously injured, but Mummy and Daddy both explained to Alex that Molly's ears were hurting because of the 'pips' in them, which the kind vet had taken out. The little boy would not forget this early lesson in being mindful of others' feelings.

In the desolate early days following Rachel's murder, Alex came up to his father while he played at home. Apropos of

---

17 Hanscombe, A. (1996). *The Last Thursday in July: The Story of Those Left Behind*. London: Century Books.

nothing, the child picked up the nozzle of the nearby vacuum cleaner and took it across to Daddy. Imitating the noise of the machine as though it were switched on, Alex began moving the nozzle back and forth across his father's chest. André wondered what imaginary game his son might be playing but, with a child's charming enthusiasm for being in charge, Alex told him to sit still because he was going to use the Hoover to get the pip out of his daddy's heart.

André was astonished that a tiny child could be aware that the heart is regarded as the seat of emotion; moreover, he had chosen just the right site in the body to target. Alex was obviously, just as his father thought, a bright little boy, but the poignancy lies in his crystal innocence. His actions were as touching as his attempt to use a makeshift plaster to help his mummy get better, and just as heartbreakingly ineffectual. Would that someone could use a vacuum cleaner to suck up human pain and emotional trauma. Most remarkable is the loving care that motivated Alex. Amidst the horror of what had befallen him, the child just kept going and tried to make things better. In so doing, he showed the essence of what makes us human: he connected with another person. In this, the little boy was a symbol of hope for the future.

Robert Napper and his ilk intrigue us because we try to fathom their behaviour and struggle to reconcile their deeds with our concept of just what it means to be human. This curiosity is natural enough, but the authors have no wish for him to remain in the spotlight as this book nears its end.

In this final chapter, we will consider the people he affected. Giving pause to examine the impact that one person's dreadful crimes can have is vital. The consequences ripple outwards across ever increasing pools of humanity and downstream along entire lifetimes. The most direct impact is obviously on those who lost their lives. Rachel and Samantha ought to have had decades ahead of them, stuffed full with experiences of family and friends, their natural share of sadness and tears, work, love and laughter. Jazmine did not even complete her childhood. All were utterly robbed of life.

The impact on those left behind after the death of a loved one is well charted. Academics and practitioners alike work to understand grief. The stages and processes that the bereaved may expect to undergo are predictable: denial; anger; depression; acceptance. Some models list different stages, and there are many academic discussions over what constitutes 'normal' stages of grief. What happens to people who do not conform to what is normal? As if bereavement itself is not enough, must they then feel a sense of failure for not passing to the next stage quickly enough? Should grief for an elderly aunt who lived a long and happy life be regarded as the same process as grief for your own child?

It is a complex area and its details are beyond the scope of this chapter but, suffice to say, such knowledge can be used to assist people in eventually renewing an interest in their own lives. Individual experience differs, as do circumstances.

A loved one's murder is a very particular set of circumstances that propels relatives into an extraordinarily intense grieving process. Psychological studies have shown that the mental distress (e.g. feelings of guilt and hopelessness about the future) of parents whose adolescent or adult child has died violently tends to diminish by the end of the first year. In the second year after bereavement, the mother's mental distress declines further while that of the father actually increases in some respects.

As with all statistical results, however, they mean little without interpretation and the devil is in the detail. The mother's distress was higher than the father's to begin with, and so women are not necessarily any better off by the time the second year of grieving gets underway. Interpreting the 'whys' of this is the most important part. It is possible, for example, that men suppress their most acute distress as part of their culturally expected role to stay strong or to support their child's mother; they may feel able, by the second year, to relinquish some control and permit themselves to admit their pain as the mother's initial anguish declines.

Sadly, there are few crumbs of comfort in the statistics. The decline in mental distress is relative. The figures compared to the rest of the (non-bereaved) population are the most revealing in terms of the impact of losing your son or daughter in violent circumstances, standing in stark contrast to the well-being of most people. Even two years after the death of a child, its mother displays distress levels five times higher than average mothers. For fathers, the distress is four times that which is considered normal. Parents are commonly plagued by recurring images of the (imagined) scene of their child's death. They feel intense anger not only – as may be expected – towards the murderer, but also towards the criminal justice system. Anxiety, depression, panic attacks and posttraumatic stress disorder (PTSD) are also common among parents whose child has been murdered.

Moreover, parents – in particular, mothers – recover more

slowly than other close relatives, such as siblings or partners. This is, to some degree, unsurprising. Reaching old age is a reasonable expectation in the western world and early death is therefore a shock; a violent death is a greater shock still. However, where loved ones are near peers, people have usually contemplated that one will predecease the other at some stage. Albeit one cannot predict who will live longer, the possibility is at least accepted that it could be either sibling or partner who will be first to pass away.

Naturally, this in no way diminishes the grief of others whose loved one has met a violent death. Rather, it is the case that parents bear an extra burden. Since the advent of modern medicine, it is not typical for western parents to even contemplate losing a child. In this context any death is shockingly unexpected, a murdered child is rarer still. It seems to be beyond what we have culturally defined as the natural order of events. Parents expect to be outlived by their children and anything contrary is a major violation of their view of the world. That they will have to organise their child's funeral does not bear thinking about, and so parents tend not to think about it ever. If it happens, they are utterly unprepared.

Many parents feel themselves to be socially isolated, or even alienated, from others. How can this be otherwise? They have undergone an experience which, fortunately, the great majority of us will never have to endure. It is entirely logical that they perceive themselves as different and set apart from most other people. This may be reflected back by some erstwhile friends, or relatives who regard the bereaved as somehow different now and choose not to embark on a newly revised relationship. On the day Robert Napper was convicted at the Old Bailey, Rachel Nickell's father put it this way: "You are avoided by so-called friends who think some bad luck will rub off on them."

Others may be extremely well intentioned but not know how to show support. Parents cite misplaced expressions such as, "I understand how you feel" as hurtful and thus themselves make the choice to withdraw. There are many features which can influence and transform relationships after this kind of bereavement. Certainly, revisions are necessary. Things cannot go back to how they were. One bereaved parent said succinctly, "Grief re-writes your address book."

This notwithstanding, staying connected with others in a practical 'keeping active' sense – regardless of the internal perception of isolation – is known to help adjustment. It at least offers the opportunity to talk about the experience, whereas parents who 'clam up' or numb the pain by seeking solo comfort in alcohol or drugs (known as 'repressive coping') are more likely to show symptoms of PTSD. What's more, these symptoms may still be in evidence even five years on after the loss of the child.

Specialist researchers who study death are known as thanatologists. One area of interest is to examine which factors predict recovery from bereavement, thereby informing the first step in devising treatment programmes. Put another way, if Jane copes better than John, we need to determine exactly what advantage Jane possesses and see if it can be administered to John and others like him.

But it is important to know that not all others will be like John or Jane. Some deaths are different, and some thanatologists have looked very specifically at the factors that predict which parents will cope with the violent death of a child (whether by accident, suicide or murder). Self-esteem is an important factor. Having a solid belief in your self-worth is centrally important. Perceiving the world as benevolent and meaningful also helps people to cope after the violent death of a loved one. At first glance, this may seem strange. How can a parent possibly hold onto the belief that the world is a benevolent place when their child has been killed?

Some people have the capacity somehow to see the world as generally good, though the most dreadful thing has happened to them. Others may find meaning in their religious beliefs by attributing the causes to different sources. For example, believing the Devil was behind your child's death helps to quarantine the perception that nothing has any meaning anymore. From this viewpoint, someone can still retain a separate faith that God made a world full of kindness.

The puzzle that someone in such dire circumstances can see the world as a benign place is explicable. They can incorporate the death of the child into their world view (known as their 'assumptive world'). Certainly, this does not happen quickly; indeed, they may have to rebuild entirely a view of the world that has been completely shattered, but eventually they will compartmentalise what happened to their child and, thus, learn to cope. (Once again, this is relative. Life is obviously irrevocably changed.)

Many parents feel continuing guilt, which is a component part of mental distress. We may attribute this to the idea that a central feature of the parental role is to protect your child. This makes intuitive sense, yet it persists in parents whose primary role as a caregiver and protector has been fulfilled.

Their adult children have left home and gone to live their own independent lives, and it is no longer a parent's job to protect them.

This sense of guilt and self-recrimination may have a couple of possible explanations. It may simply be because parenting in general and protection in particular have been such a significant defining role in the parent's life. Most adults will attest to the sometimes irritating ways of parents who continue to treat them, grown men and women, as if they were small children. Adult visits to parental homes commonly include regressive reminders to wrap up warm, as if an adult cannot decide for him/herself whether s/he needs a scarf. Thus the difficulty of relinquishing the role of parent is one explanation.

Some thanatologists suggest another possibility, that the feeling of guilt because they did not protect their child helps parents to cling to the notion that the world is a predictable place. Things could have been different 'if only' they had protected them. 'If only' allows some semblance of control; 'if only' grants them the notional power to have made things happen otherwise. The alternative view is that the murder was an entirely random event. If the world is so utterly random, then murder can happen again just as suddenly and no one is safe, ever. Far better, the reasoning goes, to accept guilt and stick with the worldview of events as predictable, manageable, controllable if one is only more vigilant. The 'random world' alternative is rejected because it is just too terrifying a prospect to contemplate.

Other factors that bear on parents are the relationship between mother and father, the characteristics of the child they have lost and the environment they contend with after

PIPS IN THE HEART

their child's death. For Rachel Nickell's family, that environment included the ever-present media. Returning from holiday on receiving the news of their daughter's death, her parents and brother transferred immediately from the plane which had flown them back to the UK to a car that would drive them to a press conference. They were denied the cocoon of home to which people naturally retreat in times of adversity and suffering.

Andrew Nickell, accompanied by his wife and son and flanked by police, made an eloquent plea for people to assist in finding the murderer. Rachel's partner, André, had already spoken. His appeal followed his official identification of Rachel's body. He was driven by police straight from one venue to the next, from the bland, functional space of St George's Hospital to the warren of functional offices that make up New Scotland Yard.

Leaving his traumatised son in the capable hands of his own mother to play with stickers and crayons in a back office, André was ushered out to face the banks of cameras. Expecting to encounter what he described as something akin to "a firing squad", he found himself instead facing a roomful of tears. He had not expected that strangers would be affected by the tragedy, but the detective beside him shrugged off British notions of masculinity to hold André's hand.

Marshalling the family into making media appeals is standard investigative practice. The police need to ensure that it is done while a case is still at the forefront of the public's mind, even though it intrudes on grief at its rawest. Catching the offender understandably takes priority, and the family would be the last to wish it otherwise.

Notwithstanding the immense difficulty of facing such a task in such awful circumstances, they sometimes bring retrospective benefits for those involved. Families may feel just that bit less powerless in the face of a situation where they can change nothing about the death. Alex was the only person exempt from full participation in the investigation, his welfare instead considered paramount. However, the psychologist who treated him after his mother's death advised that his welfare and the investigation's needs were not mutually exclusive. She reminded everybody that, despite their concerns about questioning Alex over his ordeal, it would one day prove important for him to look back and know that he had done his best to help. Allowing him to assist in the investigation was beneficial to his well-being.

Some thanatologists argue that part of the struggle of bereavement is in managing simultaneously the desire to hold onto the person lost and the need to let them go. This is tangibly manifested for some. When murder has forced close relatives to let go of their loved one, they are expected also to surrender such belongings as are necessary for an investigation. If tests are required to determine which fibres belong to the victim's or family's clothes and which have come from a stranger's, relevant items need to be given to police. You may wish to breathe in the remnants of perfume from the sweater which first framed a happy face on Christmas morning; you may want to hold the gloves which enfolded the hands you clasped, but they have to go. Personal possessions which were once suffused with memories metamorphose into mere materials for the lab. Someone's life is bagged, numbered and tested.

PIPS IN THE HEART

Loved ones must submit to the swabs and syringes to establish whose DNA was the legitimate partner's and whose was the stranger's. André Hanscombe had to endure questions about the most intimate aspects of his life with Rachel. This was mirrored sixteen months later when Conrad Ellam had to furnish police with the smallest details of his love-life with Samantha Bisset. Victims of the Green Chain rapes had to likewise offer up their privacy. Offenders will likely use the defence that someone else is responsible for bruises or other injuries – a partner, perhaps. Contemporaneous records of victims' sexual experiences in the days before the offence help to undermine such claims, exposing guilty defendants as liars. Police have to gather the information while memories are fresh, painting as full a picture as possible in preparation for every eventuality.

At a time when families wish to retreat into their sorrow, they must allow access to their homes, and permit their bank accounts, address books, routines, relatives and friends to be raked over in the search for clues.

Bereavement made public can be an odd and disturbing experience. In high-profile cases, members of the public who feel touched by the death wish to be involved in some way. They may find ways to offer condolences by sending messages, flowers or, in the case of Alex, roomfuls of toys. This widespread support from strangers can be moving and positive, but it also has the potential to become strangely intrusive.

André wrote of the dislocation he felt at a public gathering on Wimbledon Common after Rachel's death. He was at once touched by people's concern yet upset at the 'otherness' of the vigil. The event was organised by a church, but Rachel had not been a religious person. It is impossible to know, of course, but to try to key into the oddness of this experience, choose a relative of your own and then imagine turning on the news to hear strangers suddenly announcing their memorial for your Aunt _____ or your cousin _____, whom none of them ever knew.

High-profile crime victims become appropriated by the public; it is one more aspect that makes the bereavement extraordinary. The normal desire for privacy in grief is not honoured and the bereaved are forced to let go of their loved one, as private citizens become public property. Mr Nickell spoke of the pain – "like a kick in the stomach" – every time home videos of Rachel appeared on the news. On the day his daughter's killer was convicted, he appealed to the media directly: "Please, after today, do not use them. Please give her some peace."

The protracted legal process is an important feature of the environment endured by those whose loved one has been murdered, and it is well established as a 'secondary stressor' over and above what is suffered by anyone who has to adjust to bereavement. Samantha Bisset's stepfather, Jack Morrison, reported that the prospect of attending Robert Napper's trial was the element that proved too much for his wife. Samantha's mother, Margaret, collapsed with a fatal heart attack the night before she was due to face in court the man who had savagely killed her daughter and granddaughter.

Samantha's mum was only fifty-three years old but, in the words of her husband, she "changed overnight and went

PIPS IN THE HEART

downhill" after the deaths of Samantha and Jazmine. Even without knowing her medical history, this is one occasion where it is not necessary to be a dispassionate scientist. One simply has to be human to agree with her husband's claim that his Maggie "died of a broken heart". Three generations of one family had succumbed to Napper's crimes and left Jack Morrison alone.

Some bereaved parents change their aims throughout the stressful legal process. What some may initially wish in the immediate red heat of their loss is not attainable. Eventually, the fury they cannot vent on the murderer typically becomes reconciled with what the criminal justice system can provide. Studies have shown that being able to modify these types of goals (i.e. the search for justice) is a predictor of coping reasonably well. Of course, these findings were drawn from parents who had come to accept that the offender was facing a punishment of sorts, even though it may not be as harsh as they might have wished. Whatever the sentence, there has at least been a conviction.

Victims' families face enormous struggles to accommodate the fact that power is held by the criminal justice system, not themselves. It is clearly immensely difficult to accept. Reconciling one's own idea of justice, or the desire for revenge, with what the system allows, ceding control to lawyers, judges and juries, can be a horribly arduous task but it is at least straightforward.

For the Nickells and the Hanscombes, it was not such a straightforward matter. In the mid-1990s, Rachel's family faced a court trial. At some point, like other families, they must have had to tailor their anger and put their faith in the system we have – because there is no other. But then they faced the trial of Colin Stagg and he was found not guilty.

The perception that a guilty man had gone unpunished would have had an enormous impact. It can only have been compounded by subsequent events, as the new investigation into Robert Napper made it clear that Stagg was in fact innocent. A bereft family found that they had somehow been knitting fog. The anger and despair created by the misguided first investigation had somehow to be unravelled and knitted up again, to weave a different man into the narrative of their collective loss. And all the while, the media attention did not abate. Their task was truly Herculean.

Central to everybody's concern was Alex, the child who had borne witness to his mother's death. Studies that explore the impact of homicide paint a bleak picture. Children who merely live in a community where murders have occurred are affected by the events, showing increased levels of anxiety, having trouble sleeping and seeking the reassurance of a parent's bed. These are the responses of children who have not even had any direct connection to the crimes themselves, though the fear does tend to disappear within a year of the events in their neighbourhood.

Children who have lost a family member to murder are, naturally enough, far more directly and profoundly affected. Like their adult relatives, they are at increased risk of PTSD and likewise have to cope with all the different aspects of grief. All must incorporate the murder into their life experience. Adults may have to rebuild a shattered worldview whereas children's have yet to develop.

It is an ongoing process throughout childhood to learn of

PIPS IN THE HEART

right and wrong, to build an understanding that actions have consequences and so on. These normal developmental patterns are seriously violated by the injustice of murder. The most well-adjusted, securely attached children grow up able to depend on the stability of a family. This is the place where they are kept safe and protected. Being able to meet these bereaved children's normal developmental needs is extraordinarily difficult.

The family is not permanent when the focal point is lost. Few would argue that the person most willing to lay down their own life for another is the person who gave us life to begin with – our mother. These bereaved children cannot rely on such a certainty; they are not safe when their fiercest protector has already been defeated. Reassuring them that the world is a safe place is facile and futile. It is in direct conflict with their lived experience.

What is more, their idea that the world is unsafe is rational, grounded and entirely logical. It may be unwise, therapeutically, to try to disabuse them of the idea. After all, they are facts. This is their reality. Nevertheless, their normal child-like need for safety remains and needs to be managed, their sense of security nurtured, if they are not to be overwhelmed by anxiety. It is the most delicate balance to acknowledge their reality and still keep them from tipping over into disabling fear.

Proximity to the event increases the risk of problems later on. Those who witness the murder are especially vulnerable. Children as young as three do remember the details, though there is some evidence that some children's memories are slightly distorted by the fact that they misunderstand what happened. As small children try to fit the event into what they know, their own experience of the world, they may sometimes offer an altered interpretation. For example, a four-year-old who described how, "Mummy cut herself shaving" had actually witnessed the babysitter killing her mother with an axe. It seems she tried to squeeze the horror into a framework she understood, and the only prior awareness she possessed referred to bathroom razors and the accidental cuts they make.

In many respects, however, small children's memories are reliable. A girl of three who survived attempted murder was able to explain in great detail exactly what had happened to her during the time spent with her abductor. When it came to identifying him, she had no problem picking out the photo of 'the bad man' who threw her down a hole (her abuser had disposed of her in a sewage drain). Her police interviewer and therapist repeated the exercise to make sure she hadn't chosen that particular photo by chance; they showed her the batch minus the suspect's picture to see what she would do. The child picked none and stated clearly that he wasn't there. When they finally pretended they couldn't find the picture, the child picked up the whole lot and plucked his photo out.

Growing up with an enhanced sense of vulnerability interferes with the normal process of adolescence, whereby young people become increasingly independent. Any adult will recognise as typical the foolhardy activities of young people (males in particular) who engage in dangerous pursuits to show off. Whether a lad climbs to the top of a rickety scaffold, pulls stunts racing a motorbike or simply challenges another to a fight, what seems pointless danger to adults is a 'buzz' to teens. Evolution has hardwired them so that young people on the cusp of adulthood engage in risk-seeking behaviour. The swagger of youth comes complete with a sense of invulnerability that leads young people to confidently take the risk of leaving the nest.

By contrast, homicide survivors are more likely to feel they cannot take care of themselves, while society impels them to do just that. These types of conflicts may manifest behaviourally in many ways, not all of them with an obvious or direct link. For example, a teen who flatly refuses to complete schoolwork might simply be unable to do the task, could be indulging in some very ordinary teenage rebellion, or else might be striving to be expelled so he can stay home with his remaining parent in an attempt to feel safe.

Eighty-seven percent of children who experience the murder of a parent also lose their home. Friends, familiar surroundings and routines all disappear suddenly. Given that most parental murders are the result of domestic violence, the remaining parent is the offender and is lost to prison. Few children stay in their former accommodation. Even those fortunate enough to avoid the care system usually move into grandparents' or relatives' houses, rather than vice versa.

Alex, too, lost his home when he lost his mother. Besieged by the press in the early days, he and his father had to decamp to his grandmother's home. André eventually felt forced to leave the country. He took Alex to a new life in Europe – first France, then Spain – where they could make an anonymous start as a family of two, causing a rupture in their relationship with Rachel's parents.

KILLER IN THE SHADOWS

It seems inappropriate to discuss Alex's 'good luck' in the context of such horror, yet to describe it any other way would be to deny the undivided love, attention and sheer toil that André invested in his son. He endured interminably lonely months cut off from support networks at home while he grieved and built a life in their rural farmhouse. Any parent who has undertaken the fulltime care of a small child will testify to the truth that love does not always compensate for the tedium of endless days spent feeding, playing, preparing for bedtime, feeding, playing, preparing for bedtime...

Much stimulation is gladly sacrificed for children's benefit, but it can be an isolated existence. Toddlers — notwithstanding the sheer joy they can bring — are no substitute for adult company, and Alex was a traumatised child whose care was an even greater responsibility. For weeks he clung to André like a limpet, terrified to let go. Formerly a little boy who had been confident enough to greet and talk to adults, to wander from his bedroom to the toilet in the middle of the night without needing a parent, he became a child for whom, in his father's words, "only a few seconds alone was enough to plunge him into terror. He had so little trust left in the world."

As André woke every day to meet his own grief, his alarm clock for the whole first year was a child who screamed as he struggled to emerge from his nightmares. Alex was fortunate indeed to still have his father.

Alex's adolescence was admirably untroubled, given his history, though it was certainly not uneventful. In his early to mid-teens he was unable to concentrate and underperformed in school, threatened with expulsion several times for his challenging behaviour. He hung around with a local gang responsible for graffiti and general antisocial behaviour. His choice of friends culminated in his arrest on suspicion of the theft of a motorbike, though he was eventually cleared of blame.

How are such incidents to be interpreted? It is, as we mentioned earlier, almost obligatory for teens to test the boundaries by pushing at them. In this sense, it is perfectly normal to misbehave. This does not mean that adults should do nothing about it, but there is no need to think society is ready to collapse because teenagers get up to no good. Adolescents are supposed to misbehave, adults are supposed to manage it, and then everyone settles down again when the phase ends.

Trouble at school is common enough. The teenager of impeccable behaviour and academic performance is the extraordinary one. Many young people even have a brush with the law, which usually ends when youth does. The worry for parents, of course, is that they cannot predict whether it is a short-lived, youthful indiscretion or the start of a negative path towards criminality. Before adulthood proper delineates their path, parents fret about whether their sons (most often) are normal teens in a rebellious phase or young men destined for big trouble.

Alex was troubled enough that his father had to physically wrestle him to the ground to calm his anger. He also knew how to wound, by declaring to André, "I haven't got a family," but his father's support has been steadfast, and a supportive family is one of the biggest protective factors for young people who might be at risk of offending. During his early to mid-teens, Alex's behaviour at school and beyond was by no means perfect but it was within the bounds of normality for young people. On the whole, his behaviour seemed fairly unremarkable, which is remarkable in itself.

But the murder becomes a benchmark against which everything is measured. It cannot help but be the fulcrum around which all subsequent events pivot. All behaviour, all relationships, are redefined by it. André strived hard not to have the murder of Rachel become the defining event in the eyes of other people. It was admirable that he did not want his son to be treated with kid gloves, and he is justly proud that he did not overcompensate, but the very fact that it took sustained effort to do so points to the permanent, constant presence of the crime.

Each decision needed to be weighed against what is normal, and then life had to be recalibrated so it conformed as closely as possible to what everyone else experiences. How others are likely to react always has to be weighed. André did not want Alex to be in a position of being "able to get away with anything" on account of his previous suffering. However, to attain his wish, the past lives of father and son had to be kept secret from people at Alex's school.

Life as a homicide survivor is not 'normal' and this is an inescapable fact. His father has commented on the normal situation where fathers are the most powerful figure in their children's lives, astutely recognising that he was not. On the contrary, Alex had come face to face with the figure that destroyed his family; nothing could ever be a more powerful influence on his life than his mother's killer.

PIPS IN THE HEART

In later years, Alex blotted out his father's attempts to inform him of the police's renewed investigation as the case against Napper was being prepared. André strongly believes that his son has a right to know what happened, but Alex does not welcome his efforts. Unlike his father and grandparents, he chose not to attend when Napper appeared in court.

The family is still negotiating their way through the painful fractures caused by Rachel's death. Father and son continue, but the relationship between the Nickells and the Hanscombes is broken. André and Rachel's parents fell out over seemingly small incidents, such as who had the right to decide on a haircut for Alex. However, these disagreements are only trivial in an ordinary context.

There seems no harm in a grandmother welcoming her small grandson into the warmth of her bed to sleep. It can only have given her back something of her tragically lost role as a mother. But Alex's father was trying to re-instil in the child the confidence to sleep alone in his own bed. He does not see a small issue; he sees four years' hard work undone.

Grandparents give a little boy a haircut to make him comfortable as he holidays with them in the South of France. This action symbolically returns the father to a supremely painful time; he had not wanted to watch his child's baby locks fall to the floor with a snip of the scissors but, if he was to take him out in public, he had disguise him somehow after a tabloid had published his photograph.

The grandparents' decision to have Alex's hair cut was a repeat of a situation wherein the father felt his child's life was beyond his control. The grandparents' need to be closely involved with their lost daughter's child was a poignant attempt to make things normal, to reinvest in life through doing very ordinary things. No one committed a major wrong. Unfortunately, in trying to wrest control in an uncontrollable situation, small slights loomed large over people already at breaking point. Despite their valiant efforts down the years, the child effectively lost his grandparents along with his mother.

People will naturally have different opinions as to who is more or less deserving of sympathy. But if we set judgement aside for a moment and consider without prejudice, there is a simpler point to be made. The impact on so many can be traced back to one man. The reverberations of what Robert Napper did resonate through many, many lives.

Paul Britton's career was blighted by the failed Operation Edzell; the careers of other profilers were diverted by the indirect damage to their reputation. The careers of police officers were cut short. One serving detective inspector felt he was scapegoated for having allegedly procured confidential documents from which to write his own 'inside account'.

The undercover policewoman 'Lizzie James' may have been involved in a misguided operation, but her belief that she was courting an extremely dangerous killer was very real. Her courage in trying to draw out a murderer finished her career.

We have covered in detail the impact on Colin Stagg. Even after his acquittal, he continued to endure years of tabloid vilification and was spat on in the street. Mr Justice Ognall, the judge who refused to admit the honeytrap evidence against Stagg, bore, in his own words, a "vendetta pursued

PIPS IN THE HEART

against me by certain newspapers in the aftermath of the trial"; some sections of the press believed he had let a guilty man literally get away with murder.

Lest we forget, many of the relatives of murderers bear a deeply unenviable stigma, though they have committed no crime. Napper's sister, Gillian, has expressed her fervent wish that the years of intrusion will cease and she and her family will be left alone to get on with their lives, now that her brother has been convicted of killing Rachel.

It is as if the stain of the offences can rub off. For relatives, this often amounts to a dirty secret, a life of lies where care is exercised daily to make sure that the notorious sibling or son is never mentioned for fear of misdirected reprisals; if discovered, some families attract such opprobrium that they have to up-end their lives and start over.

Rape victims seldom recover their previous confidence or the feeling of security they had before they were attacked. Their fears can intrude on marital relationships and their anxieties can be passed down to children. But the biggest burden presses on those affected by Napper's murders.

The knowledge that the person responsible is safely locked away can bring some degree of relief. Without that conviction there is no justice, and fear remains unrestrained while the families believe that the killer is still free. The Nickells and the Hanscombes lived for years with the searingly corrosive idea that the murderer was possibly committing further crimes.

Samantha Bisset's mother, Maggie, was convinced that Napper had killed Rachel Nickell as well as her beloved daughter and little granddaughter, Jazmine. Her husband,

Jack, said she attributed it to "a woman's intuition" and, to the day she died, she would not relinquish her belief that both families had been destroyed by the same man.

The Nickells and Hanscombes, on the other hand, did not know who had killed Rachel. They did not know he had indeed gone on to kill again and taken two more lives. They did not know he had been locked away since 1995. They lived from 1995 until 2008 without certainty of any of these things. In all that time, Napper never once told anyone what he had done. He did not offer the family one shred of solace.

Yet somehow people bear such unbearable burdens and continue; they stay connected at some level. Those who retreat completely into their grief eventually re-emerge and somehow finally re-connect with others. Perhaps this connection is what matters most. Despite his desperate ordeal, André continued to devote himself to another person. He held and healed his troubled son for year upon year.

Even in the throes of the most intense distress, Rachel's father connected with other human beings. When he met the detective who, along with his son, broke the news of his daughter's death, he acknowledged the difficulty of the task and thanked the officer for telling him. Despite all, he found the compassion to put himself in that policeman's shoes. Sixteen years on, he paused outside the Old Bailey to thank, among others, the police whose misguided pursuit of Colin Stagg had intensified and prolonged his family's grief. It was, he said, "easy with the benefit of hindsight to say mistakes were made".

Samantha Bisset's partner, Conrad Ellam, admitted publicly that he still has the symptoms of PTSD from discovering the bodies of Samantha and Jazmine – a scene so horrific that a seasoned police photographer with no personal attachment to the victims could not return for work for many months. Yet this humble man has somehow distilled his horror into the simple statement: "I tried to turn my life around."

Doubtlessly, private ghosts remain, but he nevertheless firmly rejects the idea of blame on the grounds that, "It's not going to lead anywhere." He acknowledges that it was the awfulness of losing Samantha and Jazmine which made him reassess his aims, leave menial jobs behind and train for a more rewarding career in wildlife conservation. Mr Ellam has done a remarkable job of building a new life for himself.

It would be glib to think that people get over such tragedy by 'reconnecting'. They do not. Many relationships founder after the violent death of a loved one. Sometimes, those who are left behind cannot cope with the grief of a partner as well as their own and, in a bid to dilute the pain and escape the intensity of the reminders, marriages fail. Indeed, such partnerships break up more frequently than those of the rest of the population.

For some, the person who is lost has consumed the future and there is nothing left in their relationship but a common bereavement. The Hanscombes and Nickells are one such example. Sometimes, for people to move on and reinvest in life again, they must jettison relationships that have become founded on and mired in grief. Yet, somewhere along the line, people do somehow reconnect – that is the miracle of being human.

Stories of people shipwrecked or prisoners in solitary confinement testify to significant psychological changes in people separated from contact with other human beings. The experiences of the scientist Admiral Byrd in the Antarctic during the 1930s are well documented. Byrd had planned and looked forward to six months alone at a weather station. He felt lost and bewildered in four weeks, using his imagination to compensate for the absence of other humans. To soften his intense loneliness, he pretended he was with people he knew. After three months, his imagination had turned into hallucinations, which in other contexts would be regarded as psychotic. Studies have shown that most people who endure extended isolation will eventually show signs of mental illness.

Napper's descent into the most atrocious of crimes began with his isolation, his detachment from other human beings. Although it was not by any means the only factor, his separation perhaps characterises the essential distinction. He was unable to make a connection and so he could inflict dreadful pain on other humans. Those he hurt, by stark contrast, continue to connect with others.

There is no implied prescription for what the families of murder victims ought to do. Each individual responds and copes differently, yet they all reach out on some level. Some are nothing short of astonishing in their ability to do so. Dr Shaun Russell, whose wife Lin and daughter Megan were murdered by Michael Stone, eventually built a new life with Josie, his younger child who survived the attack. Before this, Dr Russell told how he had wanted to torture and kill Stone to avenge the pain that had been inflicted upon his family. Ultimately, however, he expressed his sorrow for the murderer on account of the difficult life the man had led. He also described his sympathy for the killer's family because they "have had to endure so much over the years."

Conrad Ellam, likewise, shows admirable dignity in his refusal to demonise Robert Napper. Instead, he says that he can "sympathise with his condition". This degree of connection is unusual. To reflect on what has caused another human being to suffer is human; to feel for him when he is the sole, direct cause of your most intense sorrow is amazingly, admirably magnanimous.

To research the field of psychology entails plunging regularly into the murky and oft dispiriting gloom of inhuman behaviour. Many people prefer instead to admit only happy things into their lives and instinctively turn away from harrowing events; they do not understand why or how anyone would choose such a career. And it's true that it can be emotionally harrowing, but one only need reflect on the experiences of victims and their families to appreciate who is truly affected by crime. Investigative and forensic psychology is not a job that leaves one bereft of faith in human behaviour.

On the contrary, it is impossible not to be humbled by the endless determination of victims or their families. That someone whose life has been utterly razed can plumb the depths of their sorrow and somehow dredge up the strength to rebuild it is remarkable. That others can find the sheer generosity of spirit to reject bitterness in order to move forwards is infinitely admirable. Those who can find it in themselves to feel for, or even forgive, the offenders who destroyed their lives are nothing short of heroic. They teach us what it means to be human.

FURTHER READING

The interested reader may wish to explore further some of the themes and issues discussed. The list below is intended as a springboard, so it is not exhaustive in the way that academic references usually are. It is, though, varied and includes books as well as academic articles to guide the reader in a range of directions.

Alison, L. (2005). *The Forensic Psychologist's Casebook: Offender Profiling and Criminal Investigation*. Devon, England: Willan.

Alison, L., Bennell, C., Mokros, A. and Ormerod, D. (2002). 'The Personality Paradox in Offender Profiling: A Theoretical Review of the Processes Involved in Deriving Background Characteristics from Crime Scene Actions'. *Psychology, Public Policy & Law,* 8, pp.115-135.

Alison, L. and Crego, J. (2008). *Policing Critical Incidents: Leadership and Critical Incident Management*. Devon, England: Willan.

Arndt, Jr. W. B., Foehl, J. C. and Good, E. F. (1985). 'Specific Sexual Fantasy Themes: A Multidimensional Study'. *Journal of Personality and Social Psychology,* 48, pp.472-480.

Asaro, M. R. and Clements, P. T. (2004). 'Homicide Bereavement: A Family Affair'. *Journal of Forensic Nursing*, 1, pp.101-128.

Baron, J. (2000). *Thinking and Deciding*. Cambridge, England: Cambridge University Press.

Bichard, M. (2004). *The Bichard Inquiry Report*. London, England: Stationery Office. Available online:
http://www.bichardinquiry.org.uk/report

Baudet, A. L. and Belmont, J. W. (2008). 'Array-Based DNA Diagnostics: Let the Revolution Begin'. *Annual Review of Medicine*, 59, pp.113-129.

Beauregard, E., Proulx, J., Rossmo, K., Leclerk, B. and Allaire, J. F. (2007). 'Script Analysis of the Hunting Process of Serial Sex Offenders'. *Criminal Justice and Behavior*, 34, pp.1069-1084.

Beech, A. C., Fisher, D. and Ward, T. (2006). 'Sexual Murderers' Implicit Theories'. *Journal of Interpersonal Violence*, 20, pp.1366-1389.

Bennell, C. and Jones, N. J. (2005). 'Between a ROC and a Hard Place: A Method for Linking Serial Burglaries by Modus Operandi'. *Journal of Investigative Psychology and Offender Profiling*, 2, pp.23-41.

Britton, P. (1999). *The Jigsaw Man*. London, England: Bantam Press.

Caddy, B., Taylor, G. R. and Linacre, A. M. T. (2008). *A Review of the Science of Low Template DNA Analysis*. London, England: Home Office.

Canter, D. (2005). 'Confusing Operational Predicaments and Cognitive Explorations: Comments on Rossmo and Snook et al'. *Applied Cognitive Psychology*, 19, pp.663-668.

Canter, D. and Alison, L. (1999). *Profiling in Policy and Practice*. Aldershot, England: Ashgate.

FURTHER READING

Charles, K. E. and Egan, V. (2008). 'Sensational and Extreme Interests in Adolescents'. In R. N. Koksis (editor) *The Psychology of Serial and Violent Crimes and Their Criminal Investigation*. Totowa, NJ: Humana Press.

Claridge, G., Clark, K., Powney, E. and Hassan, E. (2008). 'Schizotypy and the Barnum Effect'. *Personality and Individual Differences*, 44, pp.436-444.

Craissati, J. (2004). *Managing High Risk Sex Offenders in the Community: A Psychological Approach*. Sussex, England: Brunner-Routledge.

Egan, V., Figueredo, A. J., Wolf, P., McBride, K., Sefcek, J., Vasquez, G. and Charles, K. (2005). 'Sensational Interests, Mating Effort, and Personality'. *Journal of Individual Differences*, 26, pp.11-19.

Egan, V., Kavanagh, B. and Blair, M. (2005). 'Sexual Offenders, Personality and Obsessionality'. *Sexual Abuse*, 17, pp.223 – 240.

Forer, B. R. (1949). 'The Fallacy of Personal Validation: A Classroom Demonstration of Gullibility'. *Journal of Abnormal Psychology*, 44, pp.118-121.

Goodwill, A. and Alison, L. (2006). 'The Development of a Filter Model for Prioritizing Suspects in Burglary Offences'. *Psychology, Crime and Law*, 12, pp.395-416.

Grossman, D. (1995). *On Killing: The Psychological Cost of Learning to Kill in War and Society*. Canada: Back Bay Books.

Hanscombe, A. (1996). *The Last Thursday in July: The Story of Those Left Behind*. London: Century Books.

Knabe, S. (2008). *Geographic Profiling under the Microscope: A Critical Examination of the Utility of Geographic Profiling and Expert Geographic Profilers* (unpublished masters thesis).

Lewandowski, L. A., McFarlane, J., Campbell, J. C., Gary, F. and Barenski, C. (2004). '"He Killed My Mommy!" Murder or Attempted Murder of a Child's Mother'. *Journal of Family Violence*, 19, pp.211-220.

Macpherson, W. (1999). *The Stephen Lawrence Inquiry: Report of an Inquiry by Sir William Macpherson of Cluny*. London, England: HMSO. Available online: http://www.archive.official-documents.co.uk/document/cm42/4262/4262/htm

Mokros, A. and Alison, L. (2002). 'Is Profiling Possible? Testing the Predicted Homology of Crime Scene Actions and Background Characteristics in a Sample of Rapists'. *Legal & Criminological Psychology*, 7, pp.25-43.

Oliver, C. J., Beech, A. R., Fisher, D. and Beckett, R. (2007). 'A Comparison of Rapists and Sexual Murderers on Demographic and Selected Psychometric Measures'. *International Journal of Offender Therapy and Comparative Criminology*, 51, pp.298-312.

Pedder, K. (2002). *The Rachel Files*. London, England: John Blake Publishing.

Proulx, J., Beauregard, E., Cusson, M. and Nicole, A. (2007). *Sexual Murderers: A Comparative Analysis and New Perspectives*. Sussex, England: Wiley.

Rokach, A. (1990). 'Content Analysis of Sexual Fantasies of Males and Females'. *The Journal of Psychology*, 124, pp.427-436.

Rossmo, D. K. (2005). 'Geographic Heuristics or Shortcuts to Failure?: Response to Snook et al'. *Applied Cognitive Psychology*, 19, pp.651-654.

Sandnabba, K., Santtila, P., Alison, L. and Nordling, N. (2002). 'Demographics, Sexual Behaviour, Family Background and Abuse Experiences of Practitioners of Sadomasochistic Sex: A Review of Recent Research'. *Sexual & Relationship Therapy*, 17, pp.39-55.

Savage, S. P. (2007). *Police Reform: Forces for Change*. Oxford, England: Oxford University Press.

Shay, J. (1994). *Achilles in Vietnam: Combat Trauma and the Undoing of Character*. New York: Scribner.

FURTHER READING

Snook, B., Taylor, P. J. and Bennell, C. (2005). 'Shortcuts to Geographical Profiling Success: A Reply to Rossmo'. *Applied Cognitive Psychology*, 19, pp.655-661.

Snook, B., Taylor, P. J. and Bennell, C. (2004). 'Geographic Profiling: The Fast, Frugal, and Accurate Way'. *Applied Cognitive Psychology*, 18, pp.105-121.

Snook, B., Wright, M., House, J. and Alison, L. (2006). 'Searching for a Needle in a Needle Stack: Combining Criminal Careers and Journey-to-Crime Research for Criminal Suspect Prioritization'. *Police Practice and Research*, 7, pp.217-230.

Stagg, C. and Hynds, T. (2007). *Pariah: Colin Stagg*. London, England: Pennant Books.

Vigil, G. J. and Clements, P. T. (2003). 'Child and Adolescent Homicide Survivors'. *Journal of Psychosocial Nursing and Mental Health Services*, 41, pp.30-41.

Villejoubert, G., Almond, L. and Alison, L. (2009). 'Interpreting Claims in Offender Profiles: The Role of Probability Phrases, Base-Rates and Perceived Dangerousness'. *Applied Cognitive Psychology*, 23, pp.36-54.

Woodhams, J., Hollin, C. R. and Bull, R. (in press). 'Incorporating Context in Linking Crimes: An Exploratory Study of the Relationship between Behavioural Consistency and Situational Similarity'. *Journal of Investigative Psychology and Offender Profiling*.

Woodhams, J., Hollin, C. R. and Bull, R. (2008). 'The Sexual Offending of Juveniles'. In R. N. Kocsis (editor), *The Psychology of Serial Violent Crimes and Their Criminal Investigation*. Totowa, NJ: Humana Press.

Woodhams, J., Hollin, C. R. and Bull, R. (2007). 'The Psychology of Linking Crimes: A Review of the Evidence'. *Legal and Criminological Psychology*, 12, pp.233-249